DOMESTIC VIOLENCE

A Reference Handbook

DOMESTIC VIOLENCE

A Reference Handbook

Margi Laird McCue

**CONTEMPORARY
WORLD ISSUES**

ABC-CLIO

Santa Barbara, California
Denver, Colorado
Oxford, England

Copyright © 1995 by Margi Laird McCue

Library of Congress Cataloging-in-Publication Data

McCue, Margi Laird.
    Domestic violence : a reference handbook / Margi Laird McCue.
    p. cm.—(Contemporary world issues)
    Includes bibliographical references and index.
    1. Family violence—United States. 2. Family violence—United States—Prevention. 3. Victims of family violence—Service for—United States. I. Title. II. Series.
    HQ809.3.U5M385 1995 362.82'92—dc20 95-44080

ISBN 0-87436-762-X

02 01 00 99 98 97 96   10 9 8 7 6 5 4 3 2

ABC-CLIO, Inc.
130 Cremona Drive, P.O. Box 1911
Santa Barbara, California 93116-1911

This book is printed on acid-free paper ∞.

Manufactured in the United States of America

To the children—
to Christina, Anthony, Lance, Justin, Sydney,
and to the millions of other children
who have lost part of their childhood
to violence in their homes—
with the hope they will have the opportunity
to live all of their tomorrows in safety, peace, and freedom.

Contents

Preface

This book is intended to provide comprehensive information about domestic violence; what it is, its causes, the extent of the problem, whom it affects, available services, and possible solutions. To provide the reader with a broad and in-depth view of the issue, domestic violence is explored from historical, social, psychological, and legal perspectives. Because the problem is very old but public acceptance of domestic violence as a legitimate problem is fairly recent, there are differing perspectives and conflicting attitudes regarding the cause and possible solutions. I have tried to provide various perspectives, facts, and statistics, and enough information from actual cases to allow the reader to draw his or her own conclusions. The book should also provide readers with the tools necessary to access readily additional information on domestic violence and related topics. Chapter 5 lists nationwide organizations, each of which has statistics, journals, newsletters, and other forms of information available to the public. Chapters 6 and 7 are complete and annotated bibliographies that will allow the reader to continue to research any aspect of domestic violence he or she desires.

As stated in Chapter 1, for the purposes of this book domestic violence is defined as spousal abuse and, more particularly, the abuse of men against women with whom they have or have had an intimate relationship. This has been proven to be the case in more than 90 percent of documented incidents. For consistency the male pronoun is used when referring to perpetrators and the female pronoun when referring to victims. However, in Chapter 4 I do discuss the issue of husband battering and same-sex violence. I also initially planned to devote a segment of the book to elder abuse, but since that has become such a large and serious issue in and of itself, it deserves much more than a short discussion in this book.

In the course of my research I interviewed a number of women survivors of violence, as well as men in batterer treatment programs and children of battered women. I also interviewed many domestic violence professionals. In Chapter 1 I use vignettes from the interviews of four of the women in order to illustrate points. This was done with their permission and, although two of the women also gave me permission to use their names, I chose to change all of the names in order to protect the survivors' identities and those of their families. The stories are intended to make the nature of domestic violence easier to understand, not to sensationalize the issue. Because domestic violence cuts across all economic, ethnic, cultural, racial, and religious boundaries, it presents many issues unique to specific populations, and I discuss some of these in Chapter 4.

Like all contemporary social problems, domestic violence is a complicated issue with no simple answers. As I researched the material it felt many times as though I were peeling an onion, each layer revealing yet another underneath. Also like onion peeling, exposing inner layers produced tears. The terrible pain domestic violence causes women, children, and families is difficult, if not impossible, to describe. When hearing stories from the women—some 20 to 30 years after the fact—I was struck most by the residual pain still apparent in those survivors. Hearing the voices of the children of violence, some still young and some now grown, caused me to renew my own commitment to stopping this cycle of violence. The more I researched and read, the more I became convinced that education about the issue and hard preventive work with our children provide the only avenue toward eliminating this very tragic problem. I hope this book can contribute to that effort.

Acknowledgments

I would like to acknowledge the many domestic violence organizations, particularly the National Coalition Against Domestic Violence and the Oregon Coalition Against Domestic and Sexual Violence, who helped in my research on the issue. Their available resources and their referral to persons with information was invaluable. In addition, I would particularly like to thank Belle Bennett for her editing skills and her wise counsel on the issue and Dan McCue for his initial editing of the manuscript. Thanks goes to the women, children, and men who granted me interviews, especially Paula, Linda, Becki, and Millicent. Their stories gave a human face to the issue and provided me with a greater understanding of the problem. I wish to thank my life partner, Dennis, for his research help and, particularly, his incredible patience, encouragement, and support. Finally, I wish to acknowledge with love my children, John, Liz, Dan, Rob, and Laura, who have continually been an inspiration to me. Their encouragement (and, at times, their prodding) made the task easier and possible.

Domestic Violence 1

On a balmy June night in the Midwest, after Molly and Don had returned from a party with friends, Don took the babysitter home and Molly fell into bed. She was exhausted because this was her first evening out following the birth of their daughter in March. When Don returned from the babysitter's, he immediately woke Molly and started yelling at her for talking to particular men at the party, accusing her of flirting with them. His verbal abuse escalated and Molly kept trying to hush him for fear he would wake the baby as well as the other four children. Thinking of how bone tired she was, Molly kept telling Don she just wanted to get some sleep before the baby woke again needing a bottle. All of a sudden, when Molly tried to shut out his voice by putting her hands over her ears, Don grabbed her by the hair and jerked her out of bed. By this time his verbal accusations had moved from her behavior at the party to her incompetence as a wife and mother. Although Molly knew this was going to get bad, she had neither the energy nor the ability to

1

resist physically or get away. When Don started beating her with his fists, she put up her arms to protect her face and crouched on the floor, hoping it would end soon. Don grabbed her by the hair, turned her on her back and choked her while banging her head on the floor. When Molly stopped crying out for him to stop, Don stopped, got up, and went to bed, where he immediately fell asleep. Molly lay there for a long time in a semiconscious state.

Molly experienced this violent attack in the seventh year of her ten-year marriage to Don. It was one of many that occurred during their marriage and is typical of violence that is referred to as domestic violence.

What Is Domestic Violence?

Domestic violence has many names, including spouse abuse, domestic abuse, domestic assault, battering, partner abuse, marital strife, marital dispute, wife beating, marital discord, woman abuse, dysfunctional relationship, intimate fighting, mate beating, and so on. In a June 1994 speech, Secretary of Health and Human Services Donna Shalala referred to domestic violence as "terrorism in the home." In her book *Next Time She'll Be Dead* Ann Jones states that "we are stuck with a vocabulary too flimsy for the subject, a vocabulary powerful only in this one respect: its insidious subversion of our understanding." Whatever name we give to it, domestic violence is a grave and difficult problem.

A definition of domestic violence commonly accepted by legal professionals is "the emotional, physical, psychological, or sexual abuse perpetrated against a person by that person's spouse, former spouse, partner, former partner or by the other parent of a minor child. Abuse may include threats, harm, injury, harassment, control, terrorism or damage to living beings or property" (Hubbard, 1991).

Emerge, a batterer's treatment program in Boston, defines domestic violence as any act that causes the victim to do something she does not want to do, prevents her from doing something she wants to do, or causes her to be afraid.

Because between 91 and 95 percent of domestic abuse, as defined above, involves men hurting women, this book defines domestic violence as violence perpetrated by men against women with whom they have or have had an intimate relationship. Chapter 4 includes information about "husband abuse," the abuse of men by their wives or intimate partners.

"Abuse" vs. "Battering"

The literature about domestic violence many times uses "battering" and "abuse" interchangeably. Although domestic violence can be a single incident of abuse, it is more often a systematic pattern of abuse that escalates over time, in frequency and severity. Acts of domestic violence move from these isolated acts of violence to battering. Ann Jones's definition is that battering is "a process of deliberate intimidation intended to coerce the victim to do the will of the victimizer." Battering is a pattern of abuse that occurs over a period of time, anywhere from a few weeks to many years. The intent of this battering is to gain power and control over the victim.

As the frequency of violent episodes increases, they become more severe. Likewise, the longer that violence continues over months and years the more serious and dangerous it becomes. In other words, over time situations may progress from verbal abuse to punching the woman often to using weapons.

Different Types of Abuse

Domestic violence is classified into emotional, physical, and sexual abuse. Many times all three are going on in the same relationship; however, sometimes there may be one kind of abuse and not others.

Emotional Abuse

Emotional abuse always accompanies, and in most cases precedes, physical battering. Targeted, repeated emotional abuse can severely affect the victim's sense of self and reality. Basically, the process is the same as the brainwashing inflicted on prisoners of war.

> When Molly was pregnant with her fifth child, Don would work late and upon returning home would tell Molly that he had been with his 15-year-old girlfriend, who he said had a

beautiful body and was a wonderful and exciting partner in bed. This was always accompanied by Don's criticism of Molly's housekeeping and his derision of her for "letting herself go." Molly became depressed, especially when she looked at her bulky, pregnant body in the mirror, thinking "no wonder he has a girlfriend with me looking like a beached whale." As a result of the constant emotional abuse, punctuated by threats and regular, well-placed punches and slaps, Molly developed the sense that she had no option except to try to make Don happier by keeping the house cleaner and, once the baby was born, working hard to regain her figure.

A typical pattern of escalating emotional abuse might look like this. The abuser:

- Makes hostile "jokes" about the habits and faults of women.
- Makes insults about the victim.
- Ignores the victim's feelings.
- Withholds approval as a form of punishment.
- Yells at the victim.
- Labels the victim with insulting terms like "crazy," "bitch," "stupid."
- Repeatedly delivers a series of insults specific to the victim and crafted for maximum damage.
- Repeatedly humiliates the victim in front of family members and others.
- Blames the victim for all the abuser's troubles and failures.
- Puts down the victim's abilities as a mother, lover, worker.
- Demands all the victim's attention and resents the children.
- Tells the victim about his affairs.
- Tells the victim she must stay with him because she "needs" him and couldn't make it without him.
- Threatens to abuse the children and/or get custody of them.
- Threatens physical violence and retaliation against the victim.
- Accuses the victim of being violent if she acts in any way to protect herself or her children.

Sexual Abuse

Forms of sexual abuse are commonly a part of violence in the home, yet these are very difficult matters to discuss openly.

Barbara and Michael had only been married for a day when his sexual abuse of her began. He not only insisted on sex many times during the night, but accompanied this with vivid descriptions of pornographic acts. Barbara said she doesn't remember many individual incidents of abuse but said Michael was "obsessed" with pornography and continually told her that they needed to repeat the sexual act because she had not satisfied him. Barbara believed she was a "prude" about the pornography and was embarrassed to tell anyone about what was happening. She blamed herself for being "naive" and for failing in her duties as a wife. Although she had a demanding full-time career, Barbara got very few hours of sleep each night because of her attempt to be a "better" wife. After their daughter was born, Barbara mistakenly thought the sexual demands would decrease. Unfortunately, they not only continued but they got more threatening, feeling more like rape to Barbara each time. Finally, after three acts of physical abuse and almost continual emotional abuse, Barbara was able to escape with the help of a battered women's shelter. It was only later that Barbara realized that what she had experienced had been marital rape and that Michael's behavior was not normal.

Following is a typical pattern of escalating sexual abuse. The abuser:

- Jokes about women and sex in the presence of the victim.
- Looks on women as sex objects.
- Shows jealousy (may become extreme).
- Minimizes the victim's feelings and needs regarding sex.
- Criticizes the victim in sexual terms.
- Touches the victim sexually in uncomfortable ways.
- Withholds sex and affection.
- Attaches negative sexual labels to the victim such as "whore" or "frigid."
- Always demands sex.
- Forces victim to strip as a form of humiliation (may be in front of the children).

- Becomes promiscuous with others.
- Forces the victim to witness his sexual acts.
- Uses threats to back up his demands for sex.
- Forces victim to have sex with him or others.
- Forces uncomfortable sex on victim.
- Forces sex after beating the victim.
- Wants sex in order to hurt; uses objects and/or weapons.
- Engages in sadism, mutilation.
- Murders the victim.

Physical Abuse

Physical abuse may begin in a physically nonviolent way with neglect, which can include failing to meet the victim's needs for physical intimacy. When abuse crosses the line into overt violence, it may begin with relatively minor assaults such as painful pinching or squeezing. As the abuse is repeated, however, it grows more violent and often becomes targeted—that is, directed to a part of the body, such as the torso, where the injuries are less likely to show.

> When Lisa and Victor were first married while still in their teens, they would typically go to a local tavern with their friends on weekends and drink beer and dance. After three months of marriage, upon returning home from one such evening, Victor accused Lisa of having "made moves" on his friend. He slapped her face and told her never to do that again. Lisa felt bad, thinking he must have misunderstood something that had happened, and therefore excused his abuse. The abuse, however, escalated to the point where Lisa, still looking for answers, suggested they not drink alcohol anymore. Unfortunately, his accusations and accompanying abuse continued for a couple more months, until Lisa ran away after a particularly frightening incident involving a continual beating with his fists. She never returned and immediately filed for divorce. After he was served with the papers, Victor sought out Lisa, and when he found her at a friend's house playing cards with a group of people, he grabbed her by the hair and tried to drag her out of the house. Lisa's friends, who rescued her and physically escorted Victor to his car, later told her that there was a gun in the car. Lisa has no doubt that he would have used it on her if he had been successful in getting her to his car.

Following is a typical pattern of ongoing, escalating physical abuse. The abuser:

- Pinches, squeezes in a painful way.
- Pushes or shoves.
- Jerks, pulls, or shakes.
- Slaps or bites.
- Hits, punches, or kicks.
- Chokes or throws objects at the victim.
- Targets hits, kicks, and so on so that injuries do not show.
- Inflicts a sustained series of hitting or kicking blows.
- Restrains then hits, kicks, or otherwise attacks the victim.
- Abuse becomes bad enough to require some medical treatment.
- Throws the victim.
- Causes broken bones and/or internal injuries.
- Causes miscarriage or injuries that require a therapeutic abortion.
- Uses objects at hand, such as household utensils, as weapons.
- Denies the victim medical treatment.
- Uses conventional weapons, such as a gun or knife.
- Causes permanently disabling and/or disfiguring injuries.
- Murders the victim.

Typically, in all forms of violence—whether physical, sexual, or emotional—only intervention will prevent the escalation of the continuum.

All violence doesn't necessarily follow this pattern of gradual escalation of events and severity. Some violence goes from A to Z very quickly, without going through the intervening steps. If a man believes strongly in his role as the head of the family and maintains control through emotional means over his household, he feels great fear if he perceives a threat to that control, which he takes as a threat to his very manhood. This perceived threat can trigger an act of violence that is unexpected and seems to be out of the blue. He must bring the situation back to "normal," with him regaining what he sees as his rightful place at the head of the family. The violence can be directed at his wife or at the children if any of them challenge his control. In retrospect, battered women who suffer what seems to be unexpected violence can usually see what might have been warning signs if they had understood the dynamics of domestic violence.

Mandi and Louis had what seemed to be an ideal marriage. Mandi, who had two sons by a previous relationship, believed Louis was her "prince," the husband for her and the father for her sons. Mandi describes Louis as a very vibrant person, a physically beautiful man who was playful and had a great sense of humor. Every night he would come home from work and dance through the house singing "My family—my family—I love my little family." Louis sang romantic songs and taught Mandi how to cook. In the evening they always did things together as a family.

Before Louis and Mandi were married, Mandi was involved in numerous church activities. Shortly after their marriage, Louis started making plans for the whole family during times that conflicted with her church activities, saying now that she had him she didn't need anything else. Mandi eventually gave up all her friends and her church group and devoted herself to Louis and the boys. She did not, however, give up her job as a property manager, for she was doing well in her position. Her success in her career gave Mandi a great feeling of accomplishment.

The first violent episode occurred one year into their marriage, after an argument over their vacation destination. Louis pushed Mandi, who put out her hand to break her fall and broke her wrist. Although this alarmed her, Mandi didn't tell anyone but decided to work harder on their relationship. She dropped her one remaining church-related activity and focused full attention on her marriage.

Mandi recalls that Louis took increasing control over their relationship, and that she began to keep things from him that she thought might make him upset. After 18 months of marriage and a romantic weekend at the coast, Mandi and Louis returned to some problems in an apartment complex that Mandi managed. There were reports that one of the tenants, who was also a friend of Louis's, was beating his wife. Mandi reported the abuse to the police and the friend was arrested. As a result Louis gave Mandi the ultimatum to either quit her job or he would leave. She refused, so he gathered up his personal belongings and left.

The following evening Louis returned while Mandi was preparing dinner, saying they needed to talk. He stated, "I'm very, very upset—I'm talking to you now—you are my wife—my friends are all making fun of me—this is my house—my kids—now you sit down." When Mandi protested, saying they needed to wait until the boys were asleep, Louis yelled, "no—now." Mandi threatened to call the police and Louis grabbed a butcher knife and made the first and potentially one of the most lethal of 18 stab wounds to her body. Because she was very physically fit, Mandi was able to defend herself and Louis finally stopped just short of killing her. Although Mandi survived, she is not without both physical and emotional scars. She and her sons, who witnessed the attack, have spent the past three years recovering and working toward becoming whole again.

The Causes of Domestic Violence

When one looks into the cause(s) of domestic violence there are no simple answers, and as with many issues today, there are a number of opinions, depending on the respondent's perspective. This section explores the sociological, psychological, and feminist perspectives. The psychological perspective puts forth two theories from disciplines within the field, the psychodynamic theory and the social learning theory.

Although each theory comes from a particular philosophical perspective and discipline, each one has points that are similar to or consistent with those of other theories. Most domestic violence professionals are not purists who subscribe to only one theory, but have found that each theory has provided insight in their work with battered women, children, and batterers. A solid grounding in all of the theories aids in an understanding of the dynamics of domestic violence, its causes, and society's reaction to the issue.

The Sociological Perspective

Sociologists believe domestic violence must be viewed from a group behavior approach; therefore, a society's cultural norms are analyzed to determine the attitudes prevalent in the subcultures studied.

One sociocultural belief is that cultures that approve of the use of violence have the highest rate of domestic violence. Because we in the United States have accepted spanking as an appropriate method of child discipline and violence is portrayed on television and in our daily lives, our culture is seen as encouraging abuse.

This sociocultural perspective views violent behavior as a result of conditions that inhibit the biological, psychological, and social needs of human beings. For example, if a person is frustrated at work and feels it is unwise to react to frustration with anger in the workplace for fear of losing his or her job, it has been accepted practice to express these feelings of frustration in the home.

David Gil, professor of social policy at Brandeis University and a proponent of this theory, proposes that violence may be overcome by making a social-structural change in our society. His proposals are sweeping and include several amendments to the Constitution, some involving a universal right to work, equal rights for women, and several pieces of legislation on work sharing, public work, universal health maintenance, comprehensive education, and tax reform.

Systems Theory

Family systems theory is a psychosocial theory that focuses on the process of interactions within the family. Violence, according to the systems theory, is a product of the family system and is based on the premise that in each family there are established rules of behavior for each individual member, that each member's boundaries are defined, and the patterns of interaction have been dominant over time.

Therefore, according to this theory, if one family member challenges the established goals of that family's system, a corrective action by another family member occurs. This corrective action is taken to establish that member's own power position and is done through an increase in violent behavior. For example, when the man of the house perceives his wife as assuming too much independence in their relationship, he beats her as a means of restoring her to her position within the family system. Violence is a way for the husband to cope with tension, resolve conflict within the system, and restore the family system's equilibrium.

A couple who are locked into a systemic relationship in which they reinforce the use of violence as a "resolution" of conflict are caught up in the rules of the relationship rather than the resolution of the problem. According to family systems theorists, once established this pattern is very resistant to change.

Russell P. Dobash and Rebecca Emerson Dobash are sociological researchers and activists who have conducted numerous studies on domestic violence since 1974 and are considered foremost authorities on the issue of wife beating. They state in their book, *Violence against Wives*, "The promise of general systems theory is, according to its proponents, that it can be applied to any type of systems, human, mechanical, or biological. . . . This model is so abstract and generalized as to be of little use in the analysis of any particular type of violence between family members, even excluding the usual sociological accounts of differential roles and activities of husbands and wives."

Family systems theorists believe that an analysis of wife battering that focuses on family processes does not imply that the system processes alone are responsible for the violence. However, they believe that if we understand violence from the systems theory approach, it is possible to get an overall perspective on the pattern of violence within the family and how it became ingrained in the family system.

The Psychological Perspective

Psychological theories of domestic violence range from the psychodynamic approach, which views domestic violence as a pathological problem, to social learning theory, which focuses on learned behavior of individuals.

Psychodynamic Theory

The psychodynamic perspective suggests that there is a mental illness present in either the abuser or the abused and therapy is geared toward changing the underlying disorder.

An early Freudian theory advanced by Dr. Helene Deutsch in the 1930s describes women in abusive relationships as primarily masochistic. The masochistic woman provokes men into abusing her, thus fulfilling her need to be hurt.

In his book *Human Aggression*, Anthony Storr sees men as naturally viewing sexual intercourse as an act of aggression whose self-esteem is tied into the concept of conquest. A wife's rejection of sex may therefore result in violence from a husband who is insecure about his masculinity.

Descriptive studies emphasizing the psychopathological roots of battering trace male violence to a vulnerable self-concept (or low self-esteem); a complex mix of helplessness, powerlessness, or inadequacy; fear of being dependent; traditional attitudes regarding male dominance, particularly about sex; pathological jealousy; fear of abandonment, alternating with a desire for control over women and children; an inability to communicate feelings or to identify feelings in others (empathy); and a lack of assertiveness (Saunders, 1993).

Sociological critics of the psychodynamic theory of domestic violence say that seeking causes and sources of violence through pathological individuals or deviant relationships ignores the fact that violence is endemic to Western society.

Pathologies of the Abuser

Specific pathologies that psychiatrists or psychologists might view as the underlying cause of domestic violence include personality disorders in the abuser (or profiles that tend toward such disorders) such as:

- Asocial/borderline, in which there is instability in a variety of areas, including interpersonal behavior, mood, and self-image, combined with selfishness.
- Narcissistic/antisocial, in which there is a grandiose sense of self-importance and fragile self-esteem with intense feelings of rage or humiliation in response to criticism, combined with a disregard for rules, irritability, and aggressiveness.
- Dependent/compulsive, in which there is an inability to assume responsibility, a lack of self-confidence, and an inability to function independently combined with a need for perfection and to be dominant in relationships, insisting that people conform to his way of doing things.

These men would show clinical elevations on standardized tests such as the Minnesota Multiphasic Personality Inventory (MMPI). MMPI profiles characterize the average abuser as alienated, isolated, insecure, distrustful of others, and overly concerned about their masculine image (Bernard & Bernard, 1984).

Social Learning Theory

The social learning theory focuses on actual behavior rather than individual pathologies. According to the social learning theory, violence is learned aggressive behavior that is perpetuated by the reinforcement in our society of aggressive, "macho" behavior in men. One premise of social learning theory is that those actions that are rewarded are maintained, while those that are not decrease in frequency. Based on their clinical experience with violent men, Sonkin and Durphy note that one reason that men batter is because it works: it gets them what they want. The social learning theory maintains that an abusive man saw abuse "successfully" used by a male authority figure in childhood and as a result learned behaviors that led to his use of abuse in relationships as an adult.

The Feminist Perspective

Feminists define domestic violence as wife abuse, with the term "wife" broadened to mean a woman functioning in that capacity in an intimate relationship. According to the feminist perspective, wife abuse can be understood only if one understands that our society is one traditionally structured along the lines of gender, with men as a class wielding power over women. As the dominant class, men have had access to material and symbolic resources, while women have been devalued as secondary and inferior.

Domestic violence is rooted in the traditional belief that the husband dominates with implied power. Our social structure sets forth a pattern in the family in which the husband is in charge and both parents rule the children. According to feminists, the institutions of marriage and family encourage abusive men to use physical force to control or gain power over their wives or intimate partners. Men feel entitled to this position of authority and their position is reinforced by religious teachings and our social and legal systems.

R. E. Dobash and R. P. Dobash found in research for their book *Violence against Wives* that patriarchy contributes to wife abuse and that patriarchy is fostered in our economic and social system. Our social system has defined the husband as the dominant, strong, authoritarian, aggressive, and rational provider for the family, while the wife has traditionally been assigned to a dependent, passive, submissive, soft, and—at times—hysterical role. Our society has flourished under this model by dividing the labor force in half, encouraging women to remain at home and care for their husbands and children while husbands leave the home to provide a living for their families (Dobash, 1979).

Feminists say that early sex-role socialization conditions girls to become submissive victims while boys are socialized to become perpetrators of violence. In the preschool setting during free play, one can observe the strong sex-role identification when "playing house"—usually the "mother" is serving the "father" coffee while he makes demands of both the wife and child before going off to work. This early process sets the stage for the male figure to dominate the passive female figure.

Men have had unrealistic sex-role expectations and perceptions of their dominance through the family structure, and thus the abuser accepts the right to be abusive within the sanctity of his home. Supporters of feminist theory, citing these sex-role expectations and belief in male dominance, believe that violence is a systemic issue and any change requires a restructuring of the family unit and associated sex roles. Establishing equality will empower and enhance each member of the family unit, strengthening it and allowing honest communication. Feminists believe that as long as women are not equal in every way, domestic violence will be a problem in our society.

Within the movement, feminists have disagreed on whether the problem of domestic violence should be addressed by helping individual women who are battered or by putting energy into changing the pervasive social attitudes that allow such abuse to take place.

Although there are distinct differences between these perspectives and theories, there are some elements in most of them with which professionals from other perspectives are able to agree. While social learning theory is inconsistent with views of psychiatrists who emphasize the pathological or deviant aspects of violent families, social learning theory regarding the reasons why men abuse is partially consistent with feminist theory regarding the learned behavior of batterers. Feminists do not agree with those social learning theorists who, from a psychological perspective, hold that women learn their victim behavior either through victimization as children or by witnessing their mothers' beatings. Sociologists and feminists agree that social structure is the prime cause of domestic violence, but feminists strongly disagree with sociologists who espouse the family systems theory, believing that this is a form of victim blaming and that battered women become caught in a pattern of behavior with their abusive partners in order to survive. Feminists believe that battered women are not responsible for their battering, that men choose to batter because they have been socialized to believe they are entitled to superior rights and that society's institutions have traditionally supported men's sense of entitlement.

Domestic Violence: A History

Today's battered women's movement began in 1971 in an English town with 500 women and children marching to protest a reduction in free milk for schoolchildren. This protest led to the establishment of the Chiswick Women's Aid, a community meeting place where women could meet and discuss problems and concerns. Some women talked about abuse they were suffering in their homes and, under the leadership of Erin Pizzey, Chiswick's Women's Aid soon became known as the Battered Wives' Center. A refuge for battered women and their children was established and replicated around Britain. In 1974, Erin Pizzey's book about wife battering, *Scream Quietly or the Neighbors Will Hear*, drew media attention to the centers. The shelter movement was launched.

U.S. feminists interested in the issue of battered wives traveled to Britain, where they studied the structure of the women's refuges. They brought the ideas and basic plan back, and replicated them in a few places in the United States. Since that time the battered women's movement has grown and moved from grassroots to government-funded programs.

The women's movement brought the concerns of battered wives to the attention of the public in the 1970s, but wife beating has existed throughout the history of Western society. Women were considered subject to their husbands' rule, totally dependent upon them, with no rights as individuals. Beating them was legal, especially if they committed some offense against the husband's authority. A woman was subject to her father's rule until marriage, when she was "given" by her father to her husband. Once married she was under her husband's authority. If she left her husband for any reason, she had no property and lost her children. The subjugation of women was established by the institutional practices of the church and state and was supported by the philosophers, religious leaders, politicians, and writers of the Western world, such as Rousseau, Hegel, Kant, Fichte, Blackstone, Saint Augustine, John Knox, Calvin, and Martin Luther (Dobash and Dobash, 1979).

Prior to the twentieth century, the subjugation of women and the right of husbands to physically chastise their wives were rooted in a long patriarchal tradition. There were only sporadic attempts to alleviate the problem until the mid-nineteenth century, when the problem of battered wives became an issue of the women's rights movements in the United States and Britain. Although laws that provided some relief were passed, very little change occurred. By the twentieth century concern over the individual's right to privacy and the sanctity of the home became a barrier to intervention in the case of wife abuse. Only the strong political force of the modern-day women's movement has publicized the issue and begun to effect change.

Society's Response to Domestic Violence

The Feminist Response

Feminists are responsible for making domestic violence a public issue, for initiating the shelter movement, and for advocating laws to protect victims of violence and make batterers accountable for their behavior.

Domestic violence became an issue of the women's movement in the early 1970s, shortly after rape crisis centers were established. It had become apparent to many activist feminists that women were not only unsafe on the street, but many lived in 24-hour fear in their own homes. A group of feminists traveled to Britain to study the battered women's movement and shelters started by Erin Pizzey. When they returned they began a grassroots movement that would address a woman's right to be safe in her own home.

The first U.S. shelter was established in 1974. Shelters now number between 1,500 and 2,000 and continue to be the heart and soul of the battered women's movement. Feminists have been instrumental in promoting education of the public about the issue of domestic violence, sponsoring many media campaigns, including specialized training of professionals in education, mental health, social services, public and private health care, child development, and law enforcement. Feminists have been particularly effective in reaching politicians, an effort that most recently produced the Violence Against Women Act, which was signed into law as part of the 1994 Crime Bill. They have developed programs to train law enforcement about domestic violence so officers could respond knowledgeably to domestic violence calls, arrest perpetrators, and protect the women. Feminists have advocated training prosecutors and the judiciary about domestic violence and have served as legal advocates for battered women since the beginning of the movement.

Response by the Men's Movement

Some domestic violence coalitions have recently reported the presence of men's groups protesting at public meetings that focus on the issue of battered women. They have been particularly vocal about demanding equal funding for shelters and programs for "battered husbands." At this time only one U.S. shelter for battered men exists—in St. Paul, Minnesota—but very few men have used the facility. Advocates for abused men claim that men are afraid to tell because they feel they have an image to live up to and will be laughed at if they reveal abuse by their wives. Proponents of men's shelters are making an attempt to create public interest in the issue, saying that men won't go public with the problem as long as they feel they won't be believed.

According to some battered women's advocates, treatment programs for men, supported by men's groups, in some ways justify the abuse and provide excuses for the abuser. Many of these same programs also provide treatment for "battered husbands," which battered women's advocates say further alienates the battered women's movement.

The Psychological Community's Response

The psychological community has conducted numerous research studies on the issue of domestic violence to determine which men abuse and which women are abused. Their commitment to this effort has drawn criticism from some battered women's advocates, who believe that too many studies are made of the victims and not enough focus is placed on a social system that allows violence against women to persist. Advocates say the focus is too much on the victim and that this results in victim blaming, such as the psychodynamic theory, extended only a few decades ago, that abused women are masochists who provoke their abuse.

The value of psychological studies, however, is that they provide a detailed profile of the abuser (which generally supports both feminist and sociological perspectives on domestic violence), as well as important information regarding necessary components of batterer treatment programs and prevention programs for children. Additionally, information gained from research on the effects of battering on women has provided valuable information for attorneys providing legal defense to women who assault and sometimes kill their batterers in self-defense.

Sociologists' Response

Sociologists have completed numerous studies that have quantified the problem of domestic violence in our society, produced data regarding institutions within the society that contribute to the problem of domestic violence, and proposed needed changes within the society to positively affect the problem. Some have declared that only radical political change of our societal structure to eliminate hierarchical structure on all levels will be effective. Some have advocated change that occurs from the bottom up, in the form of education for children and adults through targeted educational programs and the mass media.

Some sociologists believe that because the problem of domestic violence has its roots in a society that is not only hierarchical in structure but that also advocates violence as a means of resolving conflict, these structures need to change in order to eliminate domestic violence. Although they applaud the efforts of the battered women's movement and their advocacy of women, many sociologists do not believe that working with relatively few women is enough. Larry Tifft, author of the 1993 book *Battering of Women: The Failure of Intervention and the Case for Prevention*, advocates prevention and education as the only way to effect positive change. He divides prevention into three types and proposes the many levels on which these prevention efforts must occur. He believes change can only occur if it is based on the premise that domestic violence mirrors our hierarchical social system and is supported by that system, which therefore allows it to perpetuate and flourish (Tifft, 1993).

The three types of prevention discussed by Tifft are primary, secondary, and tertiary. Primary prevention involves changing public attitudes about violence and includes:

- Awareness and education programs such as public education (media, public relations campaigns, and so on) directed at the general public.

- Education directed toward professional groups in disciplines such as law enforcement, legal and judicial, education, social services, mental health, medicine, ministerial, and so on.
- Education programs for adolescents, teenage mothers, and other parents. Programs for men's and women's groups.
- Education programs for preschool and elementary school–age children.
- Advocacy and political action programs directed at changing laws regarding domestic violence, issues of gender equity, and human rights.

Programs for individual women survivors of abuse to intervene and prevent their re-abuse are considered secondary prevention. Secondary education would also include counseling and group prevention programs for children at risk.

Tertiary prevention is the response to violence after it happens—helping the victims heal and dealing with abusers. Transition programs for victims as well as arrest, conviction, and diversion to treatment programs for abusers are some examples. Prevention programs for victims and abusers that focus on the individual can lead to changes in that individual and his or her environment. A positive change in that individual might have a *primary* preventive effect on his or her children. For example, if a battered woman becomes strengthened in her ability to provide for herself and her children without staying in an abusive environment, the children will no longer be exposed to violence in the home and violence as a way to resolve conflict will no longer be modeled there, and that child may learn new ways to resolve conflict.

Prevention and education need to take a prominent place among efforts to stop violence against women. The greatest impediment to the prevention of domestic violence has been the curtain of silence surrounding the issue. Domestic violence professionals and feminist organizations have attempted to bring the issue into the open, and though there has been much more media attention to the problem in the 1990s, particularly recently, education needs to continue on many levels—in the media, governmental agencies and organizations, schools, criminal justice institutions, churches, corporations, women's and men's groups, and so on.

The Media and Domestic Violence

Feminists, psychologists, and sociologists agree that the popular media in the United States perpetuates attitudes that foster domestic violence. Newspapers, magazines, television, radio, and movies—through their depiction of women, families, sex, and violence—appear to promote attitudes that support men's violence against women and relationships in which women are subservient to men.

This is not a new phenomenon. Throughout its existence, the movie industry has produced movies that both condone and glamorize violence against women. In 1931 James Cagney screwed half a grapefruit into Mae Clarke's face in the movie *Public Enemy,* a film that brought him instant stardom. Many movies of the 1940s portrayed women who seemed to enjoy domination by men. Take, for example, the line spoken by Katharine Hepburn, "I'd give anything for one good smack on the south end," from the 1948 film *State of the Union,* a reference to her yearning for the return of her husband's love. Or "if he beats you, it's because he loves you," Yvonne De Carlo says to her future stepmother in *Frontier Gal.* Clark Gable tells Greer Garson "a good crack in the jaw would do you good" in the 1948 film *Adventure,* to which she replies, "If it would, I'd love it." Some actors have publicly endorsed hitting women by making public statements such as this one made in a 1970s interview by Telly Savalas, who became a sex symbol in the television series *Kojak:* "I adore women. I am their total slave up to a certain point. I pamper them, cater to them, but when necessary, you have to bop 'em."

The depiction of women in advertising is a striking example of women portrayed as sex objects who deserve to be abused. In the late 1980s there were many fashion ads that featured women who were abused, bound and gagged, or in body bags. Some department store windows featured battered women and women stuffed into trash cans as the conquests of leather-clad men. Mainstream magazine fashion layouts featured women pulled along by corset ties, the neck in choke collars; trussed and restrained in straightjackets and straps; blindfolded and sometimes stuffed in garbage bags. One Esprit ad depicted a woman on an ironing board with a man about to iron her crotch; a Foxy Lady ad showed a woman who had been knocked to the floor and her shirt ripped open; a Michael Mann ad pictured a woman in a coffin (Faludi, 1991).

Guess ran jeans ads in the late 1980s that pictured women in bodysuits cowering under a sneering male figure. In Guess's "Louisiana Campaign," the first photo in the ad pictures a young girl hiding behind a tree and spying on a couple, the second shows the man grabbing the woman's jaw and twisting it, and the third shows an anguished young woman with her face in her hands and her clothes in tatters. Fashion photographer Wayne Maser, who shot Guess's fashion ads, said, "My work is a reaction against feminist blandness . . . women can be women again. All my girls have a choice" (Faludi, 1991).

A recent *Big Brother* magazine featured an ad for "bitch skateboards" that depicts a sign headed by the word "bitch" under which a man is pictured pointing a gun to a woman's head. In an ad for Old Spice that appeared in *Sports Illustrated* and *Outdoor Life* a tall man has a small woman pinned against a brick wall and she has her hand against his chest but is shown laughing. The large one-word heading is "No" *(Ms. Magazine)*.

Many beer ads combine images of women, sex, drinking, and violence. They imply that all of these go together, that they are all pleasurable experiences. Perfume ads have also been filled with images that imply the forcible conquest of women by men. The women depicted usually look no older than thirteen and the message is usually heavily laden with sexual overtones. This image of women being overpowered by men is pervasive in much of today's advertising.

Some song lyrics, particularly those of some heavy metal songs, also combine women, sex, and violence. In a song by heavy metal group Sarcofago, the singer laments to Tracy that she hurt him and broke his heart, that he didn't want to do it, that her dead body is so sweet it is causing him to sexually desire her. He performs sexual acts upon her cold and rotting flesh and concludes by asking her why she forced him to kill. Ted Nugent sings a song entitled "Violent Love" in which he takes "her" in a room with mirrors where he shows her his brand new whip; she screams and asks him to give her a dose of his violent love. On their 1987 album *Girls, Girls, Girls*, which reached #2 on the Billboard pop charts, Motley Crue sing a song about how the the blade of his knife turned and sliced his girl apart, but that killing her helped keep her at home (Medzian, 1991).

Many times rap lyrics encourage violent behavior and center on the subjugation of women. One by the late rapper Eazy-E says he creeped on his bitch with his Uzi, went to the house, kicked down the door, and unloaded like hell. NWA, another rap group, has released a number of songs that include violent sex, gang rape, and femicide, including "To Kill a Hooker" and "One Less Bitch" (Jones, 1994).

These songs are played on many radio stations. Even songs that don't have lyrics of obvious sadism many times have videos that depict scantily clad women in suggestive and submissive positions who are usually conquered against their will by angry-looking young men.

There are also many video games that depict violence. There are some games whose goal is to capture a woman and abuse her, at least one whose goal is rape, and some whose goal is murder. Since young boys are the most frequent users of these games, psychologists, parents, and child development specialists have expressed grave concern over the amount of sexism and violence depicted.

Some media reporters also tend to employ terms used to describe romantic love when referring to the violence that occurs in intimate relationships. In reporting a story about a batterer who shot and killed his ex-girlfriend after months of stalking her and then traveled 80 miles and killed his former wife, the television newscaster called it the tragic result of a "love triangle." Further reporting revealed there was no connection between the former wife and former girlfriend other than their relationship to the murderer. The man had battered both, which is why they had left him.

An article in a 1989 issue of the *Baltimore Sun* tells the story of a man who took his wife out of a bar, then punched, raped, and strangled her. The reporter attributed the murderer's motive to a "fit of jealous rage" and said the man had "collected" his wife from the bar and "made love" to her before strangling her. The murderer excused his action by saying his wife had told him that their youngest child was not his. When a New York police officer dragged his girlfriend into the street outside of police headquarters and shot and killed her, then killed himself, the *New York Post* ran a banner headline on the front page that read "Tragedy of a Lovesick Cop" (Jones, 1994).

Not only do the journalistic media, advertising, and entertainment industries have a profound effect on how we interpret violence against women, they also shape the public's attitudes using techniques specifically designed to persuade and influence. Probably the most enduring effect is upon the attitudes of children. According to Micheal Medved in his book *Hollywood vs. America*, more than 3,000 research projects and studies have found a connection between a steady diet of violent entertainment and aggressive and antisocial behavior. Because children watch TV an average of 28 hours a week and are the primary fans of rap and heavy metal music, they probably receive the most damage at a time when they are developing their values. What they hear and see only reinforces what many of them have learned in their homes about the acceptability of domestic violence.

References

Adams, David. "Identifying the Assaultive Husband in Court: You Be the Judge." *Response* 13, no. 1 (1990).

Browne, Angela. *When Battered Women Kill.* New York: The Free Press, 1987.

Brygger, M. P., and J. Edelson. "Gender Differences in Reporting of Battering Incidents." Paper presented at the Second National Conference for Family Violence Researchers, University of New Hampshire, Durham, 1984.

Carlson, B. E. "Children's Observations of Interpersonal Violence," in A. R. Roberts, ed., *Battered Women and Their Families: Intervention Strategies and Treatment Programs* (New York: Springer, 1984).

Conkle, Luann K., and M. K. Randolph. "Behavioral and Emotional Characteristics of Children Who Witness Parental Violence." *Family Violence and Sexual Assault Bulletin* 9, no. 2 (1993).

Dobash, R. Emerson, and Russell P. Dobash. *Violence against Wives.* New York: The Free Press, 1979.

Faludi, Susan. *Backlash: The Undeclared War against American Women.* New York: Doubleday, 1991.

Faulk, M. "Men Who Assault Their Wives," in M. Roy, ed., *Battered Wives* (New York: Van Nostrand Reinhold, 1977).

Hotaling, G. T., and D. B. Sugarman. "An Analysis of Risk Markers in Husband to Wife Violence: The Current State of Knowledge." *Violence and Victims* 1, no. 2 (1986).

Hubbard, Laurie. *From Harassment to Homicide: A Report on the Response to Domestic Violence in Multnomah County.* Portland, OR: Bureau of Community Development, 1991.

Jones, Ann. *Next Time She'll Be Dead: Battering and How To Stop It.* Boston: Beacon Press, 1994.

Miedzian, Myriam. *Boys Will Be Boys: Breaking the Link between Masculinity and Violence.* New York: Doubleday, 1991.

Schechter, Susan. *Women and Male Violence: The Visions and Struggles of the Battered Women's Movement.* Boston: South End Press, 1982.

Stark, E., and A. Flitcraft. "Woman-Battering, Child Abuse and Social Heredity: What Is the Relationship?" in N. Johnson, ed., *Marital Violence, Sociological Review.* Monograph no. 31 (London: Routledge & Kegan Paul, 1985).

Steinmetz, S., and M. Straus. *Violence in the Family.* New York: Harper and Row, 1974.

Tifft, Larry L. *Battering of Women: The Failure of Intervention and the Case for Prevention.* Boulder, Colo.: Westview Press, 1993.

Walker, Lenore E. *The Battered Woman.* New York: HarperCollins, 1979.

———. *The Battered Woman Syndrome.* New York: Springer, 1984.

———. *Terrifying Love: Why Battered Women Kill and How Society Responds.* New York: HarperCollins, 1990.

Chronology 2

The purpose of this chronicle of events, laws, and legislation is to provide a historical context within which domestic violence can be understood, to provide an understanding of the impact of particular events on the issue, and to gain an understanding of the cause and effect between events and responses to domestic violence. The history of Western civilization provides the foundation upon which our institutions are built. Our laws are based on the common law of England. I have therefore included important events, laws, and legislation in the Western world that reflect that history.

| Around 753 B.C.E. | Romulus, the founder of Rome, formalizes the first known "law of marriage." It requires married women to have "no other refuge, to conform themselves entirely to the temper of their husbands and the husbands to rule their wives as necessary and inseparable possessions" (Browne, 1987). The law of marriage reflects the double standard that seems directed at protecting the rights and |

Around 753 B.C.E. (*cont.*)	authority of men and controlling and oppressing women. The most frequently mentioned offense for which punishment of women is severe is adultery or suspected infidelity, not so much because of lost love but because of loss of control over the man's property, his wife.
200 B.C.E.	After the end of the Punic Wars a rise in a class of wealthy women is seen. Because the wars have lasted a long time, and men have been absent for a protracted period, women have assumed many of men's traditional roles, including the pursuit of politics, philosophy, attendance at military maneuvers, and joining new religious movements. Although chastisement of wives is still possible, it is done in a somewhat mediated form. A man is not allowed to beat his wife unless he has suffered a grievance sufficient for divorce. If a man is convicted of striking his wife without sufficient reason, he must give her monetary compensation.
300 C.E.	By the fourth century, excessive violence by either spouse constitutes sufficient grounds for divorce; however, a woman must prove her charge if that violence is a beating. A woman does not have to remain her husband's property in spite of his behavior, but his behavior must be terrible before she is allowed to leave.
1400s	During the "age of chivalry," *Knight of La Tour Landry* describes the correct conduct of a "chivalrous" French knight toward a "scolding" wife: "He smote her with his fist down to the earth, and then with his fist he struck her in the visage and broke her nose, and all her life after she had her nose crooked that she might not for shame show her visage it was so foul blemished. . . . Therefore the wife ought to suffer and let the husband have the work, and be the master" (Dobash and Dobash, 1979). In his *Rules of Marriage* Friar Cherubino of Siena recommends: "When you see your wife commit

an offense, don't rush at her with insults and violent blows. . . . Scold her sharply, bully and terrify her. And if this still doesn't work . . . take up a stick and beat her soundly, for it is better to punish the body and correct the soul than to damage the soul and spare the body . . . Then readily beat her, not in rage but out of charity and concern for her soul, so that the beating will resound to your merit and her good" (Browne, 1987).

1531   In Europe, Martin Luther refers to a woman's place in one of his writings: "Men have broad shoulders and narrow hips, and accordingly they possess intelligence. Women have narrow shoulders and broad hips. Women ought to stay at home, the way they were created indicates this, for they have broad hips and a fundament to sit upon, keep house and bear and raise children" (Dobash and Dobash, 1979).

1609   King James I of England states, "Kings are compared to fathers in families." Obedience to Kings is stated in terms of "Honor thy Father" and in France it is declared that "one makes Kings on the model of fathers" (Dobash and Dobash, 1979).

1641   In Massachusetts, the *Body of Liberties* is established by the Puritans. It contains the provision that "Everie marryed woeman shall be free from bodilie correction or stripes by her husband, unlesse it be in his owne defence upon her assault." This is the first American reform against family violence. Although most of the criminal laws are adapted from biblical law or from English custom, this law is not, and its origins are unclear.

Although divorce in the Puritan society is possible, physical cruelty alone is not considered enough reason; it must be accompanied by adultery and neglect of the family. A woman who asks for divorce has to show that she has been a dutiful wife who has not provoked her husband into

1641 (*cont.*)   hitting her. So, although wife beating is not generally approved of in the Puritan society, there does not seem to be any way out of the situation.

1740   In the American colonies, a concerted effort is initiated to protect people from public crime, violence that originates outside of the family. At the same time concerns about "private" moral crime, such as wife and child beating, recede into the background.

1760s   In England, *Commentaries on the Laws of England* by William Blackstone is published and becomes widely used by the legal system. Blackstone states that a crime is an act that produces mischief in civil society, while private vices lay outside the legitimate domain of law. Disharmony in the home is no longer seen as a major problem in society. In elaborating on "private" violence, Blackstone states: "For as [the husband] is to answer for her misbehavior, the law thought it reasonable to intrust him with this power of chastisement, in the same moderation that a man is allowed to correct his apprentices or children. . . ."

Further, Blackstone comments on murder of one's spouse as follows:

> Husband and wife, in the language of the law, are styled baron and feme. . . . If the baron kills his feme it is the same as if he had killed a stranger, or any other person; but if the feme kills her baron, it is regarded by the laws as a much more atrocious crime, as she not only breaks through the restraints of humanity and conjugal affection, but throws off as subjection to the authority of her husband. And therefore the law denominates her crime a species of treason, and condemns her to the same punishment as if she had killed the king. And for every species of treason . . . the sentence of woman was to be drawn and burnt alive (Browne, 1987).

Early 1800s   The temperance reform movement begins in the United States. Reformers believe there is a connection between alcoholism and wife beating, but largely ignore the effect of a man's alcoholism on his family until, in a temperance speech delivered in 1813, the image of the "trembling family" emerges as a metaphor. By 1830 the image of the suffering wife doomed to a hopeless life of misery becomes associated with the temperance movement. In 1835 the *Pennsylvania–New Jersey Almanac* prints the first drawings of family violence in the United States: drunken husbands lifting a chair or tongs to bludgeon a wife and children. By the 1840s temperance reformers regularly speak out against wife beating, as they believe it is a violation of domestic ideals and destructive of feminine virtue. Because the family is a private place, shielded from the public eye, the public is unaware of the extent of the problem. In order to appeal to public sympathy, the wife is portrayed as the anguished wife and the drunk husband as the "brute." Because it is believed that alcohol causes men to become brutes and that the family is the obvious victim of their brutishness, the temperance movement becomes a natural place for women's involvement.

1824   The Supreme Court of Mississippi upholds a husband's right to chastise his wife. The court rules that a husband should be allowed to chastise without being subject to vexatious prosecution, which would supposedly shame all parties.

1848   A new political activism within the temperance movement occurs at the same time as the growth of new ideas on the rights of women. At a convention on women's rights that meets in Seneca Falls, a Declaration of Human Sentiments identifies a series of women's grievances against "male tyranny." One of these grievances states that man "has so framed the laws of divorce, as to what shall be the proper causes, and in case of

1848 (*cont.*) separation, to whom the guardianship of the children shall be given, as to be wholly regardless of the happiness of women—the law, in all cases, going upon the false supposition of the supremacy of man, and giving all power into his hands" (Pleck, 1987).

1849 *Lily*, the first temperance journal to be edited by a woman, Amelia Bloomer, is established. Many articles on women's rights appear, as well as letters demanding divorce for the alcoholic's wife. By 1850, 19 states grant divorce for cruelty, though it is easier to obtain a divorce on grounds of drunkenness. Many judges do not recognize cruelty as grounds for divorce unless the wife is submissive, pure, and protective of the children.

1852 Susan B. Anthony attends a state temperance meeting and is drowned out by boos when she speaks out against the exclusion of women from politics. She and a few other women decide to organize a new women's temperance society. At the first convention in mid-1852, Elizabeth Cady Stanton is elected the first president of the New York State Woman's Temperance Society. Stanton, who has opened her home as a refuge for battered women neighbors, has strong beliefs about violence against women. Stanton addresses the 1852 convention and attempts to gather support for a divorce bill that is before the New York Senate. She resolves:

> Let no woman remain in the relation of wife with the confirmed drunkard. Let no drunkard be the father of her children. Let no woman form an alliance with any man who has been suspected even of the vice of intemperance; for the taste once acquired can never, never be eradicated. Be not misled by any pledges, resolves, promises, prayers, or tears. You cannot rely on the word of a man who is, or has been, the victim of such an overpowering appetite.

Let us petition our State governments so as to modify the laws affecting marriage, and the custody of children, that the drunkard shall have no claims on either wife or child" (Pleck, 1987).

Amelia Bloomer also speaks, stating that no wife should have to be the recipient of a drunken husband's "blows and curses, and submit to his brutish passions and lusts."

This convention is the first time that women publicly denounce marital rape. The convention holds that women deserve the right to life and happiness the same as any man.

London magistrate Thomas Phinn publishes statistics on the number of assaults by men against women and children in London, revealing that one in six assaults occurs within the family. As a result of his findings he advocates public flogging of abusers. Although Phinn's suggestion is not acted upon, it spawns legislation to prevent abuse of women, titled the Act for the Better Prevention of Aggravated Assaults Upon Women and Children, or the "Good Wives' Rod." This legislation punishes aggravated assault on women and children under fourteen with up to six months in prison, a fine, and an order to keep the peace for six months. The legislation passes for two reasons. First, Parliament has already passed a number of anti-cruelty to animal laws and is compelled to extend the same protection to women and children that they do to animals. Additionally, they are concerned with rising public crime and believe that punishing wife beating will help reduce other crime. They associate both criminal behavior and drunken assault on wives with the lower class, which has grown in numbers due to increased industrialization, and fear of the power of the lower class provides a greater impetus than concern for women and children.

1856   The term "wife beating" is first used in England during a campaign for divorce reform. During this

1856 (*cont.*)   same period, public shaming is an important part of English community life and used as a way of emphasizing community standards. Various forms of mockery such as "charivari," a raucous serenade using cow's horns, pots, pans, and other outlandish instruments, is performed by villagers in front of an offender's home. Although this is sometimes directed at men who beat their wives, it is more often directed at couples who deviate from the community's norms. The practice continues until at least 1862.

1857   The Society for the Protection of Women and Children, providing legal advice to victims of battering, is established in England by women's rights activists taking advantage of recently passed legislation, the Matrimonial Causes Act of 1857. They also establish the first shelter for victims of assault, set up a court for divorce, and monitor court cases involving women and child victims.

1855–1860   In the United States, Stanton and Anthony continue to work for women's rights within the temperance movement, focusing their efforts on a married woman's right to own and control property. They try to stay clear of the argument for a woman's right to divorce and remarry because it is too controversial at the time. The issue of divorce remains alive, however, and in 1855 and 1856 some New York state legislators introduce new divorce reform bills. One asks that divorce be granted on grounds of desertion, cruelty, and drunkenness. Horace Greeley, the editor of the *New York Tribune* and a proponent of women's rights, opposes the pending legislation in a biting editorial. He opposes divorce on religious grounds because of his belief that a two-parent home is the best place to raise children. However, in the case of a good wife who is the victim of a drunken and brutish husband, he approves of legal separation with custody of the children going to the wife and a provision that gives her the right to her earnings. The bill loses by only four votes in spite of Greeley's opposition, which is a much closer vote than anyone expected.

1860   Susan Anthony finds secret lodgings for the sister of a U.S. senator, who has kidnapped her daughter and fled from her abusive husband, a Massachusetts legislator. The desperate plight of this woman motivates Elizabeth Cady Stanton to introduce ten resolutions at the 1860 convention in support of a new divorce bill to go to the New York legislature. Although most people consider her stance too radical, Stanton continues to lobby for divorce reform. The onset of the Civil War in 1861 effectively kills interest in the issue.

1864   A North Carolina court declares that even though a husband has choked his wife, "the law permits him to use such a degree of force as necessary to control an unruly temper and make her behave herself; and unless some permanent injury be inflicted, or there be an excess of violence, or such a degree of cruelty as shows that it is inflicted to gratify his own bad passions, the law will not invade the domestic forum, or go behind the curtain. It prefers to leave the parties to themselves, as the best mode of inducing them to make the matter up and live together as man and wife should" (Browne, 1987).

1866   A North Carolina court rules that the actions a husband can legally take against his wife are amended, giving a man the right to beat his wife "with a stick as large as his finger but not larger than his thumb." This law is said to have been created "as an example of compassionate reform."

1869   In England, John Stuart Mill pleads in the House of Commons for women's rights to equality under the law and publishes "The Subjection of Women," an indictment of legal equality and justice for women. He states that the power over women "is

1869 (*cont.*)   a power given, or offered, not to good men, or to decently respectable men, but to all men; the most brutal and the most criminal. . . . The law of servitude in marriage is a monstrous contradiction to all the principles of the modern world. . . . There remain no legal slaves except the mistress of every house" (Dobash and Dobash, 1979).

1871   In an Alabama court, a landmark decision regarding treatment of wives by their husbands is passed, stating that the "privilege, ancient though it be, to beat her with a stick, to pull her hair, choke her, spit in her face or kick her about the floor . . . is not acknowledged by law" (Pleck, 1987).

1874   A North Carolina court follows Alabama's suit, but qualifies its ruling by limiting the cases for which the court may intervene to those cases where permanent injury to the wife has been inflicted.

1876   Lucy Stone, editor of a Boston women's rights newspaper, the *Woman's Journal*, begins publishing a weekly catalog of "crimes against women." She states that male perpetrators of violence are treated to leniency by the law and women are treated unfairly. In an effort to shock middle-class readers into action, she graphically details incidents of wife murder, rape, incest, battering, mutual suicide, etc. Stone hopes to disprove the belief that women provoke violence.

1879   "Wife Torture in England" by English suffragist Frances Power Cobbe is published in *The Contemporary Review.* Cobbe shocks readers with her graphic descriptions of the violence women suffer at the hands of their husbands. She argues that wife beating is caused by men's belief that women are their property. She also says that it is caused by poverty, drunkenness, jealousy, and the impulse to hurt that is aroused by the helplessness of the victim. She lobbies for a bill that will give an assaulted wife the right to divorce and receive economic support and child custody. The bill is pushed through Parliament by Lord Penzance, with an amendment attached stating that any wife proven to have committed adultery is to be denied child custody and separate maintenance.

1880 Encouraged by Cobbe's success in England, Lucy Stone and her husband Henry Blackwell lobby for a similar bill in Massachusetts, one that will enable a wife to apply for a separation at a neighborhood police court. The attempt is unsuccessful and Stone switches her focus to punishment of the abuser and, with Blackwell, joins the fight for women's voting rights. They believe that if women get the vote they will vote off the bench those judges who fail to punish wife beaters.

1885 A bill to punish wife beaters with whippings at a public whipping post passes the Massachusetts house but loses in the Senate. Lucy Stone, realizing that this bill has more public support than protection of victims, organizes a group of women to lobby for it, believing that the fear of pain and disgrace will act as a deterrent to potential batterers. Wife beating becomes a law and order issue, and most people favor something that will deter violent crime rather than aid the victims. The whipping post campaign lasts until into the twentieth century but results in a passage of laws in only three states—Maryland in 1882, Delaware in 1901, and Oregon in 1905. Unfortunately, in Maryland and Delaware the whipping post is used primarily to flog blacks. Very few wife beaters are ever punished, and the whipping post is rarely used after 1910; it is abolished in Maryland in 1948 and Delaware in 1952. No permanent gains for battered women are made as a result of the whipping post campaign.

The Protective Agency for Women and Children is founded in Chicago. It is established as a separate

1885 (*cont.*) department of the Chicago Woman's Club for the purpose of protection of women and children. The agency grows to include delegates from 15 associations in Chicago. Agents of the society listen to women's complaints of sexual molestation, harassment, incest, rape, wife beating, and consumer fraud. They provide legal and personal assistance to victims and monitor courtrooms to protect victims' rights. They send homeless girls or battered women to a shelter operated by the Woman's Club of Chicago, where a woman can stay for up to four weeks. After the agency merges with the Bureau of Justice, a predominantly male organization, in 1896, it continues operating on behalf of women and children. In 1905 it merges with Legal Aid and by 1912 any work on behalf of women disappears. The former motto "woman's work for women," is replaced with "men's and women's work for the wronged and helpless." By 1920 divorce is discouraged and marital reconciliation is promoted.

1900–1920 The turn of the century marks the beginning of the Progressive Era, when many reforms are instituted regarding the family, including the establishment of family courts or domestic relations courts across the United States to deal with issues of family violence. Although the purpose of these reforms is to reshape immigrant and lower-class families to look like middle-class families, they have the effect of strongly encouraging wives to become subservient, compliant, and economically dependent.

In addition, domestic violence is seen more as a domestic dispute than as a criminal matter. Judge Bernhard Rabbino, the first presiding judge of the New York Domestic Relations Court, states that "domestic trouble cases are not criminal in a legal sense" and believes that batterers of women and children do not really intend to break the law. Each spouse is believed to be equally at fault in a domestic abuse case. The belief is that families should stay together—that children should remain in the home and that couples should remain together.

Progressive reformers fail in their efforts to keep families together through social efforts due to the high cost of social services and easy access to asylums and orphanages to which women and children can be committed by their families. Additionally, women who are successful in gaining separation and enforcing child support find that life is easier away from their abusive mates.

1930s   Freudian psychoanalytic theory becomes influential in defining and understanding family violence. Helene Deutsch, a follower of Freud, presents the theory that masochism is common in women and and that it explains why women stay with their abusers: they secretly enjoy the pain of the abuse. This theory is popular during the Depression as it offers men the comfort of dominance and control at a time when their ability to support their families is threatened. Another analyst, Karen Horney, rebuts Deutsch's theory, asserting that Freud has a faulty view of womanhood and that this belief in female masochism reinforces women's subordination to men. She believes that this theory is rooted in misogyny and is able to flourish because of women's economic dependence on men and their exclusion from public life (Pleck, 160). Horney is unsuccessful in challenging Deutsch, as there is no active women's movement to provide public support and the psychiatric community does not support her belief. Deutsch's theory on the masochism of women remains the predominant psychiatric theory on this issue through the 1950s. One psychiatrist refers to the battered woman as the "doormat wife" who is unable to accept responsibility for her own participation in her battering.

1960s   The abuse of children is recognized as a problem in American families. The 1962 publication of "The Battered Child Syndrome" by pediatrician C.

1960s (*cont.*) Henry Kempe and four others and an editorial in the *Journal of the American Medical Association* sparks a renewed interest in child abuse. This leads to early policies that temporarily remove abused children from their families and place them in foster care or with relatives. Many studies are conducted on the issue, and state and federal legislation establishes laws, policies, and procedures regarding the maltreatment of children. Violence against wives and mothers is not addressed.

1964 A study of battered women, "The Wife-Beater's Wife: A Study of Family Interaction," by John E. Snell, Richard J. Rosenwald, and Ames Robey appears in a professional journal on psychiatry. It studies women who have accused their husbands of assault and finds the women "castrating," "aggressive," "masculine," "frigid," "indecisive," "passive," and "masochistic." The authors conclude that even though the women protest the abuse, it serves to fulfill their needs.

1971 Erin Pizzey, a London woman concerned about women's issues, establishes the Chiswick Center, a neighborhood center offering advice to women. She soon realizes that many of the women who come for advice are suffering abuse in their homes and, along with a group of women, she establishes child care and a refuge for homeless women. These shelters soon become established throughout England and the "shelter movement" is born.

1972–1973 Many women from the United States visit the shelters in England and bring back the Chiswick model to replicate in this country. Although there are a few safe house programs for battered wives of alcoholics, Women's Advocates in St. Paul becomes the first shelter for battered women established in the United States based on a feminist collective model. It starts as a legal aid collective in the early 1970s and in February 1973 moves to a one-bedroom apartment so that minimal shelter to battered women can be provided when necessary. In April 1974 the group is able to buy a house and names its shelter program Women's House, and in October the doors are opened to women needing refuge.

A women's shelter, Rainbow Retreat, is opened in Phoenix, Arizona, on 1 November 1973. Admission is limited to families who are either abused or displaced by alcoholic husbands. In 1974, Haven House in Pasadena, California, opens its doors for abused families with alcoholic husbands.

Also in 1973, Nancy Kirk-Gormley, a survivor of a violent ten-year marriage, establishes the first National Organization for Women (NOW) task force on battered women, the Pennsylvania Task Force on Household Violence. The members act as advocates for battered women, accompanying them to court and assisting in pressing assault charges against husbands.

In April 1974 the Women's Center South in Pittsburgh, Pennsylvania, is immediately filled to capacity when it opens its eight-bed refuge for battered women and their children. In January 1976 two more shelters open in California, La Casa de las Madres in San Francisco and the Women's Transitional Living Center in Fullerton. There are 20 shelters in the United States by the end of 1976, 300 by 1982, and approximately 1,200 in 1994.

1974   The first newspaper article on wife abuse appears in the *New York Times* and is syndicated in newspapers across the country. The article originates with New York attorney Marjorie Fields and tells the story of her clients, battered women who are unable to get the police to respond to their calls for assistance. Fields recommends that women police officers be included in special units to respond to domestic abuse complaints. Efforts are made

1974 (*cont.*)   across the country by feminist attorneys to change police practices. In 1976, women attorneys in Oakland, California, and New York City bring class action suits against police departments in their cities to change policies. Many women attorneys become involved in defending battered women who have murdered their batterers. The result is the creation of more public awareness of the abuse and violence these women have suffered over the years.

Erin Pizzey publishes *Scream Quietly or the Neighbors Will Hear* in England, the first book about domestic violence from the battered woman's perspective.

1976   During 4–8 March, the first International Tribunal on Crimes Against Women takes place in Brussels, Belgium. For the first time, women survivors testify publicly about the many crimes committed against them in and out of the home by husbands, acquaintances, strangers, employers, and so on. The crimes to which these women testify are ones that are either openly or tacitly sanctioned by their societies. The workshop on battered women proposes the following resolution: "The women of Japan, Netherlands, France, Wales, England, Scotland, Ireland, Australia, USA and Germany have begun the fight for the rights of battered women and their children. We call for urgent action by all countries to combat the crime of woman-battering. We demand that governments recognize the existence and extent of this problem, and accept the need for refuges, financial aid, and effective legal protection for these women."
    This resolution is sent to the governments of all involved countries and serves as motivation for those attending the tribunal to return home and take action.

In October, a Wisconsin Conference on Battered Women turns into a historic event when women from around the country begin a national newsletter, *The National Communication Network for the Elimination of Violence Against Women (NCN)*. This eventually merges with the newsletter of the Feminist Alliance Against Rape and the joint paper evolves into *Aegis, the Magazine on Ending Violence Against Women*. This publication fulfills many needs. It inspires and helps reduce the feeling of isolation many women across the country feel. It provides insight and focus, giving some of the isolated women the ability to define their community as a national rather than local one. *Aegis, Response*, published by the Center for Women Policy Studies and concerned primarily with criminal justice, hospital, social service, and federal responses to rape and battering, and *SANEnews*, published by the Community Health Center of Middletown, Connecticut, and focusing on information-sharing and legislative developments, link women in the battered women's movement nationwide.

1977   On 9 March, Francine Hughes, after having suffered more than 13 years of extreme abuse at the hands of her husband, Mickey, sets fire to the gasoline-soaked bedroom where he sleeps. In November she is found not guilty of murder, by reason of temporary insanity. Her case is highly publicized and becomes the basis for a movie starring Farrah Fawcett, *The Burning Bed*, which airs on national television in 1987.

International Woman Year's National Women's Conference in Houston is held in November and the following resolutions are passed:

The President and Congress should declare the elimination of violence in the home to be a national goal. To help achieve this, Congress should establish a national clearinghouse for information and technical and financial assistance to locally controlled public and nonprofit organizations providing emergency

1977 (*cont.*) shelter and other support services for battered women and their children. The clearinghouse should also conduct a continuing mass media campaign to educate the public about the problem of violence and the available remedies and resources.

Local and state governments, law enforcement agencies, and social welfare agencies should provide training programs on the problems of wife battering, crisis intervention techniques, and the need for prompt and effective enforcement of laws that protect the rights of battered women.

State legislatures should enact laws to expand legal protection and provide funds for shelters for battered women and their children; remove interspousal tort immunity in order to permit assaulted spouses to sue their assailants for civil damages; and provide full legal services for victims of abuse.

Programs for battered women should be sensitive to the bilingual and multicultural needs of ethnic and minority women.

In addition to the above resolutions, a Caucus on Battered Women meets and decides to develop a national coalition.

Oregon becomes the first state to enact legislation mandating arrest in domestic violence cases when it adopts the Family Abuse Prevention Act, which serves as a model for the nation. The act includes the process by which a woman can obtain a restraining order whether or not her abuser is prosecuted.

1977–1979 Domestic violence legislation co-sponsored by Maryland Republican Newton Speers and Louisiana Democrat Lindy Boggs is introduced into the House. A bill sponsored by Maryland Democrat Barbara Mikulski is also introduced and the two bills are merged after compromise. The bill is introduced during the 1977–1978 session and passes in the Senate but loses in the House. During the 1978–1979 session a similar bill is introduced but loses in the Senate and passes in the House.

1978   During 30–31 January, the United States Commission on Civil Rights sponsors a Consultation on Battered Women: Issues of Public Policy. Hundreds of activists arrive in Washington to listen and organize. The consultation results in *Battered Women: Issues of Public Policy*, which offers more than 700 pages of written and oral testimony. The National Coalition Against Domestic Violence (NCADV) is organized during this consultation.

One hundred and twenty-eight women from 13 Western nations meet on 14–15 April at the International Conference on Battered Women in Amsterdam, concluding their conference with the following press release: "Although individual refuges in different countries face different practical problems of housing, finances and government policies, we agreed to the fact that women being battered is rooted in an international acceptance of the subordination of women" (Schechter).

Florida becomes the first state to pass a law levying a surcharge on marriage licenses for the benefit of battered women's shelters. A $5 tax is levied, with $600,000 expected to be raised that year, which would raise up to $50,000 for each qualified shelter. Since then similar laws have been enacted in most states and are the primary source of funding for most shelters.

Minnesota becomes the first state to allow probable cause (warrantless) arrest in cases of domestic assault, regardless of whether a protection order had been issued against the offender.

The Law Enforcement Assistance Administration (a predecessor agency of the Office of Justice

1978 (*cont.*)	Programs, U.S. Department of Justice) awards 11 grants to family violence projects to be used to provide a range of services.
1979	President Jimmy Carter establishes the Office of Domestic Violence to serve as a national clearinghouse and center for the dissemination of information. Its 1980 budget is $900,000 for grants, research, and dissemination of materials.
	The Conference on Violence Against Women is held in Denver and another conference, Confronting Woman Abuse, is held in Chicago. They host women from across the country and provide skills training and information on topics such as organizing shelters, children's needs, police and court advocacy, and worker burnout.
	The first congressional hearings on domestic violence are held.
Late 1970s	State laws are enacted concerning wife abuse, providing funding for shelters and improved reporting procedures, repealing spousal immunity from torts, and establishing more effective criminal court procedures. By 1980 all but six states have passed such laws.
1980	On 27 February, 600 women from 49 states meet in Washington, D.C., for the first membership conference of the NCADV. Participants evaluate the meeting positively as they work with many diverse women from across state lines and use lobbying efforts for national legislation as a unifying activity. Out of this conference the Southeast Coalition, incorporating eight states, is founded.
	Domestic violence legislation is introduced in the United States Congress for a third time. Two Republican senators, Orrin Hatch of Utah and S. I. Hayakawa of California, lead the opposition. In a letter given to colleagues they state that such "leg-

islation represents one giant step by the federal social service bureaucracy into family matters which are properly, more effectively and democratically represented by the states and local communities" (Pleck, p. 196). A coalition of groups formed for the purpose of "strengthening the American Family" opposes this bill, saying that domestic violence legislation is a feminist issue that is an attack on "motherhood, the family, and Christian values"; that radical feminists will be "coming to the federal trough for a $65 million feed if the domestic violence bill becomes law"; and that "battered women's shelters make women promise to divorce their husbands in order to enter the shelter" (Pleck, p. 197). As Congress comes to a close in 1980, the bill is withdrawn when it appears headed for defeat. Although the newly formed NCADV and the battered women's movement suffer a legislative defeat, they use national organizing to educate thousands of people across the country.

The city of Duluth, Minnesota, undertakes a Domestic Abuse Intervention Project, a coordinated system of criminal justice intervention on domestic violence cases. The systems involved include police, prosecutors, civil and criminal court judges, and probation officers. In addition, the project runs batterers' treatment groups, a center for supervised child visitation, and parenting education. The project works closely with battered women's shelters, serves as a model for the rest of the country, and is rated as successful in providing safety for many women and children. At this writing, Duluth maintains an exceptionally low rate of domestic homicide year after year.

In October the First National Day of Unity is established by NCADV to mourn battered women who have died, celebrate women who have survived the violence, and honor all who have worked to defeat domestic violence. This becomes Domestic

1980 (*cont.*)   Violence Awareness Week, and in 1987 expands to a month of awareness activities.

NCADV holds its first national conference in Washington, D.C., which is attended by more than 600 battered women's advocates from 49 states. The conference gains federal recognition of critical issues facing battered women, and sees the birth of several state coalitions.

1981   Soon after Ronald Reagan takes office as president, the Office of Domestic Violence is closed due to budget cuts and lack of support.

The Family Protection Act is introduced in Congress to eliminate federal laws supporting equal education; forbid "intermingling of the sexes in any sport or other school-related activities"; require marriage and motherhood to be taught as the proper career for girls; deny federal funding to any school using textbooks portraying women in nontraditional roles; repeal all federal laws protecting battered wives from their husbands; and ban federally funded legal aid for any woman seeking abortion counseling or a divorce. The bill, supported by the Reagan administration, is defeated.

The National Coalition declares 17 October 1981 a national day of unity on behalf of battered women across the country.

1983   Domestic violence legislation calling for federal funding for shelters is attached to the Child Abuse and Prevention Treatment Act of 1983 and signed by President Reagan in 1984. Six million dollars is appropriated, less than one-fourth of the original request. A U.S. Attorney General's Task Force on Family Violence is convened.

A Police Foundation study in Minneapolis, funded by the National Institute of Justice, finds arrest more effective than two nonarrest alternatives in reducing the likelihood of repeat violence. The study findings are widely publicized and provide the impetus for many police departments to establish pro-arrest policies in cases of domestic violence.

1984   The U.S. Attorney General establishes the Task Force on Family Violence to examine the scope and nature of the problem. Nearly 300 witnesses provide testimony at public hearings in six cities. In its final report, the task force outlines four specific recommendations for prosecutors with application to wife assault:

- Prosecutors should organize special units to process family violence cases.
- The victim should not be required to sign a formal complaint before charges are filed, unless mandated by state law.
- Whenever possible, prosecutors should not require family violence victims to testify at the preliminary hearing.
- If the defendant does not remain in custody, a protective order restricting the defendant's access to the victim should be issued as a condition of release.

Florida becomes the first state to enact legislation mandating consideration of spouse abuse in child custody determinations.

The passage of the Family Violence Prevention and Services Act through grassroots lobbying efforts earmarks federal funding for programs serving victims of domestic violence.

1985   On 25 February, *The Wall Street Journal* publishes a story about the divorce proceedings of John and Charlotte Fedders of Washington, D.C. The article details events of the trial and Charlotte and John's testimony of financial and family

1985 (*cont.*)   difficulties, including over 19 years of John's battering of Charlotte. The story is important because John Fedders has a top position in the Reagan administration as chief of the enforcement division of the Securities and Exchange Commission. Late on 26 February John Fedders resigns, writing that the newspapers had greatly exaggerated allegations in the divorce trial and that there had been only seven incidents of violence in their marriage. The trial publicity is responsible for many calls and letters to Charlotte from upper middle-class women, battered wives of professionals from across the country, detailing years of abuse.

Surgeon General C. Everett Koop tells health professionals that "domestic violence is a public health menace that police alone cannot cope with."

A landmark decision is handed down in the lawsuit of Tracy Thurman against the City of Torrington, Connecticut, and 24 individual police officers. The suit alleges a violation of her constitutional rights, as set forth in the Fourteenth Amendment, regarding an individual's right to equal protection under the law. The lawsuit is filed after the police fail to respond to and take action on many calls from Tracy Thurman for protection from her ex-husband Buck over a period of two years. Buck not only batters Tracy severely and threatens her life, but does so in the presence of police officers. Tracy is permanently disfigured and partially paralyzed and Buck Thurman is eventually arrested, tried, convicted, and sentenced to 20 years in prison. The decision reminds police of their civil liability and sparks the adoption of new pro-arrest policies across the country.

1986   In April the *Washingtonian* magazine publishes a lengthy article told from Charlotte Fedders's perspective about what went wrong with her marriage and her dreams. Her story prompts many women to write and call the magazine, outlining their own stories of battering at the hands of well-educated, professional men.

1987   In April Charlotte Fedders appears as a witness before a House Education and Labor Select Subcommittee. The Reagan administration has proposed ending the Family Violence Prevention and Services Act of 1984, and these budget hearings are held to review the need and effectiveness of the Child Abuse Prevention and Treatment Act and the Family Violence Prevention and Services Act. In her testimony Fedders says she wants to "help other wives understand that no person has the right to make another afraid."

A book written by Charlotte Fedders with Laura Elliott, *Shattered Dreams*, is published. It tells Fedders's life story. After the book's publication, a New York Domestic Relations Court rules that Charlotte Fedders's alimony payments are to be reduced and John Fedders is to receive 25 percent of the royalties from the book, the rationale being that Charlotte Fedders shares equal responsibility for the ruination of the marriage and that, since the book is about the husband, he is entitled to share in the royalties. This ruling is later overturned by a higher court.

NCADV establishes the first national toll-free domestic violence hotline.

The first national conference to promote a dialogue among domestic violence researchers, practitioners, and policymakers is held at the University of New Hampshire.

On 2 November 1987, Joel Steinberg, an attorney, and Hedda Nussbaum, his live-in partner and a former children's books editor, are arrested in

1987 (*cont.*)   New York City for the beating murder of their "adopted" six-year-old daughter Lisa Steinberg. It is revealed that Joel Steinberg has systematically battered and tortured Nussbaum over a nine-year period. Prosecutor Peter Casolaro, in a 32-point "catalogue of abuse," concludes that the physical abuse continued with regularity and has become "a persistent tool used . . . to control Miss Nussbaum, or . . . to break her will" (Jones). The abuse over a nine-year period of their relationship includes broken bones, burns, permanent eye and ear injuries from blows and kicks, multiple nose breaks, damage to sexual organs, knocked-out teeth, pulled-out hair, and degrading sexual and emotional abuse. In July 1988 District Attorney Robert Morgenthau, determining that on the night Lisa was taken to the hospital, Nussbaum was too physically and mentally incapacitated herself to be capable of either injuring the girl or taking action to save her, arranges to drop murder charges in exchange for Nussbaum's cooperation in prosecuting Steinberg. On 30 January 1988 the jury finds Steinberg guilty of manslaughter, not murder, in the first degree. In post-trial interviews the jurors say they believe Hedda Nussbaum shares as much if not more responsibility for Lisa's murder, even though Steinberg is proven to have delivered the blows that resulted in the child's death. Some jurors feel that a "nice" man like Steinberg, an attorney, is really a victim of his "crazy" wife.

1988   *State v. Ciskie* is the first case to allow the use of expert testimony to explain the behavior and mental state of an adult rape victim. The testimony is used to show why a victim of repeated physical and sexual assault by her intimate partner would not immediately call the police or take action. The jury convicts the defendant on four counts of rape.

1989   Surgeon General C. Everett Koop launches a campaign to alert the 27,000 members of the American College of Obstetricians and Gynecologists to the issue of domestic violence, what he calls "an overwhelming moral, economic, and public health burden that our society can no longer bear."

1990   A social club in the Bronx burns on 25 March, killing 87 people trapped inside the building. The arsonist is Julio Gonzalez, a Cuban refugee who commits the crime two months after the woman he has lived with for eight years, Lidia Feliciano, throws Gonzalez out for "making sexual advances" to her 19-year-old niece. Gonzalez stalks Feliciano and goes to the club where she works nights, professing his "undying love." He makes such trouble that he is thrown out and later returns with gasoline and burns the club down. Feliciano is one of five persons to survive, and public sentiment, fueled by stories in the media blaming her for Gonzalez's violence, turns so against her that she and her children have to be removed from her home of 20 years and placed under special protection.

Democratic Governor Richard F. Celeste of Ohio grants clemency to 25 women who have been serving time in the state prison for killing or assaulting their abusive husbands or companions. After reviewing the cases of more than 100 women, the governor says the 25 women have been "victims of violence, repeated violence . . . [who] have been entrapped emotionally and physically." This is the first mass-release of women prisoners ever in this country.

The Violence Against Women Act is introduced in the Senate by Democratic Senator Joseph Biden of Delaware. The House bill is sponsored by Democratic Congresswoman Barbara Boxer of California. It goes to hearings in the Senate Judiciary

1990 (*cont.*)   Committee but dies with the 101st Congress. (After Boxer is elected to the Senate in November 1991, the bill is sponsored in the House by Pat Schroeder of Colorado and Louise Slaughter and Charles Schumer of New York.)

1991   The American Medical Association (AMA) announces in October the start of their campaign to combat a "public health menace," family violence. Their informational packet identifies family violence as "America's Deadly Secret." Surgeon General Antonia C. Novello commends the AMA for "bringing the topic of domestic violence to light."

1992   Roman Catholic bishops in the United States issue the church's first official statement about spouse abuse, saying the Bible does not tell women to submit to abusive husbands.

    The Journal of the American Medical Association devotes most of its June issue to violence against women. The AMA's Council on Scientific Affairs recommends that physicians initiate a routine process to screen their female patients in order to identify victims of violence. The council recommends training programs for practicing physicians and medical schools, and development of protocols for identifying and treating victims. They also recommend that the AMA launch "a campaign to alert the health care community to the widespread prevalence of violence against women."

1993   As of 5 July, marital rape is a crime in all 50 states. However, 31 states still have some exemptions from prosecution if "only" simple force is used, or if the woman is legally unable to consent due to the severity of a disability (temporarily or permanently, physically or mentally).

1994   In March, *Defending Our Lives,* a documentary film about battered women in prison for killing their batterers, wins the Academy Award for best documentary.

In May, results of a survey of 16 insurance companies reveal that 8 of the companies surveyed view victims of domestic violence as bad risks and are denying them health, disability, or life policies. These practices persist whether or not the women have separated from the batterers. A spokesperson for State Farm, one of the country's largest insurance firms, says, "It would not be prudent for us as a company to insure someone we knew was being abused any more than it would be to insure a diabetic for not taking their medication." After pressure from politicians and national women's organizations, State Farm announces it will no longer use a background of being or having been battered to deny an applicant insurance.

On 12 June, Nicole Brown Simpson and her friend Ronald Goldman are murdered in a knife attack in front of Nicole Brown Simpson's home in Brentwood, California. Because Nicole is the former wife of O. J. Simpson, the well-known 1970s football star and television/film personality, the brutal murder immediately becomes the focus of media attention. One week after the murder, O. J. Simpson is arrested and charged with the double murder. A lengthy history of domestic violence is revealed, including at least nine calls to the police in which Nicole Simpson asserted that O. J. Simpson is battering her. In a couple of reports made public, this battering is documented by the police; in fact, it is revealed that Simpson has been arrested and served two years' probation for a 1989 incident.

Because of the intense media attention given this case, Americans are confronted with the issue of domestic violence on their televisions and in

1994 (*cont.*)   their newspapers and magazines. As a result, phone calls to domestic violence hotlines surge to record numbers in the week following Simpson's arrest; in Los Angeles calls are up 80 percent. Additionally, lawmakers across the country start taking notice of the problem. In New York the state legislature unanimously passes a sweeping bill that mandates arrest for any person who commits a domestic assault. The New York bill includes domestic violence training of the police. Members of the California legislature press for a computerized registry of restraining orders and the confiscation of guns from men arrested for domestic violence. These same lawmakers pass a bill that will increase state funding tenfold for California shelters and domestic violence prosecution. Colorado's package of anti–domestic violence laws, one of the nation's toughest, goes into effect. Colorado's law not only compels police to take abusers into custody at the scenes of violence but also requires arrest for the first violation of a restraining order. Subsequent violations bring mandatory jail time.

When asked by a reporter if the Nicole Brown Simpson case has made a difference, one resident of Sojourn, a program for battered women in Santa Monica, says, "I feel now that if I speak out about the abuse, someone will listen." Another woman says, "in my own mind I no longer have shame." A counselor tells the reporter she hopes that domestic violence is not just a vogue issue of this season, "for when the cameras are gone and the reporters are no longer in our office we'll still be in the business of saving women's lives" (Cable News Network, 19 August 1994).

An article by Francine G. Hermelin appearing in the November 1994 issue of *Working Woman* states that although publicity from the Simpson case has increased awareness among battered women, causing demand for shelter space to increase, private donations to shelters have actually decreased.

A backlash results from the sudden surge in the media attention to the issue, and articles in print media and people on radio talk shows and television programs challenge some of the statistics quoted by domestic violence organizations. An attempt is made to discredit the current wave of concern for battered women and to refocus attention on battered husbands, with some calling them the forgotten victims of domestic violence. Headlines similar to this, on page one of the 7 July 1994 issue of the *Oregonian*, the largest daily newspaper in the state of Oregon, appear: "Twisted 'Facts' of Domestic Violence Fizzle under Scrutiny." Only one statistic is challenged in this lengthy story, and this challenge is used as a basis for stating that too many funds go to battered women. Some of the research into this story is subsequently shown to be flawed by a number of domestic violence professionals; however, such stories continue to appear across the country in newspapers and on television, all emanating from two syndicated columnists, Joe Hallinan and John Leo.

Late in 1994, Denise Brown establishes the Nicole Brown Simpson Charitable Foundation in memory of her sister. The foundation provides information on stopping domestic violence and will function primarily for the purpose of educating and informing the public on the issue.

A Massachusetts court determines that a man accused of abusing his wife and three girlfriends over a period of three years was motivated by hatred or bias against women as a class. A superior court judge issues a preliminary injunction barring Salah Aboulaz from contacting the women. If the injunction is violated, Aboulaz can face up to ten years in prison.

The court, in this case, believes that a clear pattern of hate-motivated behavior has been established. Two years ago, Massachusetts added "gender" as a class to their Civil Rights Act. Only eight other states and the District of Columbia

1994 (*cont.*)   currently have civil rights statutes that address gender-motivated violence. Boston has adopted a policy of checking all domestic violence cases for civil rights violations.

The Violence Against Women Act is passed in both the House and the Senate and made part of a sweeping crime bill. The act includes funds for a National Domestic Violence Hotline, an increase in Family Violence Prevention and Services Act funds for shelters, interstate enforcement of protective orders, training for state and federal judges, and funding for school-based rape education programs. The civil rights provision that recognizes that assaults motivated by the victim's gender are bias crimes in violation of a person's right to be free from discrimination, and that the targeting of a woman for assault and violence because she is a woman is an act of discrimination and therefore a violation of an individual's civil rights, is removed from the House version of the bill but remains in the Senate version. The comprehensive crime bill passes in the House on 21 August and in the Senate on 25 August 1994. It is signed into law by President Clinton on 13 September 1994.

1995   On 2 March, a Kirkland, Washington, man shoots and kills three women in the King County courthouse during a break in a hearing on his petition for annulment of his marriage. The three women are identified as his pregnant wife and her two friends. He claims he was duped into marrying his Filipino wife so she could enter the United States legally. The wife had claimed abuse within days of the 1993 marriage. The Asian and Pacific Islander Women and Family Safety Center states, "This is a domestic violence murder," not simply a case of lax courthouse security.

On 21 March, President Clinton officially opens the Violence Against Women Office at the Department of Justice and appoints Bonnie Campbell as its first director. While serving as Iowa's first female attorney general, Campbell helped enact strong domestic violence and antistalking laws in that state. The newly created office is designed to help states and communities deal with domestic violence. According to the president, $26 million is to be made available immediately to help the states open rape crisis centers, staff domestic violence hotlines, provide victims' advocates, and pay for more officers and training. The allotted money is to be the first installment of a six-year commitment of $800 million for these purposes.

On 24 May, a jury in West Virginia finds Chris Bailey guilty under the new federal law in the Violence Against Women Act that makes crossing a state line to assault a spouse or domestic partner a federal offense. His crime includes severely beating his wife and then driving around two states with her locked in his trunk. There is a history of prior beating inflicted by Bailey upon his wife, who survives this attack but suffers permanent brain damage. Bailey could get 20 years in jail under the federal law as well as life imprisonment for kidnapping. On 1 September Bailey is sentenced to life plus 20 years in prison.

On 14 June, the *Journal of the American Medical Association* publishes results of a 1992–1993 study conducted in Denver emergency rooms. According to the study, of the 648 women who made emergency room visits, 11.7 percent visited because of abuse from male partners. This was lower than the anticipated 25 to 30 percent, although 54 percent said they had suffered from either physical or emotional abuse at some time in their lives. Dr. Carole Worshars, codirector of the Cook County Hospital Crisis Intervention Service in Chicago, says the 11.7 percent figure does not reflect the overall number of women who seek medical treatment for domestic violence, as the greater majority of victims seek treatment not for acute battering, but for complications of long-standing abusive relationships. Such complications include hypertension, diabetes, and psychiatric problems as well as other chronic diseases.

On 4 September through 15 September, the United Nations Fourth World Conference on Women is held, drawing 4,000 delegates from 189 nations and speakers including Prime Minister Benazir Bhutto of Pakistan and Hillary Rodham Clinton. On the final day of the conference, the delegates ratify a Platform for Action, which calls on governments to improve the economic status of women worldwide and decries marital rape, genital mutilation of girls, dowry-related attacks against women, domestic battering, and sexual harassment in the workplace, calling all these abuses violations of women's' human rights.

On 3 October, the jury in the O. J. Simpson double murder case returns verdicts of not guilty on both charges of murder. In a post-verdict interview, one of the jurors comments that the domestic violence evidence presented by the prosecution during the trial was a waste of the jurors' time and that the case was about murder and not about domestic abuse.

References

Browne, Angela. *When Battered Women Kill.* New York: The Free Press, 1987.

Cable News Network (CNN), Prime Time News, 19 August 1994.

Dobash, R. Emerson, and Russell P. Dobash. *Violence against Wives.* New York: The Free Press, 1979.

Pleck, Elizabeth. *Domestic Tyranny: The Making of American Social Policy against Family Violence from Colonial Times to the Present.* New York: Oxford University Press, 1987.

Schechter, Susan. *Women and Male Violence: The Visions and Struggles of the Battered Women's Movement.* Boston: South End Press, 1982.

Biographical Sketches 3

Abigail Adams (1744–1818)

Abigail Adams, the wife of the second president of the United States, exemplified the principles of patriotic womanhood for which citizens of the new nation expressed admiration. Although she was concerned and involved in the new society her husband was helping to create, she revealed a concern that all women be freed from the unlimited power given to husbands so as to be assured of some protection from those who might inflict "cruelty and indignity" upon them.

Born in Weymouth, Massachusetts, Adams, like many women of the era, received no formal education. She married John Adams in 1764. Living in Braintree (now Quincy), Massachusetts, the couple had five children over the next decade; in 1764 John Adams moved to Philadelphia where he became a delegate to the first Continental Congress. Abigail wrote many letters to her husband during the Revolution in which she gave him much personal support and political advice. In one such letter, written in 1776, Abigail Adams asked her husband to "Remember the Ladies." She wrote,

> . . . and by the way in the new Code of Laws which I suppose it

59

will be necessary for you to make I desire you would Remember the Ladies, and be more generous and favourable to them than your ancestors. Do not put such unlimited power into the hands of the Husbands. Remember all Men would be tyrants if they could: If particular care and attention is not paid to the Ladies, we are determined to foment a Rebellion, and will not hold ourselves bound by any Laws in which we have no voice, or Representation. That your Sex are Naturally Tyrannical is a Truth so thoroughly established as to admit of no dispute, but such of you as wish to be happy willingly give up the harsh title of Master for the more tender and endearing one of Friend. Why then, not put it out of the power of the vicious and the Lawless to use us with cruelty and indignity and impunity. Men of Sense in all Ages abhor those customs which treat us only as the vassals of your Sex.

In spite of Abigail Adams's plea for the "Ladies," no effort was made to grant an equal status to women in the Constitution of the United States. Abigail Adams continued to speak out to her husband about the rights of women, but her voice did not go beyond his ears until her letters were made public after her death.

Susan B. Anthony (1820–1906)

Susan B. Anthony, a nineteenth-century feminist, had a lifelong concern for women's rights and was a leader of the women's suffrage movement, working at one point for women's divorce rights.

She was born into a liberal family in Massachusetts, and her father was actively involved in working for human equality. When Susan was in her late teens her family's cotton mill business failed, and everything, including their personal possessions, had to be sold at auction. The family moved to a farm outside of Rochester, where Susan got a job as a teacher and earned $2.50 per week, 25 percent of a male teacher's salary.

This was the time of the abolition movement, in which her family was active, and Susan joined them in the struggle to end slavery. Anthony's mother and sister attended the 1848 Women's Rights Convention in Rochester, and their enthusiasm motivated Susan to become involved with the women's movement and with

Elizabeth Cady Stanton and Lucretia Mott. Anthony met the women and was enthusiastic about their work, and at the age of 30 she stopped teaching and began spending all her time on women's rights issues. Her activism was directed primarily at holding meetings where she gathered signatures for women's rights reform measures on petitions to the legislature. Anthony traveled from place to place and gave speeches to gatherings of people, where she was ridiculed, vilified, and called a home-wrecker, and as a result she was the subject of many unflattering newspaper cartoons that made her look ugly and foolish. People came to her speeches, heckled her, and threw rotten eggs. Her alliance with Stanton was a good one, however, for Anthony was an excellent organizer and Stanton excelled as a speaker and writer. They worked in New York State toward a stronger married women's property bill, which passed in 1860, and they proposed liberalized divorce laws so women could survive freedom from their abusive husbands. After the Civil War, however, they opposed the Fourteenth and Fifteenth Amendments because they extended civil rights and the franchise to black males but excluded women.

In 1868 Anthony and Stanton started a women's rights weekly, the *Revolution*, in New York City. In 1869 she and Stanton founded the National Woman Suffrage Association to work for the passage of a federal women's suffrage amendment. They believed that if women were granted the right to vote, they would receive equal rights in all areas under the law. Anthony worked for women's rights until she died at age 86 in 1906. The amendment granting women the right to vote was passed in 1920.

Joseph Biden (1942–)

Joseph Biden, a U.S. senator from Delaware, cosponsored the Violence Against Women Act in the Senate, carrying it through from its introduction in 1990 to its adoption as part of the crime bill of 1994.

Born in Scranton, Pennsylvania, Biden completed his undergraduate work at the University of Delaware and received his law degree from Syracuse University. After practicing law in Wilmington, Delaware, from 1968 to 1972, he ran for and was elected to the U.S. Senate.

When he won the election he was only 29 years old, not old enough to take his seat; however, he turned 30 before his swearing in. Just six weeks after his election his wife and infant daughter were killed and his two sons were injured in an auto accident. He had to be cajoled into taking the Senate oath of office. Fifteen years later, in the middle of confirmation hearings that he chaired on the nomination of Robert Bork to the Supreme Court, he was forced into a humiliating withdrawal from a race for the Democratic nomination for president. It was discovered that in a campaign speech he had used the works of Neil Kinnock, a British Labour Party leader. In addition, he was accused of plagiarizing from a text to write a law school paper. Although he had actually footnoted the text, it proved to be the end of Biden's campaign. Not long afterward, he underwent emergency neurosurgery for a brain aneurysm that almost killed him.

Biden is known as a likeable man, an excellent orator, and one who tries hard to be fair to all sides. This was apparent at Senate Judiciary Hearings on the Clarence Thomas Supreme Court nomination, when he was seen as making such an effort to be fair that he actually gained the respect of Republicans over Democrats. His views are sometimes confusing, a strange mix of liberal and conservative. Biden won his first election on an anti–Vietnam War platform and his second on an anti-busing platform. He has endorsed the right to abortion but has been tough on crime issues. Biden sponsored the Violence Against Women Act in the Senate in 1990 and has pushed for its passage since that time. He has taken an active part in hearings on domestic violence in Washington and has been a strong supporter throughout his political career in all areas of women's rights.

Sir William Blackstone (1723–1780)

Sir William Blackstone was important to the perpetuation of social attitudes regarding family life from England to the United States. An English jurist, Blackstone wrote *Commentaries on the Laws of England*, designed as an introduction to the law for the layman, in which he reduced the laws of England to a unified and rational system. *Commentaries* was widely used by the U.S. legal system into the nineteenth century and, because this country's common law is derived from English law, Blackstone's work strongly influenced decisions made by jurists.

Blackstone was born in London and received a classical education at Oxford University, earning his bachelor's degree in civil law in 1745. From 1746 to 1753, Blackstone had a private law practice and provided legal services at Oxford University. In 1750 he received his doctor of laws and in 1761 was elected to Parliament. In 1765 he wrote the first of his *Commentaries* and upon their completion served as Judge of Common Pleas until his death in 1780.

Although he was an accomplished scholar, Blackstone was very conservative in his views and interpretation of the law. He did not understand social elements underlying the legal systems, and glossed over his inconsistencies with generalizations. Unfortunately, when he discussed "private" violence, which he maintained was outside the domain of the law, he said that because the husband is responsible for his wife's behavior, he should have the power to chastise. Blackstone's work was relied upon by lawyers and cited as authority in thousands of decisions by eminent jurists in the nineteenth century. It heavily influenced the way domestic violence was treated by our legal institutions.

Barbara Boxer (1940–)

Barbara Boxer, a Democrat, is a U.S. senator from California elected in November 1992 to a six-year term. She served as representative during 1983–1992, and while in the House she sponsored the Violence Against Women Act and continued to work for the bill's passage during the four years it was under consideration.

Born in Brooklyn, Boxer graduated from Brooklyn College in 1962. She married Stewart Boxer that year; they have two children. Boxer worked as a stockbroker in New York City until 1965. After moving to California she worked as a newspaper journalist before joining the district staff of Congressman John L. Burton in 1974. In 1976 she won election to the Board of Supervisors of Marin County, California, and in 1981 became the first woman president of the board. When John Burton retired from Congress in 1982, Boxer ran for his vacated seat with Burton's endorsement over five other Democratic candidates. She won the election from California's sixth district and was reelected four times before running for the vacated seat of Senator Alan Cranston in 1992. As a representative, Boxer served on the Budget Committee, the Armed Services Committee, the Select Committee on Children, Youth, and Families, and was co-chair of the Military Reform Caucus. She promoted congressional oversight of executive branch spending, particularly in defense programs, and played a leading role in the exposure of Pentagon procurement scandals. Other legislative priorities include health care, AIDS funding, and women's rights. Boxer ran for the Senate in 1992, capitalizing on pro–Anita Hill and anti–Clarence Thomas sentiment when saying, "If there had been only one woman on the Judiciary Committee, things would have been different." Boxer has continued as an outspoken advocate for women's rights in the Senate.

Susan Brownmiller (1935–)

Susan Brownmiller published the most comprehensive study of rape ever undertaken, which brought the problem to the close attention of the feminist movement, the police, social workers, and the public.

Born and raised in Brooklyn, Brownmiller went to Cornell University in 1952, intending to study law. At a time when her generation was politically passive, Brownmiller was drawn to radicalism and joined the Students for Peace and the Cornell chapter of the National Association for the Advancement of Colored People. After three years Brownmiller left Cornell to study acting in New York City, got few parts, and began anew to work for radical causes. She studied briefly at the Jefferson School of Social Science, spent two summers in the mid-1960s as a civil rights worker in Mississippi, and joined the staff of the *Village Voice.* Then, as a freelance writer, Brownmiller became known for her interview articles in the *New York Times* with public figures such as Senator Eugene McCarthy and Congresswoman Shirley Chisholm.

In the late 1960s, Brownmiller became active in the women's liberation movement, founding the New York Radical Feminists (NYRF). In 1970 she published an article on the movement called "Sisterhood Is Powerful" in the *New York Times Magazine.* With NYRF she picketed the Miss America pageant and participated in a sit-in at the offices of the *Ladies Home Journal,* calling it "one of the most demeaning magazines toward women."

Brownmiller's studies on rape took four years and culminated in her best-selling book *Against Our Will: Men, Women, and Rape* in 1975. Examining rape as a weapon to subjugate women in the male-female relationship, Brownmiller wrote that rape should be dealt with through reform of law enforcement procedures and the law. Creating a public awareness and dialogue about rape became important to the development of a process for dealing with domestic violence, which immediately followed. She has led the fight in denouncing pornographic magazines and films that brutalize and dehumanize women. Brownmiller continues her career as a writer, lecturer, and teacher campaigning against the abuse of women.

Helene Deutsch (1884–1982)

Helene Deutsch is considered one of the "mothers" of psychoanalysis. Her writings greatly influenced beliefs regarding victims of domestic violence from the 1930s into the 1950s.

Deutsch was born in Poland and educated in Europe. She was trained in psychoanalysis by Freud and was the first woman he psychoanalyzed. She was appointed director of the Vienna Psychoanalytic Institute in 1923. As a Jew in anti-Semitic Austria, Deutsch chose to emigrate to the United States in 1935. Subsequently she became the preeminent woman psychoanalyst in the United States and was sought out as a leader in her field until her death in 1982. Although Deutsch was a social activist who was against the Vietnam conflict and worked for women's rights, she has been attacked by feminists for the beliefs expressed in her book *The Psychology of Women*. She stated that the three essential female traits are passivity, masochism, and narcissism. She believed that masochism is the elemental power in feminine mental life and that what women want is rape, violation, and humiliation.

Charlotte Fedders (1943–)

In April 1987 Charlotte Fedders, the former wife of John Fedders, the chief law-enforcement officer of the Securities and Exchange Commission in the Reagan administration, testified in front of a House Education and Labor Select Subcommittee hearing to review the need and effectiveness of the Child Abuse Prevention and Treatment Act and the Family Violence Prevention and Services Act. She talked once again about the beatings she had received from her husband over 17 years of marriage, as well as the emotional abuse to which she and her five sons had been subjected throughout the marriage.

Charlotte Fedders was the first of five daughters born to an ambitious medical student and his wife, a nurse who had given up her career and converted to Catholicism when she married. Charlotte lived a sheltered and pampered life, attending Catholic girls' schools through college and rarely dating. She met John Fedders while she was in college and, in her own words, was "swept off her feet." John was a senior in law school, an outstanding scholar, business editor for the law review, administrative editor of the law school newspaper, president of the student bar association, and former basketball all-American at Marquette University. They married in August 1966 and settled in New York, where John had secured a position with a law firm. After that they lived first in Dallas and then in a suburb of Washington, D.C., where John Fedders was hired at a prestigious law firm and earned over $150,000 annually. Within a few years John was appointed chief law-enforcement officer of the Securities and Exchange Commission.

By this time the Fedders family and its expenses had grown considerably. Charlotte and John had five sons and their expenses included private school tuition, country club fees, a large mortgage, and entertainment expenses for lavish parties that John considered important to his position. John's salary with the federal government was only half his prior salary with the law firm. As the pressure grew, so did John's need for control over his home. His attacks on Charlotte, which had begun early in the marriage and included punches, slaps, and continual verbal abuse, escalated in frequency and severity. She finally filed for divorce in 1984. The ensuing publicity forced John Fedders to resign his position. Charlotte Fedders and her sons now live in a small house and Charlotte works in a flower shop to support herself and the family.

Karen Horney (1885–1952)

Karen Horney, a pioneer in the field of psychoanalysis, was partially responsible for the movement away from the belief in women's masochism as the cause of domestic violence. Although Horney was unsuccessful in overturning Dr. Helene Deutsch's view during the period that masochism was in favor, her writings have since been widely acclaimed and quoted, casting light on reasons for this once-popular theory.

Horney was born in Hamburg, Germany, and received her doctor of medicine in Berlin in 1913. She practiced medicine and became a prominent psychotherapist in Germany. In 1932 she moved to Chicago to become the assistant director of the Institute for Psychoanalysis. In 1934, Horney joined the faculties of the New School for Social Research and the New York Medical College as a teacher and working analyst in the practice of psychotherapy.

Horney helped to establish the American Institute for Psycho-analysis.

Breaking with traditional Freudian views and refuting the views of her contemporary, Helene Deutsch, on the psychology of women, Horney stressed instead the importance of environment and social factors in establishing personality.

Francine Hughes (1947–)

Francine Hughes became known after she set fire to her abusive husband's bedroom, where he was asleep, and was found not guilty by reason of temporary insanity. Her story was told in a 1980 book by Faith McNulty that was made into a television docudrama in 1987, the first sympathetic film portrayal of the problems facing battered women.

Francine Hughes was born to a poor family living on a farm outside of Stockbridge, Michigan, the third child in a family of six children. When she was eight, the family moved into a house in Jackson when her father switched from farmwork to a factory job. From that time on the family moved frequently, her father started to drink and gamble, and life became increasingly difficult. Francine started dating Mickey Hughes when she was in ninth grade, quit school in 1963 at the beginning of her sophomore year, and married Mickey in November 1963 when she was 16 years old. Mickey and Francine had four children and their life together was punctuated by many moves, Mickey's lost jobs, little money, and Mickey's violent beating of Francine. Although Francine managed to leave Mickey a couple of times, she was coerced by his family to move back so that she could give Mickey the physical care he needed during his rehabilitation following a serious auto accident.

The beatings and terrorization of the family intensified after his accident. Finally, on a night when Francine had planned to escape with the children and possibly get out of state, Mickey came home early and beat her for the last time. When he had passed out drunk in bed, she soaked his bedroom in gasoline and set it on fire. Hysterical, she drove with her children to the police station, where she was arrested and charged with first degree murder. Her subsequent trial and acquittal became national news.

After her release from jail, Francine Hughes rebuilt a normal life for herself and her children. She supported the family with a series of factory jobs and enrolled in nursing school. Although Francine Hughes initially felt tremendous remorse and guilt, which caused depression, she gradually regained her emotional strength. According to persons close to the family, her children have done well in school and show no signs of permanent damage from their early years.

Dorothy L. (Del) Martin (1921–)

Del Martin wrote what is considered a classic and required reading on the issue of domestic violence, *Battered Wives*, published in 1976.

Born in San Francisco, Martin was married and divorced, has one daughter, and lives in San Francisco with her partner of over 40 years, educator and writer Phyliss Lyon. Martin says her writing career began in 1934, in her junior high school journalism class, and she has been writing ever since. Martin attended UC Berkeley for one year and San Francisco State University for two years. She received her doctor of arts in 1987 from the Institute for Advanced Study of Human Sexuality in San Francisco. Her interest in politics began when listening to Franklin Delano Roosevelt's fireside chats and became firm when she was chosen from student reporters to witness election night in the *San Francisco Chronicle* newsroom. In her youth Martin wrote poetry and short stories. Since then her writing has reflected her social and political activism.

Martin has founded a number of political and social action organizations for lesbians and gays. She is a prominent and in-demand national speaker and consultant on gay and lesbian rights and women's rights. Her writings primarily reflect Martin's experience in this political and social arena and are represented in numerous anthologies and periodicals. Martin is currently working on an autobiography and research on violent pornography and censorship.

Barbara Mikulski (1936–)

Senator Barbara Mikulski of Maryland, an ardent feminist, has always taken a strong position on women's rights. She speaks to women's rights issues not only as a woman, but also from her wealth of experience as a social worker. Mikulski has advanced steadily from her beginnings in Baltimore politics, when she first became involved in a citizens' lobbying effort in the 1960s, to her election to the U.S. Senate in 1986, the first woman Democrat to be elected to that body.

Mikulski attended parochial schools in Baltimore and received her B.A. from Mount St. Agnes College in 1958 and her master's in social work in 1965 from the University of Maryland. She taught college, worked at a Vista Training Center, and was a social worker for the Baltimore Department of Social Services and the York Family Agency and Association of Catholic Charities. Mikulski was elected to the Baltimore City Council, where she served from 1971 until 1976, when she was elected to the U.S. House of Representatives from Maryland's third district. She served there until her election to the Senate in 1986. When it looked as though there would be no Senate judiciary hearings on allegations of sexual harassment made against Clarence Thomas, then a nominee for the Supreme Court, she said,

If you talk to victims of abuse the way I have, they will tell you they are often doubly victimized, by both the event in which they are abused and then subsequently by the way the system treats them. And what now has occurred is that they say that this could not be taken seriously enough to be brought to our attention. . . . To the private sector, who now has to enforce these laws on sexual harassment, whether we call it sexual humiliation or whether there's overt physical aggression, sexual terrorism, the message to the private sector is: Cool it, guys. Even the Senate takes a walk on this one.

As a senator, Mikulski sits on the Appropriations Committee, the Labor and Human Resources Committee, and the Small Business Committee. These assignments and her positions as chair of the Appropriations Subcommittee on Veterans Affairs, Housing and Urban Development, and Independent Agencies allow her to continue her legislative work on social issues.

John Stuart Mill (1806–1873)

John Stuart Mill's chief work on women's rights, *The Subjection of Women*, which was originally a plea in the House of Commons for women's right to equality under the law, was published in 1869. This work became an important cornerstone of the nineteenth-century women's movement. In it Mill states that the "law of servitude in marriage is a monstrous contradiction to all the principles of the modern world."

Mill, a distinguished philosopher and economist, was born in London and educated completely by his father. He began studying Greek at the age of 3 and by 14 had mastered Latin, classical literature, logic, political economy, history, and economics. Mill served as editor of the *Westminster Review* from 1835 to 1840. He became the leader of the Utilitarian movement in England and was elected to Parliament in 1865. Considered one of the most advanced thinkers of his time, Mill tried to help the English working people by advocating an equal division of profits, a cooperative system of agriculture, and increased rights for women.

Lucretia Coffin Mott (1793–1880)

An American reformer, Lucretia Mott worked for women's rights and the abolition of slavery. She worked with Susan B. Anthony and Elizabeth Cady Stanton in founding the very important women's rights movement in nineteenth-century America.

Mott, born to Quaker parents on the island of Nantucket off Cape Cod, grew up in a strong tradition of female equality. Her father was the master of a whaling ship and her mother ran a store. Lucretia became a teacher while still in her teens and learned early that women received far less compensation than men for the same work. When she married James Mott they settled in Philadelphia. At the age of 28, Lucretia Mott was ordained a minister by her Quaker "meeting" and thereby gained an opportunity to perfect her public speaking skills, which would prove helpful to her as a women's rights activist. She began speaking at Quaker meetings in 1817 and was noted for her eloquence and leadership. She went as a delegate to the World Anti-Slavery Convention in London in 1840 and started the women's rights movement when she and other women were refused seats there because of their gender. In 1848 she and Elizabeth Cady Stanton called the first National Women's Rights Convention, at Seneca Falls, New York. Mott had the total support of her husband, a businessman who was also interested in reforms.

Elected president of the third National Women's Rights Convention in 1852, Mott was widely beloved both within and outside the movement. She was strong and sure in her beliefs in reform, but she had a gentle manner and soft voice that commanded respect immediately. Mott was invaluable to Stanton, helping to free the younger woman from organizational chores. It was thanks in part to Mott that Stanton eventually became the leading intellectual force in the emancipation of American women. Mott continued to work for women's rights—and for freedom of worship, suffrage for freedmen, and peace, as well—until her death in 1880.

Erin Pizzey (1939–)

Erin Pizzey is the founder of the twentieth-century battered women's movement in England.

Born in Tsingtao, China, Pizzey was educated in convent schools. In 1971 she established the Chiswick Center, a neighborhood center offering advice to women. As women gathered to talk about their concerns, Pizzey was struck by many of the terrible tales of wife abuse. In response, Pizzey and a group of other women established child care and a refuge for homeless women. Pizzey wrote of the women's experiences in her book *Scream Quietly or the Neighbors Will Hear,* published in 1974. Her book and the shelters Pizzey established formed the basis for the current shelter movement in the United States. Pizzey continues to write, saying, "I am concerned about the need to understand human relationships. I work mostly with violent relationships and the needs of the women, children, and men, which have to be met. All my writing reflects this search and helps me think ahead to how we can see the family in the future." Pizzey currently resides in London.

Phyllis Schlafly (1924–)

Phyllis Schlafly, a leading spokesperson for the conservative viewpoint on women's rights, played a major role in defeating the Equal Rights Amendment (ERA) to the Constitution. An articulate and outspoken leader of the conservative movement, she believes that women belong in the home as helpmates to their husbands and full-time mothers to their children.

Born into a family with strong conservative values, she attended parochial elementary and secondary schools, Maryville College of the Sacred Heart, and Washington University, where she graduated in 1944. She earned a master's degree in political science at Radcliffe College, served briefly as researcher for several Washington congressmen, then helped run the successful campaign of Republican Congressman Claude I. Bakewell. In 1949, Schlafly married a successful lawyer from Illinois and together they had six children.

Schlafly has served as a delegate since the 1950s to the Republican National Convention and conducted research for Senator Joseph McCarthy. In 1958, Schlafly helped found the Cardinal Mindszenty Foundation to publicize the threat of communism. Her involvement with the Goldwater campaign led to her first book, *A Choice, Not an Echo*, published in 1964. Also in 1964, Schlafly was elected first vice president of the National Federation of Republican Women and in 1972 launched her first attack on the ERA, an article in her own *Phyllis Schlafly Report*. Schlafly contended that the ERA, which demanded equality of rights for women under the law, represented a serious threat to women and the family because it would thrust mothers into military combat and make wives responsible for providing 50 percent of the financial support of their families. She founded a Stop ERA organization and, in response to the women's movement, founded the Eagle Forum. She spoke against the ERA amendment in 30 state legislatures, and made excellent use of the media to promote her views. In 1978, Schlafly received her law degree from Washington University. Due largely to her efforts, along with other antifeminist organizations, the ERA was defeated in 1982.

Patricia S. Schroeder (1940–)

U.S. Representative Patricia Schroeder has been an outspoken advocate for women in the House of Representatives. When Barbara Boxer, the House sponsor of the Violence Against Women Act, was elected to the U.S. Senate, Schroeder took over the act's sponsorship in the House.

Born in Oregon in 1940, Schroeder received her B.A. from the University of Minnesota and her law degree from Harvard in 1964. Schroeder passed her bar exam in Colorado in 1964 and has worked as a field attorney for the National Labor Relations Board, hearing officer for the Colorado Department of Personnel, and was in private law practice for six years. She has served on the faculty of two community colleges and was elected to Congress in 1973.

The longest-serving woman in the U.S. Congress, Schroeder has also earned national recognition as a proponent of women's and family issues. Among her legislative achievements are the Family and Medical Leave Act and a block grant to fund day-care centers for school-age children. She is a passionate advocate for gun control legislation. Schroeder, a long-standing member of the Armed Services Committee and a member of the Committee on the Judiciary, is a member of the Select Committee on Children, Youth and Families. Schroeder serves as co-chair of the Congressional Caucus for Women's Issues, which she helped found.

Elizabeth Cady Stanton (1815–1902)

Elizabeth Cady Stanton, one of the more radical of the nineteenth-century suffragists and women's rights leaders, sought to free women from the legal obstacles that kept them from achieving equal status with men. In the nineteenth century, Stanton, Susan B. Anthony, and Lucretia Mott laid the foundation for women's rights advocates of this century. Their work for divorce reform, though unsuccessful in their time, helped advance today's efforts to stop domestic violence.

Born in New York where her father was a successful lawyer and judge, Stanton determined to prove she was as good as a boy after her father's extreme grief following the death of her only brother. Although Stanton wanted to attend Union College, where her brother had studied, she was sent to Emma Willard's all-female seminary. As a young adult Stanton was exposed to the abolition movement at her cousin's home and also met Henry Stanton, an abolitionist orator ten years her senior. They were married in 1840 in a ceremony from which the promise to obey was omitted.

The Stantons attended the World Anti-Slavery Convention in London on their honeymoon, where Elizabeth Cady Stanton met Lucretia Mott. Together they decided to hold a women's rights convention after they were prohibited from speaking or voting at the convention because of their gender. The women's rights convention was finally held in July 1848, and Stanton drafted the Declaration of Sentiments, modeled after the Declaration of Independence, which declared that women were created equal to men. After Stanton met Susan B. Anthony in 1851, the women worked as a team in the movement. While writing and speaking out on women's rights, Stanton gave birth to six children and worked in her home as a wife and a mother.

The year after Stanton and Anthony started their paper, *Revolution*, they founded the National Woman Suffrage Association to work for the passage of a federal woman suffrage amendment. For the next 20 years Stanton served as president of this organization. Stanton and Anthony traveled all over the country to promote women's rights and in 1888, Stanton unsuccessfully attempted to vote. At the age of eighty Stanton published *The Woman's Bible*, in which she tried to correct what she considered a degrading view of women in the Scriptures. The book was bitterly attacked by clergy, the press, and many of her colleagues. She continued, however, to set forth her views on religion, divorce, and woman suffrage in newspaper and magazine articles, complaining about the state of the women's rights movement and attempting to get President Theodore Roosevelt's support. Stanton died in her sleep at the age of 86.

Gloria Steinem (1934–)

Gloria Steinem, feminist activist and founding editor of *Ms.* magazine, has become a symbol of the twentieth-century women's rights movement.

Born in Toledo, Ohio, Steinem spent her early childhood traveling around the country in a house trailer while her father tried to make a living. After her parents divorced, Steinem cared for her ailing mother in a poor neighborhood in Toledo. In 1952, Steinem went to Smith College, where she majored in government and graduated magna cum laude. She continued her studies in India on a fellowship and worked as a researcher after returning to the states. In 1960, Steinem moved to New York and began her career in journalism. She wrote articles for *Esquire, Vogue, Glamour, and Cosmopolitan;* helped put together a coffee table book, *The Beach Book;* and worked as a scriptwriter on "That Was the Week That Was." In 1968, Steinem began writing a weekly column for *New York* magazine. She joined in many social causes, including the farm laborers with Cesar Chavez and the Committee for Legal Defense of African American radical Angela Davis. Steinem worked on the political campaigns of Eugene McCarthy and Bobby Kennedy, and with Shirley Chisholm helped found the National Women's Political Caucus in 1971.

When *Ms.* magazine was launched in 1972, it was promoted as a magazine that would be informed by feminist concerns and would be owned, operated, and edited by women. Gloria Steinem was the first editor and continued in that position for 15 years, until the magazine was sold due to heavy demands of advertisers. The August 1976 issue of *Ms.* was devoted to domestic violence and its cover featured a woman's bruised face and was captioned "Battered Wives." *Ms.* was one of the first periodicals to publish an entire issue on the subject, and it continued through the years to publish articles about domestic violence. In 1990 a new *Ms.* was started without advertising and with Steinem as consulting editor. Steinem has actively promoted awareness of domestic violence through the format of *Ms.* and from her position as a spokesperson for the feminist movement. She is the author of *Outrageous Acts and Everyday Rebellions; Marilyn: Norma Jean* (co-written with George Barris); *Revolution from Within;* and *Moving beyond Words.*

Tina Turner (1939–)

In 1992, popular rock-and-roll singer Tina Turner wrote, with Kurt Loder, *Tina: My Life Story,* a book from which the movie *What's Love Got To Do with It* was made. This autobiographical piece documented Ike Turner's abuse of Tina over their years together. Her story contributed to the public's understanding of the dynamics of domestic violence.

Tina Turner was born Anna Mae Bullock in 1939 in Brownsville, Tennessee. She sang gospel music in her church as she was growing up. She first performed in front of an audience in 1956 with Ike Turner's band, The Kings of Rhythm. In 1960, a son was born to Ike and Tina Turner and the couple was married in Tijuana. They toured together throughout the United States and Europe for the next 16 years. Ike Turner was very abusive, verbally and physically, and Tina was forced many times to perform and sing through badly swollen lips.

On 1 July 1976 Tina Turner left Ike after a serious beating in Dallas. Associates later said that Ike Turner had been trying to hold back Tina Turner, who was beginning to emerge as an individual star. Tina Turner continued touring, making albums, and starring in movies. In 1991 she was inducted into the Rock-and-Roll Hall of Fame and her career currently continues to be strong.

Lenore Walker (1942–)

Lenore Walker, best known for defining the "battered woman syndrome" and as an expert witness in the courtroom, is a feminist psychologist who has taught and written extensively on domestic violence.

Born in New York, Walker received her B.A. from Hunter College in 1962, her master's degree from City College of New York in 1967, and her doctorate in education from Rutgers University in 1972. Walker was on the faculty of Rutgers Medical School and Colorado Women's College. She is the director of the Battered Women Research Center and the executive director of the Domestic Violence Institute.

Walker has written the books *The Battered Woman* (1979), *The Battered Woman Syndrome* (1984), and *Terrifying Love* (1989). She has contributed numerous articles and manuscripts to anthologies and periodicals, and is in demand as an expert witness on the battered woman syndrome, which has been used as a legal defense for battered women who have killed their abusive partners. Recently the syndrome has been attacked from a number of perspectives, most particularly by feminists, who take issue with the portrayal of all battered women as helpless victims of battering. The battered woman syndrome has been used recently against some battered women to allege they are unfit to take care of their children. Walker continues to serve as a leading spokesperson and sought-after expert witness in the field. On 23 January 1995, Johnnie Cochran, the defense attorney for O. J. Simpson, announced that Lenore Walker would testify on behalf of the defense. This brought extreme criticism from many battered women's advocates and even accusations that Walker had sold out. Although the decision was highly publicized and Walker was stated to be a witness in Cochran's opening statement, she never did testify during the defense's presentation of its case.

Facts, Statistics, and Legal Issues

4

Collecting consistently accurate data regarding domestic violence is difficult, if not impossible, because it depends on victims to report incidents of violence to many diverse sources, including police, courts, shelters, medical facilities, family courts, and so on. To further complicate the collection process, reported information is buried in the data collection systems and case records of these agencies.

Studies indicate that somewhere between 10 and 60 percent of domestic violence incidents are reported to the police. Many reports of domestic violence are never documented, as many states don't require documentation of cases that don't meet certain standards of severity.

Only violence requiring medical treatment is reported to doctors or hospitals. Because so few medical practitioners or facilities have a protocol for dealing with domestic violence, much of what is treated is not recorded as abuse.

Shelters for battered women are short on space and are able to admit only 10 to 40 percent of the women who apply. Shelter personnel believe that for each woman who calls a hotline or enters a shelter there are at least ten battered women without a safe place to stay.

77

Child protective service agencies are many times the first governmental agencies to become aware of domestic violence, but because their primary concern has traditionally been the targeted abuse of children, incidents of wife abuse are buried in their case records.

Schools and day care centers may be aware of families where domestic violence is a problem, but because most states don't have mandatory reporting of domestic violence, information is generally not officially recorded.

Domestic violence data are also collected from surveys, but figures based on surveys are believed to be seriously underestimated because they do not include homes without telephones, people who are not fluent in English, or individuals who are homeless, institutionalized, hospitalized, or in prison at the time of the survey.

Even when directly asked, many women do not report acts of violence. Battered women keep silent out of embarrassment, shame, fear of retaliation, or the tendency to deny or minimize the abuse. Batterers often threaten their wives or children with harm if they tell. Women many times feel that no one will believe them even if they do report the abuse. Often there are strong social or family pressures that keep a battered woman from reporting. Because it is very difficult for a woman to admit to herself that the man with whom she has an intimate relationship is the same man who hurts her emotionally and physically, many women deny the problem even to themselves. Sometimes a woman who has suffered repeated abuse copes with the terror by underestimating the frequency and severity of the abuse she has experienced. A comparison of her assessment of the abuse with hospital records usually shows that the woman has minimized her abuse. This curtain of secrecy behind which domestic violence has been hidden makes gathering precise figures regarding the frequency and extent of the problem impossible.

What Is Known about the Extent and Seriousness of Domestic Violence?

Physical Abuse

Despite 20 years of research, estimates of the number of women severely assaulted by their partners each year vary from more than

2 million to more than 8 million. Most experts place the number of women suffering from physical abuse at between 3 and 4 million each year. None of these estimates include sexual assault or marital rape.

- The American Medical Association estimates that almost 4 million women are victims of severe assaults by boyfriends and husbands each year, and that one in four women is likely to be abused by a partner in her lifetime. The American College of Obstetricians and Gynecologists states that 3 to 4 million women are beaten in their homes every year, but this number refers to women who have called police or been so severely hurt that they required medical attention. The recent American Psychological Association Task Force on Depression in Women indicates that 37 to 40 percent of U.S. women are physically and/or sexually abused before age 21. Medical personnel in emergency rooms feel the number is more likely 50 percent or higher.
- The National Clearinghouse on Domestic Violence conducted a study in 1989 that revealed that between 3 and 4 million women are beaten each year. The study was based on statistical information provided by battered women's shelters.
- The National Crime Survey from 1978 to 1982 reported that some 2.1 million women were victims of domestic violence each year.
- The October 1992 majority staff report of the Senate Judiciary Committee, *Violence Against Women,* concluded that over 1.13 million women each year are reported as victims of serious domestic violence incidents, including crimes of assault, aggravated assault, murder, and rape committed against women in the home. The reports notes that as many as three times that number go unreported. The numbers were based upon data collected from across the United States. The report reveals the extent of the violence in such facts as:

  In 1991 21,000 domestic crimes against women were reported to police each week.

About 20 percent of aggravated assaults reported to the police are committed in the home.

- According to the Family Violence Prevention Fund, a 1993 national poll found that more people (34 percent of men and women) have directly witnessed an incident of domestic violence than have witnessed muggings and robberies combined (19 percent), and that 14 percent of U.S. women acknowledge having been *violently* abused by a husband or boyfriend.

Although the common stereotype of domestic violence tends to be that of relatively minor assaults and squabbles resulting in an occasional black eye, a substantial number of domestic assaults result in serious injury.

- Of 218 women presenting at a metropolitan emergency department with injuries due to domestic violence, 28 percent required admission to the hospital from injuries, 13 percent required major medical treatment, and 40 percent had previously required medical care for abuse (Berrios and Grady 1991).
- One study of battered wives found that the women had been punched, kicked, attacked with knives, razors, or broken bottles, beaten with belts and buckles, burned, and scalded. Forty-two percent had been assaulted with various weapons. All of these women had at some time been bruised by their batterers. Eleven percent of the women studied had suffered lacerations; 32 percent had suffered fractures, including broken noses, teeth, and/or ribs; 4 percent had experienced dislocations; and 9 percent had been beaten to unconsciousness (Ewing 1987).
- The 1991 Department of Justice statistics reveal that 85 percent of intimates' violent crimes reported by female victims were assaults, 11 percent were robberies, and 3 percent were rapes. Approximately 25 percent of the assaults were aggravated, meaning that the offender had used a weapon or had seriously injured the victim. The remaining assaults were simple, indicating either a minor injury—bruises, black eyes, cuts, scratches, swelling, or undetermined injuries requiring less than two days of hospitalization—or a verbal threat of harm.

- Abuse may be the single most common etiology for injury presented by women, accounting for more injury episodes than auto accidents, muggings, and rape combined. A review of 3,676 records randomly selected from among female patients presenting with injury during a year revealed that 40 percent of the women's injury episodes were identified as resulting from a deliberate assault by an intimate. Nineteen percent of the women had a previous history of abusive injury (Stark and Flitcraft 1985).

Emotional Abuse

Battered women suffer extreme emotional abuse. Almost all women who are physically abused also suffer emotional abuse. One reinforces the other. However, many women who are emotionally abused don't experience physical or sexual assault. Though often not reported, emotional abuse can produce devastating results.

- In 1993, the Commonwealth Fund National Health survey found that 7 percent of American women (3.9 million) who were married or living with someone as part of a couple were physically abused, while 37 percent (20.7 million) were verbally or emotionally abused by a spouse or partner.
- In a survey of 234 women with a history of physical abuse, 229 (98 percent) reported emotional abuse as well; 174 (74 percent) had received threats, 211 (90 percent) were ridiculed, 170 (73 percent) experienced excessive jealousy and possessiveness, 133 (57 percent) were threatened with changes to the marriage (i.e., divorce or abandonment), 184 (79 percent) were restricted (isolation from social or financial support), and 137 (59 percent) had property (sentimental or personal objects) damaged.

  Of the six types of emotional abuse, 101 (45 percent) of the sample rated ridicule the worst and 159 (72 percent) of the battered women reported that the emotional abuse had a more severe impact on them than the physical abuse. Women who rated emotional abuse as having a more severe impact were more likely to believe that the man would carry out his threats, or that his behavior or claims were sometimes justified. Of the 229 women who suffered emotional abuse, 54 percent (123) could use the emotional abuse to predict physical abuse (Follingstad et al. 1990).

- One study of abused women reported that nearly half of the women studied were forbidden by their abusers to have personal friends or to have such friends in the home. Another found that 30 percent of the 420 abused women studied had actually been physically imprisoned by their abusers. These women reported having been locked in closets, locked in or physically confined to their homes, and tied to furniture.
- Many times battered women are financially isolated. Lenore Walker found that 34 percent of the 435 battered women she studied had no access to checking accounts, 51 percent had no access to charge accounts, and 27 percent had no access to cash. Even battered women who are employed outside of the home are often denied access to their financial resources by the batterers (Ewing 1987).

Sexual Abuse

Battering can often involve a substantial amount of sexual abuse, including marital rape and sexual mutilation. Marital rape is rarely discussed with others or reported to law enforcement authorities, and only a few of those reported are prosecuted. It is common for battered women to have sexual intercourse with their husbands to avoid being battered. While this type of coercive sexual activity is considered in many states' laws as spousal sexual assault, many women do not consider it to be so and many fear they will not be believed if they report it. Some statistical findings:

- Diana Russell asked a random sample of 930 women in San Francisco if they had been sexually abused by strangers, husbands, or other family members. She found that 1 of every 7 women who had ever been married reported rape by a husband or ex-husband. More women reported sexual assaults by husbands and ex-husbands than by acquaintances or strangers. Finkelhor and Yllo reported similar findings in a representative sample of 326 women in Boston (Browne 1987).

- Forty percent of battered women are forced into sex against their will by their partners or husbands. Vaginal rape is the type most frequently reported. However, anal rape, violence during sex, and forced use of objects also occur. Many women have described being forced into sex after being physically abused. Rape in combination with battering is associated with an increased risk of domestic homicide (Holtz and Furniss 1993).
- A National Institute of Mental Health–funded study (based on urban area hospitals) estimated that over half of all rapes of women over the age of 30 had been perpetrated by an intimate partner (Browne 1990).

Although family pressures, including number of children, are frequently cited as risk factors for battering, battered women seen in medical facilities have no more children than non-battered women. Still, battered women are pregnant nearly twice as often and are significantly more likely to have a miscarriage or abortion.

Pregnancy is no protection from abuse and may even incite batterers to greater violence. The propensity of battering husbands to punch and kick their pregnant wives in the stomach, with resultant miscarriages and injuries to their reproductive organs, has been noted by medical professionals. There is an increased chance of pre-term labor and low birth weight in infants of mothers who are battered during pregnancy, and women often suffer injuries to the breasts and genitals.

Between 25 and 45 percent of battered women have experienced battering during pregnancy, with some studies putting the figure as high as 63 percent. One retrospective chart review of 2,676 women with injuries at an emergency department found 21 percent of the women's injuries positive, probable, or suggestive of battering. Because there are many battering incidents that never reach official medical records, the actual number of incidents is probably at least twice that number.

What Are the Characteristics of the Battered Woman?

Many studies have been done of women survivors of domestic violence, with very few commonalities having been found among the women studied. Feminists believe the only common characteristic is that they are all women and that looking for the cause of domestic violence by studying women is another example of victim-blaming. Social learning psychologists theorize that women who grow up in a home where they witness their mothers being beaten are more likely to become victimized themselves as adults. Without effective intervention, the damage done to them as children carries over into adulthood. Some studies report that girls who witness their mothers' abuse or who are themselves abused suffer low self-esteem that may contribute to their own later abuse. Sociologists believe that growing up in a traditional home and retaining a belief in the family model of male superiority can contribute to the likelihood of a woman being victimized in adulthood.

In 1986, researchers Gerald T. Hotaling and David B. Sugarman remarked:

> the search for characteristics of women that contribute to their own victimization is futile. . . . It is sometimes forgotten that men's violence is men's behavior. . . . What is surprising is the enormous effort to explain male behavior by examining characteristics of women. It is hoped that future research will show more about the factors that promote violent male behavior and that stronger theory will be developed to explain it (Hotaling and Sugarman, 1986).

Economic Status

It is difficult to find much consistency among data regarding economic status and abuse. Because statistics are generally gathered from the police, hospital emergency rooms, social service agencies, and shelters, domestic violence professionals believe the statistics are skewed, overrepresenting the economic underclass—those persons most likely to turn to public services for help. The results of the following study illustrate this problem.

- The National Woman Abuse Prevention Project reports that "domestic violence happens to people of all racial, economic, and religious groups. For example, police in the mostly white, upper-class Washington, D.C. suburb of Montgomery County, Maryland, received as many domestic disturbance calls as were received in the same period in Harlem, New York City. However, low-income battered women are more likely to seek assistance from public agencies, such as shelters and hospital emergency rooms, because they have fewer private resources than middle- and upper-income women. They are therefore more likely to be counted in official reporting statistics" (NWAPP, "Answers to Some Commonly Asked Questions about Domestic Violence," *Domestic Violence Fact Sheets,* 1989).

- "Studies consistently report an inverse relation between income and domestic violence although certain high stress, white-collar occupations or occupational environments may be associated with elevated risk. Despite early reports that domestic violence is common in upper and middle-class communities, numerous studies, including the national representative survey, find substantially higher rates of domestic violence among the poor and working class. *The extent to which reporting bias explains these differences is unclear"* [author's italics] (Stark and Flitcraft 1988).

- The psychologist George Levinger studied applicants for divorce and learned that 40 percent of the working-class applicants cited abuse as the reason they were seeking the divorce. Of the middle-class applicants, 23 percent also mentioned violence as the motivation for wanting to end the marriage (Gelles and Cornell 1990).

The "Affluent" Battered Woman

The battered woman who is from upper middle-income or affluent circumstances faces a unique set of problems. She is generally married to a man who is climbing to or has reached the top of his profession. She is active in the community, entertains regularly, has children, and manages the home and family activities. For her, however, the "American dream" has turned into a nightmare.

Affluent women are the least likely to report their abuse. Many feel the shame and embarrassment all battered women feel, but they also feel a certain class-based shame, having internalized the belief that domestic violence only happens to "poor and ignorant" women.

The public perception is that this wonderful professional man, who provides so well for his family and who obviously loves them so very much, couldn't possibly do such a thing. This perception makes it very difficult for the victim to confide in friends or obtain assistance from law enforcement. The upper middle-class abuser, usually educated and affluent, is often articulate and able to convince the victim that she is overreacting or crazy. A woman who is educated is quite likely to blame herself, asking How could I *let* this happen to me?

Many affluent battered women are totally dependent upon their husbands for financial support. The house, the credit cards, and the bank accounts are either in his name or jointly owned. If these women do leave, they become destitute, yet many times are ineligible for services because they share valuable assets with their husbands. Most feel they cannot turn to family or friends and they often have a difficult time finding an opening if they are able to contact a shelter.

The woman in this population who works is usually professionally employed and in constant danger of losing her job. In many cases the corporate hierarchy does not permit employees to have personal problems, and a woman who is harassed at work by her abuser or who has to tell her employer there is a restraining order in place often faces imminent unemployment.

Because the affluent abusive husband has the ability to hire high-priced attorneys, it is difficult to prosecute him for wife abuse. He may use his wealth during custody disputes to show the court he is better able to provide for the children. Thus, when a woman runs from her abusive husband, she many times loses her children as well as her home and social status.

Race, Ethnicity, and Culture

Most studies have found that domestic violence cuts across racial, ethnic, and cultural lines and affects families in all communities. Due again to the difficulty in gathering accurate statistics, results of studies are dependent on many factors, including where and how the study was conducted. Because of pervasive racism in the United States, the handling of domestic violence reports by law enforcement has been uneven. Battered women from communities that are not part of mainstream America due to specific cultural and/or language differences experience particular difficulties accessing resources and breaking free of the violence.

The special characteristics of domestic violence—the denial, the isolation, and the invisibility of the problem—are intensified in many ethnic communities. English language competency is often the biggest obstacle faced by victims. Women in particular may have a poorer command of the language than either their husbands or children, for they many times have no immediate need or the opportunity to learn English. Men have to learn English in order to get a job and the children learn at school. Unfortunately, this means that the abused woman does not know her rights or her legal options or have access to community resources. She many times depends on her husband or children to act as translators. If a woman is able to make a call to a hotline and reaches a person who cannot understand her, it may discourage her from reaching out for help again.

The belief that the woman's role in the family is strictly that of wife and mother is still very strong in many cultures. Women from these cultures have been raised to be obedient and subservient to men in the family and to put their family's needs before their own. Abused women often experience extreme pressure to remain silent and not reach out for help. In addition, to reach out and make public one's family problems is regarded as a violation of the sanctity of the home. The victim, the nuclear family, and the extended family lose face in the community. To report domestic violence could cut off a woman from her own community as well as her family.

Many women are afraid to report abuse because they fear law enforcement. Some women come from countries where the police were viewed not as friends, but as thugs or members of death squads. An abuser may threaten the woman by saying that if she reports his abuse he will be deported and therefore unable to provide support. If there are children, the abuser may threaten to leave and take the children back to their country of origin. The problem is compounded if the woman is an undocumented immigrant, for she is sure she will be deported if she is discovered, and she may not be eligible for any kind of public assistance. The laws regarding battered women who are not citizens or legal residents are complex, although some safeguards are in place for battered women who are married to citizens or legal residents and have begun the process to obtain resident status. These women require special advocates who understand their culture, language, and immigration laws.

Different kinds of problems face Native American women living on reservations who are victims of domestic violence. Indian reservations can be found all over the United States, but most are in fairly remote areas and spread out over many miles on prairies, mesas, canyons, deserts, and so on. Public transportation does not exist, highways are few, and law enforcement is not a phone call away, but can be hours or even days away. There are a limited number of law enforcement officers, and other crimes are given higher priority. If there are any services for abused women on the reservation, they may be almost impossible to access. Some of the problems facing Native American women are similar to those of other cultures. The woman may be reluctant to take action against the abuser because reporting him may be considered a betrayal by family members; strong kinship ties often exist and seeking help outside the extended family may be taboo. In addition, for some victims language can be a barrier that prevents them from seeking help.

Although there is a growing recognition that women from diverse cultural communities face unique problems, the development of adequate services is difficult due to lack of funds, the fast-growing numbers of diverse cultures in the United States, and the complexity of the problem. In addition, because of the growing resentment toward immigrants and the prevalence of racism in this country, services for this population are given increasingly low priority.

Age

Results of the National Family Survey indicate that all forms of marital violence occur most frequently among those under 30 years of age. The rate of marital violence among those under 30 is more than double the rate for the next older age group (31–50). Studies that examine women who seek help from agencies or shelters also find that the mean age is 30 or younger (Gelles and Cornell, 1990). The large numbers of abused women under 30 may be because many abused women in their 30s have left their abusive mate; it's possible that their children are in school and they are therefore able to work, or their earning capacity has increased, or after a number of tries they have been successful in breaking free. Another factor that might skew survey results, however, is the particular problem that older women face when confronted with the problem of domestic violence.

Older Battered Women

Older battered women have unique issues and needs. An older battered woman is generally one whose socialization occurred in the 1950s or earlier. They grew up in a time when women rarely got divorced, as the social stigma was too intense. They were raised with the idea that some abuse was normal and a woman just learned to live with it. Career options for women were few in number; a woman worked as a secretary, nurse, or teacher until she got married and became a wife and mother.

When women of this generation were young, it was relatively easy to commit people to mental hospitals against their will. An abusive husband was able to convince a doctor or a judge that his battered wife was crazy or delusional. Once she was committed, the abuser had the legal authority to make decisions about her treatment, such as whether she should receive electro-shock treatments. Even though the law has since changed, a woman who was previously committed by her abusive mate lives in terror that he can and will do it again.

A woman who has invested 30, 40, or 50 years in a relationship has more to lose if she leaves her abuser. If she and her abuser own or are close to owning their home free of mortgage payments, it may be hard to leave. She has spent many years in her home—furnishing it, tending the garden, planting trees that are now grown. She has probably raised children in that home, and it holds many happy memories that make leaving it difficult.

Her adult children may put tremendous pressure on her to stay with their father, telling her he won't be able to make it without her, at which point the focus shifts from his abuse to her selfishness in wanting to leave him alone.

The fear of being alone is particularly intense for older women, who worry about aging and becoming ill with no one to care for them. This may also compound the worries of their children, who many times fear that the responsibility will fall upon them if their parents aren't together.

While the battered older woman may be very angry and bitter toward her abuser, she generally needs to end the relationship in a way that preserves her dignity and integrity. This means that she has no wish to humiliate him or hurt him professionally.

Women from older generations were brought up to keep family problems private and they are therefore much less able to reach out for help. Because these women were brought up believing they were responsible for the happiness of the family, this issue of violence in the home causes them intense pain.

Dating Violence

Another group that deserves attention in this section is women aged 14–22 who are victims of dating violence. Although most institutions deal with this separately, it is considered a prelude to domestic violence and needs to be addressed.

Young people also experience violence in their intimate relationships. Recent investigation has found at least as high a prevalence of physical assault among dating and cohabitating couples as among married couples. Because studies on dating violence are limited almost exclusively to students in high school and college, little is known about individuals between the ages of 14 and 22 who are not attending school.

Dating violence seems to be a problem in all classes, communities, and ethnic groups. Although both men and women can be victims of dating violence, data reveal that women are the primary victims and men are hit only when women fight back. However, young single women seem more likely than married women to fight back in a violent episode with an intimate partner or date.

Dating relationships are rehearsals for marriage, and young people many times act out their parts as they perceive they should be in a committed relationship. They are just beginning to explore their roles in relationships at this stage in their development, and many times these roles are based primarily on gender role stereotypes. Young men and women experience peer pressure to follow the norm—they fear being labeled *different,* so many of them stay within the parameters of what they define as normal male and female behavior. This behavior is often based on the stereotyped roles of the dominant male and the submissive female.

Dating violence is even more hidden than violence in adult relationships. Many times this is due to isolation—the victim has given up friends and activities upon the jealous insistence of her boyfriend—or it can be because of shame and fear. Violence may be a new experience for a young woman and she may feel confused and not know where to turn. It may be difficult for a young person to admit that she has made a mistake in her choice of a boyfriend, and she may attempt to hide the problem from her parents for fear they will restrict her activities or confront the issue openly in a way that might be embarrassing to her.

Research shows that attitudes and emotions such as jealousy, guilt, fear, insecurity, or confusion are cited most often as the cause of abusive incidents. Arguments and lack of communication within the relationship seem to precipitate many incidents. The pattern of abuse is similar to adult abuse: control is enforced by verbal and physical abuse.

Most of the research on violence in dating relationships does not include date rape as a form of violence, or the statistics would be much higher. Unfortunately, little is said about the sexual coercion and assault that take place repeatedly in abusive dating relationships. In this case, the young man coerces the woman into having sex, threatening to leave her if she doesn't, telling her she needs to prove her love or to be a real woman, or forcing himself on her sexually if all else fails. This kind of violence can cause the victim to feel worthless, degraded, humiliated, and shamed, gradually making it almost impossible for her to escape.

As with adult violence, substance abuse and dating violence often occur together, though there is no causal relationship. If someone is prone to anger or violent outbursts, alcohol or drug intake may increase the likelihood of that happening. Using alcohol and drugs may impair a woman's ability to protect herself from assault.

Battered Women with Disabilities

Battered women with disabilities face special obstacles in getting help escaping their abusive home and living in safety. Not only are many shelters ill-equipped to handle women with disabilities, but the justice system and the medical system may provide further obstacles.

The Americans with Disabilities Act of 1990 defines disability as (1) a physical or mental impairment that substantially limits one or more of the major life activities of an individual, (2) a record of such an impairment, or (3) being regarded as having such an impairment.

Many shelters are in large, converted houses and few had wheelchair access until recently. Due to a lack of resources, many shelter workers still lack the training to address adequately the needs of women with disabilities. Not only are there battered women in wheelchairs, there are battered women who are hearing- and sight-impaired, who have a mental impairment, or who have other special needs.

The justice system, including law enforcement, may provide obstacles, as they may be neither equipped nor educated to handle the needs of the disabled. A woman with a history of emotional disorders many times refrains from reporting domestic violence to law enforcement for fear that the courts will not take her seriously.

Women with disabilities are more likely to have medical complications when they are physically injured. Because battered women often do not receive medical treatment for their injuries, this could result in very costly complications for the battered woman with disabilities.

Aside from the problems a battered woman with disabilities has with the system, she is more vulnerable and less able to defend herself against her abuser. She is much more dependent upon her abuser for her basic physical needs. Economic and physical dependency issues for the battered woman with disabilities may be very severe, and can only be addressed satisfactorily with resources that will provide training for law enforcement, medical, and shelter personnel, as well as funds to make shelters and transitional programs accessible.

Are Men Victims of Domestic Violence?

Since domestic violence against women has become a mainstream topic and has received increasing media attention, there has been an increase in newspaper articles and statements made on radio and TV talk shows about the problem of "battered husbands," including articles with such headings as "Husbands Are Battered as Often as Wives" (*USA Today*, 23 June 1994).

Most of these articles and statements are based upon a family violence survey conducted by Murray Straus, Richard Gelles, and Suzanne Steinmetz in 1979 that used the Conflict Tactics Scale (CTS) to measure the extent of violence in the home. The CTS does not consider context or severity of violence and is organized into categories that combine threatened, attempted, and actual violence. The "high-risk of injury" category includes "trying to hit with something" and excludes "slapping"; yet, there is no injury if a person throws an ashtray and misses, while a slap can result in anything from a red mark to a broken nose, tooth, or jaw. This survey also provides no way of knowing whether the act of violence was initiated or a defensive response. Finally, only couples who were together were surveyed, and there was no attempt to survey both members of the couple. Because the survey did not include separated or divorced men or women, those who had experienced abuse that year and had separated or those who had experienced abuse by the spouse after separation were not counted.

Even so, Susan Steinmetz coined the term "battered husbands" in response to the survey results, saying these men are hidden victims, that battered men are too ashamed to come forward with the problem. Her remarks have fueled claims of "mutual combat" and that spouse abuse equally affects both wives and husbands.

Richard Gelles and Murray Straus, who worked with Steinmetz on the survey and with her published the results in *Behind Closed Doors: Violence in the American Family* (1980), have since qualified the study's results. In their 1988 book *Intimate Violence,* Gelles and Straus state that women more often act in retaliation and self-defense and are disproportionately injured. In the 1994 paper "Domestic Violence: Not an Even Playing Field," Gelles states,

> Research shows that nearly 90 percent of battering victims are women and only about ten percent are men. . . . Men who beat their wives, who use emotional abuse and blackmail to control their wives, and are then hit or even harmed, cannot be considered battered men. A battered man is one who is physically injured by a wife or partner and has not physically struck or psychologically provoked her. Despite the fact that indeed, there are battered men too, it is misogynistic to paint the entire issue of domestic violence with a broad brush and make it appear as though men are victimized by their partners as much as women. It is not a simple case of simple numbers. . . . [One] cannot simply ignore the outcomes of violence, which leave more than 1,400 women dead each year and millions physically and/or psychologically scarred for life.

Gelles estimates that 100,000 men are battered in the United States each year, compared with 2 to 4 million battered women.

Another assertion made to support the theory of violent wives is that there are nearly equal numbers of male and female victims of spousal homicides. This argument was made in the article "The Truth about Domestic Violence: A Falsely Framed Issue" by R. L. McNeely and Gloria Robinson-Simpson in the professional journal *Social Work*, in which the authors stated that "Steinmetz observed that when weapons neutralize differences in physical strength, about as many men as women are victims of homicide." This was based on a statement by Steinmetz that data from a 1958 study—which found that 53 Philadelphia men killed their wives and 47 women killed their husbands between 1948 and 1952—suggested that almost an equal number of wives kill their husbands as the reverse, with Steinmetz theorizing that the difference in number was equalized by the availability of weapons to women.

Law enforcement statistics contradict this conclusion, however, and these statistics are almost impossible to misrepresent (see Tables 1 and 2). Between 1976 and 1985, 10,529 wives and 7,888 husbands were killed by their mates. A U.S Department of Justice report indicates that 383 men were killed by their wives and

TABLE 1 Domestic Violence Killings of Men Annually

	Husbands Killed	Boyfriends Killed	TOTAL
1983	753	290	1,043
1984	598	299	897
1985	569	266	835
1986	557	309	866
1987	543	281	824
1988	475	289	764
1989	516	301	817
7-year average =	858/year		

TABLE 2 Domestic Violence Killings of Women Annually

	Wives Killed	Girlfriends Killed	TOTAL
1983	1,062	425	1,487
1984	972	339	1,421
1985	1,006	474	1,480
1986	989	536	1,525
1987	1,045	462	1,507
1988	1,075	517	1,592
1989	881	559	1,440
7-year average =	1,493/year		

Source: Bureau of Justice Statistics, *Uniform Crime Reports* (Washington, DC: U.S. Department of Justice, 1983–1989).

913 women were killed by their husbands in 1992. Studies also show that most women murder their husbands in self-defense, while most men who kill their wives do so after lengthy periods of battering.

Does Domestic Violence Occur in Same-Sex Relationships?

Although studies show that the majority of violent incidents between intimates involves heterosexual couples, there is growing awareness of battering in homosexual relationships. Due to public attitudes about homosexuality in our society, it has been difficult for victims of lesbian or gay battering to get help. Some shelters do not admit victims of lesbian battering, and there are very few resources available to gay men.

The lesbian community has had a difficult time with the issue. Because many women have perpetuated the belief that women are not violent to one another, battering remained a secret in the lesbian community for a long time. Many times the violence has been blamed on drug abuse, mental instability, or personality flaws. The theory of "mutual abuse," which holds both partners responsible for the violence, has become another way to deny lesbian battering. According to Barbara Hart in *Naming the Violence*, "Battered lesbians describe the patterns of violence as terrorism and control. . . . The same elements of hierarchy of power, ownership, entitlement and control exist in lesbian family relationships. Largely this is true because lesbians have also learned that violence works in achieving partner compliance." The issue of lesbian battering is being dealt with increasingly within the battered women's movement.

Just as lesbian women are openly dealing with the issue, gay men are also confronting battering in their own communities, though much of their focus is on treating the batterers to effect behavioral change. Because there is no equivalent to the battered woman's movement and shelters organizing and advocating for them, much of the support for gay men has come through men's treatment programs. In some communities, domestic violence consortiums or coalitions of local programs have helped the gay men's community develop needed resources in response to the problem.

What Are the Effects of Domestic Violence?

Effects on the Women

Domestic violence is devastating to the women who are its victims. Aside from the obvious physical effects, some of which can be severe and last a lifetime, women suffer emotionally, socially, and financially from domestic violence. They may endure economic hardship; lose their homes, possessions, employment, self-esteem, and children; and be isolated from family and friends.

Psychological Effects

Some of the psychological problems that have been associated with victims of domestic violence are temporary and are *effects*, not *causes*, of the violence. They often enable the woman to survive the abuse and, though they leave emotional scars such as low self-esteem, the problems generally disappear with the cessation of the abuse and the beginning of positive emotional support.

Learned Helplessness In his book *Helplessness: On Depression, Development, and Death* (1975), M. Seligman advances the social learning theory of learned helplessness, which asserts that when a person feels helpless as a result of repeated abuse he or she has a distorted perception of reality. Lenore Walker calls upon this theory in explaining why women find it difficult to escape an abusive relationship, saying they are unable to see any way out. This feeling of helplessness leads battered women to use various defense mechanisms, such as minimizing, denial, and dissociation (splitting of the mind from the body during violence in order to cope). Walker stresses that this is not passivity, but use of highly developed sets of coping skills.

In her book *Terrifying Love* (1989), Walker cites the factors in an adult's battering relationship that are associated with the development of learned helplessness:

1. A pattern of violence, particularly a "cycle of violence" consisting of at least three stages:
   • The tension-building stage, in which the abuser's tension mounts at perceived irritations (housekeeping, children acting out, dinner not ready on time, food not to his liking, and so on). He displays hostility and dissatisfaction and usually employs

demeaning acts such as name-calling. The woman feels as if she is "walking on eggshells" and attempts to placate the abuser, using interventions to control the situation and prevent an explosion.
- The explosion stage, which occurs when the tension builds to the point where the abuser's rage spills over in the form of verbal, emotional, and physical abuse. This is the violent and dangerous phase and is usually brief, lasting from a few minutes to less than 24 hours.
- The honeymoon period, during which the abuser is typically apologetic, kind, or simply stops abusing for a short period and thus reinforces the woman's false belief that he will change, which in turn reinforces her decision to remain in the relationship.

2. Sexual abuse of the woman
3. Jealousy, overpossessiveness, and intrusiveness of the batterer and isolation of the woman
4. Threats to hurt or kill the woman
5. Psychological torture of the woman
6. The woman's awareness of the man's violence against others, including children, animals, pets, or inanimate objects
7. Alcohol or drug abuse by the man or woman

The Battered Woman Syndrome   The battered woman syndrome is a psychological diagnosis that is generally employed when a plea of self-defense is entered in the case of a woman who has killed her abusive partner or who, with her abuser, has committed a criminal act. The assignment of this diagnosis does not imply that victims of domestic violence have a mental illness that causes the violence, but rather that they suffer psychological trauma as a result of the violence. According to Dr. Walker, who first identified this syndrome, "the Battered Woman Syndrome is a terrified human being's normal response to an abnormal and dangerous situation" (1989).

A woman who suffers from battered woman syndrome does so as the result of a combination of learned helplessness and depression. She exhibits such symptoms as lack of energy and motivation, feelings of incompetence and powerlessness, and an inability to perceive alternatives to her situation. This immobilizes the woman and makes it psychologically "impossible for her to initiate responses which might bring about an end to the abuse she is suffering" (Ewing 1987).

Post-Traumatic Stress Disorder In 1987 it was determined that some battered women meet the criteria established by the American Psychiatric Association under the diagnosis of post-traumatic stress disorder (PTSD). According to this diagnosis, several criteria must be met, including:

1. Experiencing a severely distressing event outside the range of human experience, such as a serious threat to one's life or physical integrity
2. Re-experiencing the event in either recurrent recollections or recurrent dreams, a sudden sense of reliving the event or flashbacks, or intense psychological distress at events that symbolize an aspect of the traumatic event
3. Persistent avoidance of stimuli associated with the event
4. At least two symptoms of increased arousal not present before the event, including sleep disturbance, outbursts of anger, difficulty concentrating, hyper-vigilance, exaggerated startle response, physiological reaction when exposed to events reminiscent of the original event
5. Duration of the symptoms for at least one month

The Stockholm Syndrome Some psychologists believe that women who are victims of domestic violence can suffer a syndrome that most nearly resembles the Stockholm syndrome, which was identified in 1973 after four people held captive in a Stockholm bank vault for six days became attached to the robbers. The hostages began to perceive their captors as their friends and the police as their enemies.

Four conditions lead to development of the syndrome in battered women: the abuser threatens the woman's survival; she cannot escape, or thinks she cannot; she becomes isolated from others; and the abuser shows some kindness.

Because there is an imbalance of power between the abuser and his victim, the woman develops a "traumatic bond" with her abuser, feeling totally dependent on him. He isolates her from others, which only increases her dependency. In addition, the woman suffers from low self-esteem, the abuse is intermittent, and there are periods when everything seems normal. This combination renders the battered woman psychologically unable to leave.

The four long-term psychological effects of the Stockholm syndrome on the abused woman are displaced rage (focusing rage on herself or others instead of her abuser), seeing her abuser as either all good or all bad, losing her sense of self and believing she deserved the abuse, and getting caught up in the push-pull dynamic (her impulse to simultaneously push the man away and keep him close).

Some battered women's advocates have objected to the use of the Stockholm syndrome, saying there is a distinct difference between hostages and battered women. They point out that hostages are usually male, their captivity is not lifelong, there is not and has not been an intimate relationship between hostages and their captors, and hostages know that someone is advocating for their release.

"Crazy" Behavior Some law enforcement and social service professionals have reported witnessing women who are in abusive relationships acting "crazy," displaying disturbed and bizarre behavior. Dr. Lenore Walker has found in her work with abused women that those women who do exhibit behavioral disturbances or personality disorders while in a violent relationship generally cease to exhibit any bizarre behavior once they are free of the violence.

Psychoanalytic Self Psychology Proponents of Psychoanalytic Self Psychology evaluate the battered woman's sense of self as it relates to her abusive environment rather than seeing women as masochistic and inviting abuse, as has been the psychoanalytic theory of the past. H. Kohuts, the psychoanalyst who first advanced this theory, refers to "fragmentation" and "disintegration anxiety." Disintegration anxiety is just as it sounds, intense anxiety about the breakup of one's self. Symptoms include serious loss of initiative, profound drop in self-esteem, and a sense of total meaninglessness. Unchecked disintegration anxiety can lead to permanent disintegration or psychosis. C. Ewing uses Kohut's Psychoanalytic Self Psychology theory when describing the moment a battered woman—whose self-esteem is extremely damaged, who sees few alternatives to her abusive situation, and who has difficulty removing herself from the abusive situation—must decide to stay and risk "psychological death" or assert herself and kill her batterer, saying that a woman at this point sees killing her mate as the only way out (1987).

Other Effects of Domestic Violence on Women

Victims of domestic violence are survivors and find various ways to endure the abuse until they are able to leave the relationship. The coping strategies they work out enable them to put their feelings on hold so that they can deal with the day-to-day challenges of a violent and dangerous life. In addition to those psychological defenses already described, women learn other coping strategies, the most common of which are denial, minimization, anger, nightmares, shock, and dissociation.

Denial and minimization enable a woman to live with what is happening and avoid feelings of terror and humiliation (although, as has been shown, denial and minimization can also be counterproductive, as they cause the victim to deny the seriousness of the problem). Anger enables her to take strong action in an emergency. Nightmares provide a way to experience strong feelings of fear, anger, panic, and shame that she may not be able to share with anyone at the time. Shock and dissociation can numb the woman's mind and body while the assault takes place and for a time afterward, enabling her to avoid dealing with immediate feelings until she is safe.

Some survivors may develop one or more dangerous, unhealthy, or ineffective coping strategies, such as substance abuse, frequent job changes, promiscuity, eating disorders, prostitution, troubled relations with others, physical problems and illnesses, stress reactions, low self-esteem, and child abuse.

Battered women may suffer a range of psychosocial problems, not because they are sick but because they are battered. According to the American Medical Association, battering may account for 25 percent of women seeking emergency psychiatric care. Battering precipitates one of four suicide attempts by women. A three-year study by the National Task Force on Women and Depression, organized by the American Psychological Association, found that in many women depression may be the result of PTSD or undiagnosed head trauma from battering.

Statistics from the 1985 National Family Violence Survey show that women who were severely assaulted spent twice as many days in bed as other women, reported being in poor health three times as often, suffered twice as many headaches, suffered four times the rate of depression, and attempted suicide 5.5 times more often. More than 9 percent of the women reported taking time off from work because of domestic violence and 19 percent who were severely assaulted spent time away from work.

Many battered women develop such stress-related illnesses as hypertension, ulcers, allergies, skin disorders, chronic fatigue, chronic back ailments, or migraine headaches. Because generalized stress can affect the immune system, reducing the body's ability to fight off disease, battered women may be susceptible to such diseases linked to this change in the immunological system as cancer, respiratory illnesses, cardiovascular problems, and so on.

Women generally need ongoing support for a period of time after becoming free of the violence, to work through the denial, minimization, anger, low self-esteem, and other effects of the violence. Some of the coping strategies that enabled them to survive while in the relationship can impede their growth once they are independent. If they have developed more severe psychological problems or very negative behaviors such as substance abuse or child abuse, they may need professional help.

The Effects of Domestic Violence on the Children

"I feel sad when my mom and my dad fight . . . he hit my mom with the electric fan."—7-year-old

"My mom and dad don't fight anymore . . . the last time it happened was last night."—9-year-old

"When I grow up I'm just going to get a knife and kill him."—8-year-old

"I get really mad when my dad hits my mom. I yell at him and I say, do not touch my mom."—7-year-old

"I told him to leave and never come back. I feel sad."—10-year-old

"I told mom not to worry. I won't let it happen again."—4-year-old

"I don't want my mommy to hurt her head again."—3-year-old

"We're in a place that's safe now. My daddy can't find us."—7-year-old in a shelter

All of the above quotes came from children interviewed by the author who are living or have lived with domestic violence. They are just a few of the more than 3.3 million children between the ages of 3 and 17 who witness domestic violence in this country each year (Jaffe et al., 1988).

In the vast majority of families, women are the primary caretakers of children, and the battering of their mothers affects the children in many ways. Studies of children who witness violence against their mothers indicate that the children are at considerable risk physically, psychologically, and emotionally. These children face the dual threats of witnessing traumatic events and of physical abuse. Children of abused women may be injured during an incident of parental violence, be traumatized by fear for their mother and their own helplessness in protecting her, blame themselves for not preventing the violence or for causing it, or be abused or neglected themselves.

The presence of domestic violence is the single most identifiable risk factor for predicting child abuse (Johnson 1987). The battering of mothers usually predates the abuse of children. Several national studies have found that children are victims of physical abuse or neglect in 70 percent of families where the woman is battered. Nearly half of the children had been physically or sexually abused. Five percent had been hospitalized as a result of the abuse.

Although abused mothers often parent amazingly well under the circumstances, a woman is eight times more likely to hurt her children when she is being abused than when she is safe from violence (Walker 1984). Some mothers release their anger and extreme stress on their children, or they may overdiscipline their children to placate the batterer or protect the children from his rage.

Women who have been battered repeatedly are sometimes unable to be psychologically responsive to their children. They may display the following behaviors:

- unresponsiveness to the child's emotional needs
- passive rejection of the child
- detachment or lack of involvement with the child
- interaction with the child only when necessary

- lack of display of pleasure when interacting with the child
- lack of positive response toward the child's attempts to elicit interaction
- poor ability to comfort the child in times of distress
- lack of sharing in the positive experience of the child
- withdrawal, emotionlessness, or depression
- inability to derive pleasure or satisfaction from a relationship with the child

Children in homes where domestic violence occurs may receive injuries indirectly: children may be struck by thrown items or weapons, infants may suffer injuries if being held by their mother when the abuser strikes out, or older children may receive injuries while protecting their mother. Many fathers inadvertently injure children while throwing about furniture and other household objects while abusing the woman. The youngest children sustain the most serious injuries, such as concussions and broken shoulders and ribs. A very young child, held by his mother in an attempt to protect him, is hurt when the abuser continues to beat his mother without any regard for the child's safety. In a 36-month study of 146 American children ages 11 to 17 who came from homes where wife beating was a major problem, all sons over the age of 14 attempted to protect their mothers from attacks and 62 percent of them were injured in the process (Roy 1988).

Children in violent homes are at considerable risk of developing a range of psychological problems. The psychological and emotional effect of witnessing domestic violence is very similar to the psychological trauma suffered by direct victims of child abuse. The most frequently reported psychological disturbances suffered by these child victims include depression, anxiety, suicidal tendencies, phobias, withdrawal, and overt psychoses. According to a 1988 study done by the National Women Abuse Prevention Project, emotional effects include:

- taking responsibility for the abuse and for resolving the problem
- lowered self-esteem
- constant anxiety
- guilt for not being able to stop the abuser or for loving the abuser
- fear of abandonment

Commonly reported psychosomatic complaints include headaches, abdominal pains, stuttering, bed-wetting, and sleep disturbances. Children exhibit behavior problems, particularly aggression, and have difficulty in their relationships with peers.

Preschoolers show signs of terror, as evidenced by their yelling, irritable behavior, hiding, shaking, and stuttering. They often experience insomnia, sleepwalking, nightmares, and bed-wetting, or suffer such psychosomatic problems as headaches, stomachaches, diarrhea, ulcers, and asthma, as well as regressing to earlier stages of functioning.

Studies of children who witness domestic violence reveal many problems related to school experiences. Most of them exhibit a below-average self-concept and less ability to empathize than children who have not witnessed violence. They may also experience learning problems due to an inability to concentrate, stress-related physical ailments, and hearing and speech problems. They may become anxious overachievers in school in an effort to be the perfect child who will save the family. School phobias may develop because the child fears that if mother is left alone she may be hurt or killed.

Because domestic violence is the major cause for homelessness of women and children, it both contributes to the emotional, psychological, and physical problems of the involved children and causes further problems and interruptions to their school experience. Children suffer physical and emotional consequences when they are forced to leave their home, friends, and community when the mother flees her abuser. They suffer the effects of frequent dislocation when the mother moves to a shelter or to crowded temporary housing. They face economic hardship if the abusive father refuses to provide adequate financial support to meet basic physical needs.

As these witnesses to violence become teens, their problems not only interrupt their learning, but they can become a problem for the community. Children from violent homes are high risks for drug and alcohol abuse and juvenile delinquency, including committing such crimes as burglary, arson, prostitution, running away, drug use, and assault.

The Department of Youth Services of Boston reports that children of abused mothers are six times more likely to attempt suicide and 74 percent more likely to commit crimes against another person. They are 24 times more likely to have committed sexual assault crimes and 50 percent more likely to abuse drugs and/or alcohol.

Their aggressive behavior and belief in the resolution of conflict by violence spills over onto the streets of our communities. According to the National Organization for Men Against Sexism, 79 percent of violent children in institutions reported that they had witnessed extreme violence between their parents. In a television interview with Bill Moyers over the Public Broadcasting System in October 1993, U.S. Attorney General Janet Reno said that many of the young people committing violent acts today first witnessed violence in their homes, when as babies and toddlers they saw their mothers being beaten.

Children learn that anger equals violence, and that violence is normal behavior. They also learn that violence works. The victim usually complies with the abuser's demands to avoid further attack. Children learn rigid views of gender roles. They may believe that it is appropriate for men to be aggressive and domineering. Women may be viewed as powerless and deserving of abuse.

Some retrospective studies have indicated that adults who witnessed violence in the home as children were significantly more likely to engage in interpersonal aggression and to remain in an abusive relationship. These adults, particularly the males, expressed approval of wife abuse and were less able to resolve conflict constructively.

Many men who abuse their partners grew up in homes where they were physically abused or where they witnessed the beating of their mothers. In fact, witnessing domestic violence as a child has been identified by sociologists and social learning theorists as the most common risk factor for becoming abusive toward a wife or lover in adulthood. The perpetrator of the violence learned as a child that violence solves problems and is the way men get what they want.

In a study set in an abusers' program in Washington State, 63 percent of the participants had either experienced physical abuse or had witnessed physical abuse involving their parents when they were children. A 1983 Baltimore study found that 75 percent of men seen in a batterers' program reported witnessing their fathers beat their mothers and 50 percent reported being abused as children.

Boys who witness violence against their mothers are ten times more likely to abuse their female partners as adults than are boys raised in nonviolent homes (Hotaling & Sugarman 1986). In the review by Hotaling and Sugarman, 94 percent of the empirical studies found a significant relationship between men having witnessed parental violence and later abusing a partner, whereas 69 percent found being the victim of child abuse to be associated with partner abuse and 31 percent did not. As adolescents, these boys may also assault their mothers or siblings.

Due to the consistency of reports concerning the negative impact on children who witness violence in their homes, most professionals agree that prevention and intervention programs need to be implemented in order to stop the replication of the problem from generation to generation. Children living in violent homes need ongoing protection and specialized treatment to overcome the effects of their victimization.

Other Effects of Battering

Cost to Society

According to a 1992 National Organization for Women report, 30 percent of all women seeking treatment in hospital emergency rooms are victims of battering by a husband or boyfriend. Medical costs related to domestic abuse are estimated to exceed $100 million a year.

A 1987 report by the New York Victim Service Agency states that harassment on the job by the batterer, as well as the burden of time spent waiting to appear in court, reduce battered women's ability to maintain or secure employment. On a national level, domestic violence costs employers $3 to $5 billion annually due to worker absenteeism. Abusive husbands and lovers harass 74 percent of employed battered women at work, either in person or over the telephone, causing 56 percent of them to be late for work at least five times a month, 28 percent to leave early at least five days a month, 54 percent to miss at least three full days of work a month, and 20 percent to lose their jobs.

Homelessness

Domestic violence has been cited in numerous studies as the primary reason for homelessness among women and children in the United States. The statistics are startling and of course only include those homeless who have successfully obtained shelter. The following statistics range from 1987 to 1992 and do not reflect the enormity of the problem.

- The New York State Office for the Prevention of Domestic Violence found that in 1987 battered women and their children made up 40 percent of that state's homeless shelter population.
- According to a 1988 study by the Department of Housing and Urban Development, half of all adult clients staying in American shelters primarily serving families with children have been involved in domestic violence.
- In Oregon in 1988, domestic violence was the main reason that most homeless families with children were on the street (Sohl 1988).
- The Senate Judiciary Committee notes that, according to a 1990 report prepared for the Ford Foundation, 50 percent of all homeless women and children in this country are fleeing domestic violence.
- According to a 1990 report by the Pennsylvania Bar Association, domestic violence is the reason 42 percent of homeless families in Philadelphia are on the street.
- A 1990 Victim Services Agency Study in Los Angeles found that 35 percent of women living in city homeless shelters were there to escape men who beat them.
- Woman abuse is the most common cause of homelessness at Wellspring House shelter in Massachusetts.
- In a case-control study on family homelessness in Boston, researchers discovered that 41 percent of the homeless mothers willing to respond had lived with battering mates before becoming homeless (Morgan 1992).

Homelessness not only has a negative impact on the women and children, but places an enormous financial and physical strain on our social services system.

Who Are the Abusers?

Men who abuse women come from all educational and economic levels, races, religions, and backgrounds. They may be professionals, tradesmen, executives, or unemployed. They may be substance abusers or abstainers. Those who abuse wives and lovers represent all personalities, cultures, family backgrounds, and levels of education. Many do not have criminal records and have been believed to be violent only with their female partners. These men appear to be law-abiding citizens outside of their own homes and do not come across as abusive individuals in public, but maintain an image as friendly and devoted family men. However, a recent study in Quincy, Massachusetts, revealed that 50 to 80 percent of the abusers studied had prior criminal records ranging from arrest for disorderly conduct to murder.

Lydia Martinez, a domestic violence specialist with the New York City Police Department, describes batterers as "extremely manipulative and charming. Many are handsome. Socially, they cross all lines of education, color, ethnic background, religion, etc. We're talking about men who are not stupid, not mentally ill, and generally are not lawbreakers. They do have rigid, stereotypical thinking about men's and women's roles and feel it is their male right. Often they are stunned when they are arrested."

Although the abuser may present himself well to the outside world, he is often lacking in self-esteem. In her book *The Battered Woman* (1979), Lenore Walker notes the following traits as typical of the abuser:

- low self-esteem
- belief in male superiority
- tendency to blame others for their actions
- pathological jealousy
- dual personality
- severe stress reactions
- frequent use of sex as an act of aggression
- refusal to believe that their actions should have negative consequences

The abuser many times has negative attitudes toward women in general, and adheres to a stereotypical model of masculine, or macho, behavior, expecting his wife to act as a submissive and subservient housewife and mother. The abuser becomes dependent upon his partner to maintain her expected role in order to keep him in this superior position.

A common trait seen in most abusers is the tendency to deny or minimize their abuse and its effect on the victim and other family members. This tendency occurs because few abusers characterize themselves as men who beat their wives and lovers. Many abusers contrast their abuse with "brutes who beat their wives every day." They don't see themselves as brutes. They count most violence—even choking, punching, and beating—as an act of self-defense. In reality, it is usually retaliation for an act they have perceived as an attack by their wives, an attempt to regain control over a situation they perceive as threatening.

According to a 1990 American Society of Criminology report on the attitudes and behavior of batterers, one researcher noted that perpetrators emphasize loss of control and blame the victims for their (the perpetrators') behavior. They minimize the impact of their violence and redefine their behavior as something other than violence. And, while some abusers minimize and rationalize, others simply lie about their violence. A poll of clients of Emerge, a Massachusetts men's program, found that many men had lied about their violence when they were asked about it by neighbors, relatives, and police.

Abusers commonly blame their violence on the victims. They make such statements as "she drove me to it," "she provoked me," and "she really knows how to push my buttons." Or they refuse to accept responsibility for the problem by blaming the abuse on some outside factor, such as job stress, money problems, pressures of parenthood, or the effects of alcohol.

Marriages that are traditional (male-dominant) in structure seem to be at greater risk for domestic violence. Data on 2,143 couples from across the country were used to study the relationship between marital violence and the power structure of marriage, power norm consensus, and the level of divided power. Egalitarian couples were found to have the lowest percentage in the high-conflict category. Male-dominant couples were most likely to have experienced a high degree of conflict during the year of this study. In fact, they were almost twice as likely to experience a high level of conflict as egalitarian relationships were (39 percent versus 20 percent). Divided power and female-dominant couples are in the middle of the range and have about the same frequency of conflict (33.8 percent and 33.1 percent). Each study of domestic violence and its cause conducted at the Family Research Laboratory found that male-dominated marriages have the highest level of violence (Straus and Smith 1993).

In his 1990 study of wife abuse in Toronto, based on quantitative survey data gathered by telephone and interviews with female respondents, Michael Smith concluded that husbands who adhere to an ideology of "familial patriarchy" (male head of household) are more likely to beat their wives than men who do not espouse patriarchal beliefs and attitudes.

Although no one can be certain why individual men batter, psychological studies show that power and control are important factors. Many abused women report that their partners exhibit extreme jealousy, possessiveness, and a need for control in the relationship. The resulting accusations and threats generally serve to socially isolate the victim. Women typically curtail their activities with friends, co-workers, and relatives so as not to invite any accusations. For some abusers, the possessiveness has an obsessive quality, resulting in monitoring their partner's activities, eavesdropping, surveillance, and/or stalking. Abusers may take control of finances and monitor car mileage and telephone calls. This type of activity usually escalates when the woman attempts to leave the relationship.

Researchers who have conducted extensive research on batterers say that jealousy/rejection is a key to why many men abuse their wives. This jealousy is generally unfounded, but the jealous abuser believes his wife is having affairs. His wife's perceived behavior signifies rejection of him, which is threatening to his manhood. Since he believes that the man must "wear the pants" in the relationship and that violence will restore order and balance, he becomes violent and blames it on his wife's behavior with other men. Many experts consider men who exhibit this type of behavior as among the most dangerous types of abusers.

In a study of domestic violence cases, Daniel Saunders determined that the most severe violence was perpetrated by men who were severely abused or witnessed abuse in childhood, who abused alcohol and other drugs, and who were violent outside as well as inside the home (Saunders and Browne 1991).

In a University of Washington study of married couples published in July 1994 in *The Journal of Clinical and Counseling Psychology*, violent husbands were found to fall into two categories. The following chart illustrates the study's results:

	Type 1	*Type 2*
Physiology during arguments	Heart rate goes down as the argument proceeds, making his violence more deliberate	Heart rate climbs as he becomes more angry, making his violence more impulsive
Level of emotional abuse	In arguments, is highly belligerent and contemptuous, insulting and threatening the wife	In arguments, is less emotionally abusive

	Type 1	*Type 2*
Motive for violence	A general strategy of controlling the wife by instilling fear	Fear of abandonment or rejection, or jealousy
Violence outside marriage	Violence toward other family members, friends, and co-workers occurs in 44 percent of this type	Only 3 percent are violent outside marriage
Violence in childhood home	56 percent had fathers who abused their mothers	13 percent had fathers who abused their mothers
Divorce over a two-year period	None divorced	28 percent divorced or separated

According to this study, the Type 1 group is considered the more dangerous of the two, the abusers most likely to inflict serious injury on victims.

What Is the Relationship of Alcohol and Drugs to Domestic Violence?

There is some disagreement about the role alcohol and drugs play in domestic violence. The controversy is over whether individuals drink, lose control, and then beat their wives, or whether they use alcohol or drugs to gain the necessary courage and ready excuse to beat their wives. Most experts agree that alcohol does not cause the battering but becomes an excuse, a justification. They believe it may exacerbate a situation by blowing real or imagined problems out of proportion and by lowering inhibitions, but the propensity for violence must be there in order for a man to batter. There are many men who drink to excess and don't beat women, and there are many men who beat women but don't drink.

Studies show that alcohol is present in anywhere from 48 percent to 70 percent of battering incidents. As with all studies, the data reflect the source and the circumstances of the study as well as other factors. According to David Adams, co-founder of the Massachusetts men's program Emerge, the police are more likely to arrest a batterer if there is evidence he is under the influence of alcohol or drugs. Most experts do agree that alcohol and/or drugs are present in about half of all domestic violence situations.

Those cases where alcohol and/or drugs are a factor are many times more serious and potentially lethal. In her study of women who kill their batterers, Angela Browne found that 79 percent of the husbands who had been killed became intoxicated every day or nearly every day. The incidence of drug abuse was also significantly higher in the homicide group as compared to the control group.

Unfortunately, when sentencing drug and alcohol abusing batterers, courts many times will mandate substance abuse treatment and overlook batterer treatment. Because probation officers and judges have been more sensitized to alcohol and drug problems, there is a danger of focusing exclusively on the substance abuse, though the batterer's violence-prone personality is the crux of the problem and treatment to enable him to learn how to become nonviolent is crucial.

Why Doesn't She Leave?

Historian Elizabeth Pleck notes that the question "Why does she stay?" or its reverse, "Why doesn't she just leave?," was first asked in the 1920s, as the popularity of modern psychology was on the rise. In the 1920s it was believed that women of low intelligence stayed; in the 1930s and 1940s it was believed that battered women were masochistic; and since the mid-1970s the experts have asserted that women stay in abusive relationships because they are isolated, have few economic or educational resources, and have been terrorized by repeated battering into a condition of learned helplessness. Even this more humane response is less revealing than the need to pose the question, which reveals society's refusal to do anything to stop violence against women (Jones 1993).

However, the question persists. Studies reveal many reasons why some women don't leave their batterers. There is no single generalized reason, for each case is different.

- One study of women in shelters found that the length of relationship, their employment status, and the subjective measures of love and economic hardship were related to reasons for staying or leaving. It was also found that women who left the relationship were more likely than were those who remained to have brought assault charges against their partners or to have obtained a protection order. They were also less likely to have said that they were staying because they had nowhere else to go (Strube 1988).

- Some women living with violence eventually find themselves trapped in situations that may make it difficult, if not impossible, to leave. They may hope their partners will change, or may concentrate efforts on trying to keep the environment as stress-free as possible. They are often certain that things will be better if they only try a little harder. Battered women often develop skills of survival rather than escape. They focus on what they need to do to make it through today rather than making long-term plans to leave. They develop coping strategies based upon their evaluation of what method of coping will subject them to the least amount of danger (Thyfault 1984).

- Women who stay with abusers sometimes say they want to help men solve the problems that make them abusive (e.g., substance abuse), attribute battering to external causes (e.g., job pressure), define their situations as normal, blame themselves for the violence, or invoke higher loyalties, such as a commitment to marriage as an institution (Steinman 1991).

- Some women stay for economic reasons. When a battered woman leaves her abuser, there is a 50 percent chance that her standard of living will drop below the poverty line (Senate Judiciary Committee 1990). Half of all married women with children do not work outside the home, and therefore have no separate income. Even those women who are employed full-time earn only two-thirds the income of their male counterparts (Straus and Smith 1993).

- An early shelter study found that those battered women who returned to their homes had been married the longest. They also had considerably less work experience and were mostly unskilled compared to the group that did not return home. The latter group was made up of women who had professional or skilled backgrounds (Martin 1977).

Many domestic violence professionals are becoming convinced, however, that the primary reason women stay is out of *fear.* Battered women who try to leave the relationship are increasingly becoming the victims of "separation assault," a term coined by law professor Martha R. Mahoney to describe "the varied violent and coercive moves" a batterer makes when a woman tries to leave him (Mahoney 1991). "Separation assault is the attack on the woman's body and volition in which her partner seeks to prevent her from leaving, retaliate for the separation, or force her to return. It aims at overbearing her will as to where and with whom she will live, and coercing her in order to enforce connection in a relationship. It is an attempt to gain, retain, or regain power in a relationship, or to punish the woman for ending the relationship. It often takes place over time. . . ." (Jones 1993).

Statistics regarding the danger women face when they attempt to leave support this fear of assault:

- Separated or divorced women were 14 times more likely than married women to report having been a victim of violence by a spouse or former spouse. Although separated or divorced women constituted 10 percent of all women, they reported 75 percent of the spousal violence (Department of Justice 1991).
- Married women are the least likely and single, separated, and divorced women the most likely to experience assault by a male intimate. Early surveys assessed domestic violence only among intact couples, reinforcing a widespread belief that wives were the exclusive target of battering. The National Crime Survey data, however, indicate that separated women are the most vulnerable group, with divorced women next and married women last. Further, 75 percent of the clinical population of battered women (the documented population receiving health, legal, and social services) are single, separated, or divorced, and a woman's risk of abuse increases with separation. Whereas only 15.6 percent of all assaults among married women are domestic, fully 55 percent of assaults among separated women are by a male intimate (Stark and Flitcraft 1988).
- In Jones's 1980 study of 37 battered women, nearly one-third of them had managed to leave their batterers despite threats, physical control, and isolation, but in each case the batterers forced them to return. Two of

these women were forced back home at gunpoint, and another returned when the batterer put a gun to her child's head and ordered her back. Threats to kill their loved ones forced two women to return. In two other cases, the batterers tracked the women across state lines to get them to return. One batterer found his wife seven years after she left him and "cut her up" (Ewing 1987).

- According to domestic violence professional Barbara Hart, battered women seek medical attention for injuries sustained as a consequence of domestic violence significantly more often after separation; about 75 percent of the visits to emergency rooms by battered women occur after separation. In addition, about 75 percent of the calls to law enforcement for intervention and assistance in domestic violence situations occur after separation. One study revealed that half of the homicides of female spouses and partners were committed by men after their separation.

- In Browne's group of women who had killed their partners, many of the women stayed as long as they did because they had tried to escape and been beaten for it, or because they feared their partners would retaliate with further violence if they attempted to leave. Almost all of the battered women Browne studied thought their abusers could or would kill them; and many, especially in the homicide group, were convinced that they could not escape this danger by leaving (Browne 1987).

- Ironically, a sizeable proportion of women are killed because they have made genuine efforts to leave their relationships, which are characterized in many cases by long histories of violence and abuse. The act of leaving an abusive relationship is often followed by an increase in violence. Jealousy and fear of being abandoned are the most frequent reasons given for the murder of women by their intimate partners. In a study of spouse murder in Florida, 57 percent of the men who had killed their wives were living apart from them at the time of the incident (Steinman 1991).

- One study of police reports of spousal homicide found that the most common motivation for the killing of wives by husbands was the husband's feeling of abandonment, or fear that he was losing control over his wife (Casanave and Zahn 1986).

Recent research has demonstrated that the majority of battered women eventually leave the abuser. Women leave when circumstances make it possible. However, abuse increases in severity and frequency over time, and may culminate in homicide if the woman does not leave or the man does not receive either treatment or incarceration for violence. Women are also often at high risk to be killed after they have left the abuser, or when they make it clear to him that they are leaving for good.

What Help Do Battered Women Seek?

Of the 192 women at Bedford Hills Correctional Facility who said they had been the victims of abuse, 5 percent had requested family court intervention, 8 percent had sought a court order of protection, 8 percent had gone to a women's shelter, 2 percent had obtained a court advocate from a domestic violence agency, 16 percent had been hospitalized, 19 percent had received medical treatment due to abuse, 10 percent had a documented history of abuse, 22 percent had turned to social services, and 12 percent had used other services (Grossman 1985).

In 1988 Barbara A. Wauchope presented a paper at the meeting of the Sociological Society entitled "Help-Seeking Decisions of Battered Women: A Test of Learned Helplessness and Two Stress Theories." In her study she found that 68 percent of female victims sought help one or more times after being assaulted by their spouses. She further noted that the women were more likely to seek help as the violence increased. This would tend to indicate that the women were not being cowed into accepting the role of the victim (Siegal et al. 1989).

Bowker and MacCallum, two social work researchers, found that as violence continued, women turned increasingly to informal, interpersonal sources of help such as friends, as well as to formal help. The use of lawyers rose from 6 percent to 50 percent between the first and last violent incident, while the use of social service agencies increased from 8 percent to 43 percent (Schechter 1982).

What Help Is Available to Battered Women?

Shelters

Since 1974, when the first shelter in the United States was opened for battered women and their children in St. Paul, Minnesota, the number of shelters has grown to between 1,500 and 2,000 in all parts of the country. Prior to 1974 there was no organized domestic violence movement in the United States. Crisis services for battered women were provided as part of social service or religious institutions, but these institutions did not provide a basis for effective domestic violence intervention.

Since the mid-1970s, shelters have been at the heart of the system designed to provide safe space and supportive services to women and children who are fleeing their homes to escape violence. Shelters provide an environment where women and children can obtain food, shelter, and emotional support, as well as helpful information, advocacy, and services. They offer a wide range of services and benefits that help abused women sort out their options and begin the process that will enable them to take control of their lives.

Shelter Programs

Shelters generally are time-limited, allowing women to stay for an average of four weeks. Most shelter programs offer safety, education, peer support, advocacy, and professional support.

Physical safety is the most important benefit a shelter can offer abused women. A woman must know that she is safe from violence if she is to begin the process of healing. To ensure the safety of women and children residing in the shelter, most shelters keep their locations confidential from the public and other agencies. Women are asked to maintain this confidentiality as a condition of residence.

While in a shelter women receive information about resources available to them and education about domestic violence, that they are not to blame, and that they do not deserve to be hurt. Shelters offer an environment of understanding and support. Women find others who share their experience, confirming that they are not alone. Residents usually participate in groups for peer support and cooperative problem solving. Instead of the denial and isolation experienced in the past, they receive empathy and support from their peers and staff.

Shelter staff members act as advocates for the women as they work through the maze of legal and social institutions that are critical to a future independent and free of violence. This advocacy is necessary for survivors who must create order out of chaos in a very short time.

Other professional support provides a wide range of services to women and helps them make positive changes in their lives. Individual counseling is usually available to women and their children. Other services may include employment preparation, tutoring, nutrition counseling, and parenting skills. Upon entering the shelter, women and children are assessed, an individual plan is developed, and progress is monitored by their case managers. Those services important to the success of each woman and child are usually provided.

Most shelters have a children's program, which may include cooperative child care, support groups, group outings, and referrals for medical and other social services. When necessary, the shelters make arrangements with the local school system to ensure that the children are able to continue their education while at the shelter.

Many shelter programs also offer their basic services on a nonresidential basis, away from the confidential shelter site. Such services as crisis counseling, support groups, advocacy, and referrals can help abused women make decisions about whether they will leave their abusive partners. Most shelters have 24-hour hotlines that women can call for crisis counseling, referrals, and information.

Prevention and education programs have historically been a part of all shelter residential programs. The educational effort ranges from educating women about abuse in an attempt to prevent their re-abuse to educating their children in order to break their learned patterns of violent behavior. Many shelter programs also include a community education component. Although they have very limited funds, they go into the community to educate and create awareness about domestic violence. Community education ranges from volunteer speaker's bureaus to educational programs in the schools.

Transitional programs, to which women coming out of shelter can move, are increasing in number, offering women and children a place to go between shelters and total independence. They are particularly valuable in high-rent areas and for those women who need ongoing services. Women usually stay in these programs for 6 to 18 months. Some shelter programs that do not have resident transitional programs offer transitional services to women after they leave the shelter. These services include legal counsel, group support, job placement, and continued advocacy.

The Availability of Shelters

Although there has been a steady growth in shelters, there are not nearly enough available to provide beds for all the battered women who need a safe haven. In the United States, there are nearly three times as many shelters available for homeless animals as there are for homeless women.

In her testimony on the Family Violence Prevention and Services Act Re-authorization Hearing in July 1991, Barbara Hart, one of the founders of the battered women's movement, gave the following statistics regarding Pennsylvania shelters:

- Twenty-five of the sixty-seven counties in Pennsylvania offer shelter facilities. There are rural counties where an abused woman must travel over 100 miles to reach the shelter to escape her abusive situation.
- Thirty out of fifty-seven programs cannot afford staff to run children's programs.
- Twenty-seven programs have no legal advocate and 10 have only a part-time advocate.
- In the first year that domestic violence statistics were collected in Pennsylvania (1980), the number of victims receiving assistance from domestic violence programs totaled 11,328. Between 1989 and 1990 the number totaled 74,669. This 518.22 percent increase is not unique to Pennsylvania, but is the norm across the nation.

Other statistics from across the country tell the same story:

- In 1990, 12,433 women and children were denied shelter in New York State according to the state's Department of Social Services. Of all requests for emergency shelter, 71 percent were denied, primarily due to a lack of space (Huling 1991).
- "In Massachusetts, where 60,000 women are beaten so severely each year that they flee their homes and all their belongings, taking only their children, the state's

battered women's shelters reject five women and two children for every two people that they accept, because of space limitations" (*Boston Sunday Herald Magazine,* 29 January 1988)

- "When poor, battered women leave home, they cannot rely on the availability of affordable public housing or shelters. Space in shelters is extremely limited: in 1989 a Los Angeles county grand jury found that 90 percent of the battered women and children who sought safety were turned away; in Washington D.C. eight in ten women are told there is no room" (*LA Times,* 18 November 1990).

The Funding of Shelters

Shelters are costly to operate, due partly to the number of staff required to operate a 24-hour program and the extensive amount of time required per woman for advocacy. Shelter workers are highly committed, and work long, intense hours for very little pay. Many of them live at the poverty level. Many shelters are able to continue because of the dedication of their staff and the many hours of service performed by volunteers. Little has been expended by either state or federal governments on programs for battered women.

During 1989–1990, the Family Violence Prevention and Services Act funded domestic violence at the following rates:

State	$ per recipient	State	$ per recipient
Alaska	20.12	Mississippi	23.13
D.C.	11.10	New Hampshire	12.19
Florida	23.61	Oklahoma	9.77
Idaho	32.46	Oregon	24.30
Illinois	10.40	Pennsylvania	4.23
Louisiana	9.78		

By contrast, the federal support in Pennsylvania for each child recipient of protective service was $1,348, while for each recipient of drug and alcohol treatment it was $1,328.63. The federal share for each homeless person in bridge housing and emergency shelter was $166.65 and federal support for each resident in a mental health facility was $8,000. However, total federal assistance for each domestic violence victim was $27. Of the $7,240,000,000 expended for child care and child welfare in the fiscal year 1991, only $10,700,000 was allocated to family violence. Thus, only .15 percent of funds to end child abuse was directed toward programs to help battered mothers end the violence in their lives and protect their children (Hart 1991).

The Family Violence Coalition in Maryland reported in 1991 that when funding is available, it is often inadequate. For example, the state spends only $1.4 million on 18 domestic violence programs in Maryland. These programs are unable to serve many families seeking safety. One program alone was forced to turn away 800 battered women and children due to lack of space. In FY90, the Baltimore Zoo spent twice as much money to care for animals as the state spent to provide safety for women and children in all 18 shelters.

The Effectiveness of Shelters

Shelters were never intended as the solution to the problem of domestic violence, but rather as a safe haven for women who needed to flee from their abusers. Many battered women do not perceive shelters as viable options, since it means leaving one's home and family unit. Many women have a difficult time going to shelter because of the value they place on the family and marriage; they are torn between wanting to keep these things intact and wanting to end the violence. For those who do use shelters, however, there have been mixed responses regarding the effectiveness of shelter. Results vary depending on the shelter and its available services. Many times effectiveness cannot be determined until the woman has been out of shelter for a period of time. Women may return to the batterer initially, but what they have learned about domestic violence may empower them to leave the abuser later.

For the most part, battered women's shelters receive high effectiveness ratings from their clients; in a 1984 study 44 percent of the women who utilized their services rated them as very effective in helping to decrease or end the violence; 12 percent rated shelters as somewhat effective; 16 percent as slightly effective; and 22 percent as not effective. The remaining 6 percent reported that their husbands' violence toward them actually increased because of their having gone to a battered women's shelter (Bowker and Maurer 1985).

The clinical and empirical literature on shelter outcome suggests that about one-third of the residents return to their batterer upon leaving the shelter. One follow-up study found that while only 14 percent intended to leave the batterer at shelter admission and 33 percent at discharge, 55 percent were living with the batterer two months after shelter. Of these returnees, 12 percent reported having been physically abused and an additional 15 percent were verbally abused. A study of a Michigan shelter showed that 30 percent terminated the relationship directly after shelter and another 43 percent within two years, for a follow-up total of 73 percent not living with the batterer and 27 percent still living with the batterer. These findings demonstrate that many women eventually return to their batterer, despite their initial intention not to return. The women often return because of economic dependence or psychological commitment (Gondolf 1988).

The Health Care System

Again, because of the hidden nature of domestic violence, accurate statistics on the numbers of women who receive medical treatment for injuries suffered from abuse are impossible to obtain.

- According to a 1992 American Medical Association report, more than half of the victims of assaults by intimates are seriously injured. At least 25 percent report receiving medical care. One in 10 is treated in a hospital or emergency department.
- A 1993 report estimated that 35 percent of women who visit hospital emergency departments are there for symptoms of ongoing abuse. Unfortunately, as few as 5 percent of the victims of domestic violence are so identified. In studies of emergency room visits, 22 to 35 percent of women patients were there because of symptoms relating to abuse. Because one third of battered women see health professionals, health providers have enormous potential to identify and assist battered women (Holtz and Furniss 1993).
- According to 1991 U.S. Department of Justice statistics, the victim received medical care in almost 25 percent of the cases of violence by an intimate. One in 10 were treated in a hospital or emergency room; about 1 in 20

were treated in a doctor's office; and about 1 in 10 were treated at other places.

- Twenty percent of the abused population evidence mental health problems in addition to physical injury. More than one-third carry a diagnosis of depression or another situational disorder, and 1 abused woman in 10 suffers a psychotic break. Seventy-eight percent of the abused women using psychiatric services after the onset of abuse have not done so previously. At the same time, battered women are also far more likely than non-battered women to be given a pseudopsychiatric label such as hysteric, hypochondriac, and so on (Stark and Flitcraft 1988).

The Effectiveness of the Health Care System

Studies of the effectiveness of health care professionals in their response to domestic violence point to a need for training of health care professionals about the dynamics of abuse, as well as the need to develop protocols for medical care facilities handling domestic violence cases. Health care professionals need to learn the right questions to ask, recognize symptoms, refer women to appropriate services for further help, and avoid placing the woman in further danger. A woman can be placed in additional danger if the abuser is notified or if the injured woman is released to him without the notification of authorities.

- In a survey that asked 1,000 abused women to rate the effectiveness of various professionals in addressing their abuse, health care professionals had the lowest rating, ranking behind battered women's shelters, lawyers, social service workers, police, and clergy (Physicians and Domestic Violence 1993).
- One study found that in 40 percent of the cases in which physicians interacted with battered women in an emergency-room setting, the physicians made no response to the abuse. In another study, physicians attributed their failure to talk to women about violence to concerns about offending patients, to fear of opening a "Pandora's box," and to lack of time. Nationally, little information about domestic violence has been available to primary-care physicians, and although that too is

changing, the American Medical Association did not issue guidelines for physicians and their handling of domestic violence until 1992 (Knapp 1992).

- In another study, emergency department physicians identified 1 in 35 of their female patients as battered, while a review of the medical charts indicated that, in fact, 1 in 4 were likely to have been battered (*Trends in Health Care, Law & Ethics*, Spring 1993).
- In a review of the complete medical records of 3,676 women randomly selected from among female patients presenting with injury to a major metropolitan emergency room during a single year, only 1 percent of the 5,040 injury episodes ever presented by these women were identified by clinical staff as due to abuse or battering; however, a review of the adult trauma history revealed that 40 percent of the episodes were either identified by victims as resulting from a deliberate assault by an intimate partner, or that this could be surmised from the circumstances (Stark and Flitcraft 1988).
- Ninety-two percent of women who were physically abused by their partners did not discuss these incidents with their physicians; 57 percent did not discuss the incidents with anyone (The Commonwealth Fund 1993)
- In one study of 476 consecutive women seen by a family practice clinic in the Midwest, 394 (82.7 percent) agreed to be surveyed. Of these patients, 22.7 percent had been physically assaulted by their partners within the last year, and the lifetime rate of physical abuse was 38.8 percent. However, only 6 women said they had ever been asked about domestic violence by their physician (Hamberger et al. 1992).

The Police

Family disturbance calls have been labeled the "common cold" of police work. These calls, many of which involve violence between spouses, constitute the largest single category of calls received by police departments each year.

- According to a 1992 report on violence against women made to the Committee on the Judiciary, more than

21,000 domestic assaults, rapes, and murders were reported to the police each week in 1992—twice the number of reported robberies.
- Almost one-fifth of all aggravated assaults reported to the police every week are reported by victims of assaults in the home (U.S. Senate 1992).

The Police Response

Although the response to domestic violence has improved due to legislation and internal rulings in large city departments, there is still evidence of a need for training of law enforcement professionals about the dynamics of domestic violence.

- Of the 28 women killed by a husband, boyfriend, or estranged husband or boyfriend in one year in Dayton, Ohio, at least 18 (64 percent) were known to have been physically abused by that man prior to the murder. In each of 15 of the 18 documented prior-abuse cases, the police had been to the home five times. In another prior-abuse case, the two-year period preceding the murder included 12 calls made for "family violence" as part of 56 total police visits to that home (Campbell 1994).
- In their study of 2,096 battered women in Texas, Stacey and Shupe found that police failed to respond to calls from battered women in one case in three (Gillespie 1989).
- In Washington, D.C., an abusive spouse is arrested in less than 15 percent of the cases in which his victim is bleeding from an open wound, according to testimony given at hearings on "Women and Violence" before the U.S. Senate Judiciary Committee, 29 August and 11 December 1990.
- The Minneapolis Domestic Violence Experiment conducted by Lawrence Sherman and R. A. Berk in 1984 employed an experimental model to examine the deterrent effects of arrest, separation, and mediation in the police response to wife battering. For ethical reasons, the study did not include any felony assault cases. Although some theorized that arresting an offender at the scene of a violent incident may increase

the offender's hostility, especially if the offender is quickly released from custody, the Minneapolis Experiment found just the opposite to be true. Forty-three percent of those arrested were released from custody within one day, and the victim reported having a new quarrel with the offender within one day in just 6 percent of those cases. The complete findings of the study suggested that arrest was significantly superior in deterring future violence relative to the other two interventions. During a six-month follow-up period, Sherman and Berk found that men who had been arrested were less likely to assault their wives than men who were separated from their wives for a brief period of time or men who received counseling. The Minneapolis Domestic Violence experiment was employed by policymakers and activists in all parts of the United States to support legislative and policy changes in policing.

- A controversial and sometimes ambiguous 1992 report by University of Maryland criminologist Lawrence Sherman questions the effectiveness of mandatory arrests in cases of domestic violence. After comparing the use of arrest with warnings and separations in six cities, Sherman concludes that arrests can lead men to beat their wives and lovers more often after they are released. The same study found that when Milwaukee police left without making an arrest, 7 percent of the victims were again immediately assaulted. By contrast, only 2 percent were immediately assaulted by partners who had been arrested and released from jail, but over the course of a year those arrests doubled the rate of violence by the same suspects. Mandatory arrest seemed to backfire in Milwaukee, Charlotte, and Omaha, although it had a deterrent effect in Minneapolis, Colorado Springs, and Miami (Sherman 1992).
- In 1990, the Minneapolis Experiment was replicated in Omaha, Nebraska. Contrary to the evidence from Minneapolis, the major finding was that arrest and the immediate period of custody associated with arrest were not a deterrent to continued domestic violence.

The experiment was also replicated in Charlotte, North Carolina. "The results of the Charlotte experiment are decisive and unambiguous, clearly indicating that arrest of spouse abusers is neither substantially nor statistically a more effective deterrent to repeat abuse" (Gelles 1991).

- A 1989 study found that arrest without coordination with other sanctions produced greater subsequent violence. Arrest in coordination with other criminal justice efforts was a significant deterrent (Gelles 1991).
- In Maryland, about 16,000 cases of spousal assault were reported in 1990. It was estimated by the Family Violence Coalition, however, that the number of reports represented only 10 to 50 percent of the actual number of cases. Even when victims did report the assault, only 1 jurisdiction out of 24 required written reports.

When there is no mandatory arrest law, the decision by the police to arrest the abuser can be quite subjective and may depend on a number of factors, including the responding officer's attitudes, knowledge, interpretation of events, time of day, priority of other calls, and so on.

U.S. police departments have traditionally adhered to an informal rule, the "stitch" rule, whereby assault charges are not made unless the victim requires medical treatment for injuries. Many studies have found police unwilling to arrest batterers because they complain that it is a waste of their time if the prosecutors don't follow through and the courts don't convict and sentence.

There has been a persistent myth that responding to domestic disturbance calls places the responding officers in danger. A 1986 National Institute of Justice study found that the risk to officers dealing with wife assault cases was much lower than previously thought. Federal Bureau of Investigation statistics revealed that only 5.7 percent of police deaths from 1971 to 1981 occurred during domestic disturbance calls. This was lower than deaths due to burglary, robbery, traffic, and other disturbances.

The increase of arrests in low-income areas may reflect an officer's belief that individuals who live there have less right to privacy and courtesy than the middle-class suburban resident does. In addition to attitudes regarding class, officers may be affected by race and gender role stereotypes. Women of other racial and ethnic backgrounds are often seen by the police as being enmeshed in a culture of violence.

Attitudes that may be considered sexist are sometimes reflected in officers' attitudes regarding a woman's role in a relationship, marriage, and the home. Police attitudes toward arrest often reflect the officer's own identification with the husband and the belief in the sanctity of the home. Some officers believe that if the battered woman chooses to stay with her husband, she either likes the abuse or deserves it.

The more traditional their beliefs about sex roles and the more conflict these officers are experiencing in their own marriages, the more hostility they express toward battered women. Several officers who participated in a study on police attitudes toward domestic violence expressed their belief that "a man's home is his castle where he should be able to control the actions of his wife and children" (Ferraro and Pope 1993).

In some cases, it is at the victim's request that police have not pressed charges. Many women fear retaliation if an arrest is made, knowing the abuser will most probably be released within hours. Others are embarrassed and intimidated about appearing in court to testify against their partners. Studies done in California in 1977, however, found that with the help of Victim Assistance programs only 10 percent of domestic assault victims in Los Angeles and 8 percent in Santa Barbara refused to cooperate with the prosecutor (Jones 1993). A more recent study by D. A. Ford in 1991, reported in the *Law and Society Review*, found that prosecution of wife batterers was most successful when women were included in the decision-making process.

Sometimes a low priority is given to wife assault cases by officers who believe that arrests in high-profile cases will be more likely to help them in their careers. Time factors are also a consideration. Time limits are many times invoked as rationales for refusing to transport women to shelters or to search for the batterer. This again relates to priorities, as officers cite their involvement in a "domestic" as keeping them from investigation of robberies and other "more important" crimes.

In many cases the batterer fled the scene when the police were called, and thus was not available for arrest. In these cases procedure dictates that a report be written and the incident be followed up the next day, or that a search be made for the man. In many cases this is not done and, in fact, reports are not filed in some cases.

Some officers view most cases of domestic violence as "mutual combat." If they arrive upon the scene and find two violent people, even though the woman's violence may have been in self-protection, they find it difficult to determine fault. When mandatory arrest was first introduced in Washington State, officers many times arrested both parties. This necessitated a "primary clause" that required police to arrest the initiator and the most violent offender. Where mandatory arrest policies are not in place, however, the presence of two violent people usually means that no arrest is made.

In the United States, a significant stumbling block to arrest has been the need to obtain a criminal arrest warrant, unless the police witnessed the assault directly. Usually this will cause a delay between the incident and arrest. In the early 1980s warrantless arrest provisions were adopted and some states imposed additional responsibilities on police officers, requiring them to ensure the victim's safety if no arrest was made.

In 1980 the federally funded San Francisco Family Violence Project was established to change the criminal justice response to battering. The San Francisco Police Department and the district attorney's office adopted several new approaches to the issue of domestic violence, including the adoption of policies and procedures reflecting the attitude that wife battering is a crime, specialized training of the police, and a data collection system for tracking domestic violence calls, reports, and cases over time. The district attorney's office established prosecution protocols, assigning one attorney to handle a case from start to finish (vertical prosecution), establishing victim advocacy units, and providing counseling and education programs for offenders. Within the first year, domestic violence arrests increased by 60 percent. By the project's third year, the conviction rate had increased 44 percent, the number of cases in which charges were filed increased 136 percent over the first year, and there was a 171 percent increase in dispositions involving probation, jail, parole, or supervised diversion.

Another innovative project occurred in the early 1980s in Minnesota, where three suburban communities took part in a two-year project coordinated by the Domestic Abuse Project of Minneapolis. It was designed to coordinate responses to domestic violence in much the same way as the San Francisco project and also demonstrated impressive changes in police and court responses to domestic violence.

One-third of 117 U.S. police departments surveyed regarding their pro-arrest policies indicated that they had been influenced by the 1984 study of Lawrence Sherman and Richard Berk of the Minneapolis Domestic Violence Experiment. Although Sherman has since questioned the effectiveness of instituting pro-arrest policies in all cities, the results of that 1984 study suggested that batterers who were arrested were less likely to repeat the violence within the next six months, as compared to those who were briefly separated or who received counseling. There are mandatory arrest policies in most states today, although some are by jurisdiction and many have various interpretations.

What Remedies Are Available through Our Courts?

Until the 1970s, when domestic violence became a visible issue, most courts were reluctant to become involved in cases where a man physically, sexually, or emotionally abused his wife. However, the traditional belief in the sanctity of a man's home and his right to privacy so that he could control his wife and family by any means necessary is slowly evolving into the view that women have a right to be protected from abuse by their intimate partners. Most states now have a legal process through which a woman who has been the victim of domestic violence may obtain a remedy for her suffering—either through domestic violence protective orders, criminal prosecution, or civil tort litigation. Every state now has some statutory law—criminal and/or civil—dealing with the problem of domestic violence.

Protection Orders

Most states have passed statutes setting up procedures for obtaining domestic violence protective orders, which are intended to head off violent family confrontations. Most battered women are interested in stopping the battering, not in punishing their partners, and many women do not want their partners arrested because they fear retaliation. Sometimes a woman's reluctance to have her partner arrested is based on family needs—if the man receives a criminal record or is jailed, he might lose his job or the children might turn against her for sending their father to jail. These very practical reasons, as well as the need to protect themselves from further abuse, partially account for the large number of women who seek civil protection orders compared to those who file criminal complaints.

- Tucson issues about 1,000 orders a year, Milwaukee 3,000, and Portland, Oregon, over 4,000. Chicago issued 9,000 orders and extensions of orders in 1987 (Finn 1991).
- After the Pennsylvania Protection from Abuse Act was amended in June 1988 to enable victims to file *pro se* protection orders, many domestic violence programs reported startling increases in requests for protection orders (between 100 percent and 700 percent). At the Montgomery County Women's Center, for example, the number of petitioners increased from 200 prior to the amendment to almost 1,500 afterward. In Northampton County the petitioners increased by 900, from 400 to 1,300 (Senate Hearing on Women and Violence 1990). According to the Women Against Abuse Legal Center in Philadelphia, about 2,000 people filed for protection orders in 1989. The figure was nearly 9,000 in 1991. In 1992 the tally was approximately 25 percent higher.

Domestic violence protective orders provide some very specific and effective remedies for the threat of abuse. Protective orders are available to spouses, children, other family members, or even unrelated members of the household. The emphasis is on making protective orders easy to obtain.

The statutes are similar from state to state. There is no model statute from which these laws are derived, but the remedies and procedures are similar. The statutes often provide that police officers responding to domestic violence calls must inform the victim of the existence of the domestic violence protective orders and explain how to obtain them. In addition, they are responsible for supplying the victim with telephone numbers of shelters and/or support agencies that assist victims in obtaining orders. The orders may be issued with or without notice to the other party. Usually the applicant must declare in writing, under oath, that there has been past abuse. (In Arizona, an applicant must declare that one or more specific offenses have occurred, while in Florida the applicant must simply declare there have been threats of abuse or she has reason to believe she is in danger of abuse.)

The procedure usually includes the availability of an emergency or temporary order issued immediately upon application and without notice to the other party. This enables a woman to have a short period of time, usually ten days, during which she may recover from the initial trauma and obtain legal advocacy. An order of protection is effective once it is served on the abuser; however, any conditions imposed by the court are effective immediately upon issuance of the order. Once an order is obtained from the court, it is usually served by the sheriff or constable.

The primary purpose of the order is to prevent physical and psychological abuse. Abuse is prevented through an order directing the abuser from committing any further acts of domestic violence, harassment, or interference with the victim. Many times protective orders also award temporary custody of the home and personal property to the victim, ordering the abuser to stay away from the residence. Additionally, the abuser may be ordered to stay away from the victim's place of employment, school, or another place frequented by the victim.

Most protective order statutes contain penalties for violation of the order. Violation is usually a misdemeanor and is also a basis for a contempt prosecution—civil, criminal, or both. Domestic violence literature strongly suggests that protective orders are effective in deterring domestic violence *only* if the respondent believes the order will be enforced against him.

Prosecution

Prosecution is *any action* taken by the state in response to an alleged criminal violation in order to move the case toward adjudication. It can include diverting a case from trial into a treatment program. The government attorney is the prosecutor, and the process is driven by her or his discretion. The prosecutor therefore plays a primary role in determining the criminal justice response to a case of domestic violence. Prosecution involves a similar process in all courts, varying only by differing informal policies that affect prosecution.

In a victim-initiated complaint, the woman files a probable cause affidavit with the prosecutor's office. The prosecutor reviews the complaint, verifies consistency with criminal law, and determines whether the case merits court attention. If the decision is made to proceed, a summons is issued to the abuser to appear at an initial hearing, or a warrant is issued for his arrest. The defendant is arraigned and charged, and the conditions of his release while awaiting trial are determined. At this point, courts are increasingly issuing protective orders to ensure the victim's safety until the defendant's trial. Although protective orders have traditionally been associated with civil court, they have proven an effective means of reducing violence when they are consistently enforced. Once a trial is held, the possible results are the dismissal of the charges, the diversion of the abuser to a treatment program, a verdict of not guilty, or a verdict of guilty. Victim-initiated complaints are usually misdemeanor cases.

When the case involves an on-scene arrest, the officer files the probable cause affidavit, the prosecutor reviews it, the abuser is arraigned and charged, and recommendations are made to the court regarding bail and protective orders. The trial will have the same possible results. These cases are usually felony cases and are more likely to result in jail time.

How the Crime of Domestic Violence Is Classified

The decision whether to charge a case as a felony or a misdemeanor is important. Felony cases receive greater investigation by the police, are usually handled by more experienced prosecutors, and are allocated greater resources. Many times an advocate is assigned to the victim. Felonies are punishable by a year or more in a state prison, whereas misdemeanors are punishable by a fine or a term of up to one year in a city or county jail.

Research indicates that the injuries battered women receive are at least as serious as injuries suffered in many violent felony crimes, yet under state laws they are many times classified as misdemeanors. About one-third of the incidents of domestic violence against women reported in the 1986 National Crime Survey would be classified by police as rape, robbery, or aggravated assault—felonies in most states. The remaining two-thirds would likely be classified by police as simple assault—a misdemeanor in most jurisdictions. Yet based upon evidence collected in the National Crime Survey, as many as half of the domestic violence simple assaults actually involved bodily injury as serious as or more serious than 90 percent of all rapes, robberies, and aggravated assaults.

Effectiveness of the Criminal Justice System in Prosecution of Domestic Violence Cases

Studies have shown that even when arrests are made, very few domestic violence cases actually make it through prosecution and the court process and result in conviction of the batterer. According to Ann Jones, "Each branch of the criminal justice system . . . evades its duty by blaming another branch. Police say there's no point in making arrests when prosecutors won't prosecute, and prosecutors . . . say they can't prosecute when (a) police don't arrest, or (b) judges won't sentence anyway. Judges say that women waste the court's time . . . [so] . . . when you come right down to it, isn't it really up to a woman to follow through?" (Jones 1993).

Studies reveal the following:

- In one of the groups of battered women surveyed by Lenore Walker for her book *Terrifying Love,* 90 percent of the women who reported assault to the police actually did sign complaints, but fewer than 1 percent of the cases were ever prosecuted and the rate of conviction of batterers was extremely low. Only one in seven wife assaults is reported to the police and less than 1 man in 100 for whom prima facie evidence of wife assault exists is convicted in court (Dutton and McGregor 1991).

- Several cities with vigorous prosecution policies boast a high rate of success with offenders. While prosecutors file charges in only about 3 percent of Milwaukee arrests, about 70 percent are prosecuted in San Diego. Less than 5 percent of the men who have gone through San Diego's comprehensive domestic violence program are charged with domestic violence again. The program includes a year of required group counseling, with arrest and jail for failure to comply (Glazer 1993).

- Of the 781 misdemeanor cases or victim-initiated criminal complaints involving domestic violence that were heard in Philadelphia Municipal Court between October 1989 and March 1990, there were only 67 (9 percent) convictions. Of the 67 defendants convicted, two received prison terms (three months each), while 16 received nonreporting probation. Of the 67 cases that resulted in guilty verdicts, there was no record found for post-conviction supervision in 20 of the cases. Of the remaining cases, treatment was ordered by the court in only four instances. Five additional treatments were initiated by probation officers without court order (Family Service of Philadelphia 1991).

- In 1990, 4,138 incidents of family violence were analyzed based on data from the Family Division of the Connecticut Superior Court, Connecticut State Police, and 90 prosecutors' files. It was revealed that 14 percent of these defendants were prosecuted and sentenced, 79 percent were not prosecuted, and 8 percent were dismissed. Of those tried, there were no findings of not guilty; a review of prosecutors' files suggests that the decision to prosecute is identical to conviction. The most common charges brought against domestic violence offenders were Breach of Peace (29.4 percent), Assault 3 (28.9 percent), and Disorderly Conduct (22.5 percent) (American Society of Criminology 1990).

- The State of Maryland Special Committee on Gender Bias in the Courts learned that many victims believe that crimes involving domestic violence are not treated the same way as crimes in which the complaining party and the defendant are strangers. The committee attempted to test this belief in its survey of judges and lawyers by asking whether they believed that courts do not treat domestic violence as a crime. Nearly 10 percent of the judges who responded said that the statement is always true, and another 14 percent said that the statement is often true. Among the lawyers surveyed, 33 percent of female attorneys and 12 percent of male attorneys thought that the statement is always or often true. Interestingly, 51 percent of male attorneys and 68 percent of female attorneys who have a substantial domestic relations practice thought the statement is always, often, or sometimes true.

Respondents to the gender bias study were also asked to evaluate the statement, "assault charges are not treated seriously when domestic relations cases are pending." Ten percent of the judges thought the statement is always or often true, 28 percent thought the statement is true sometimes, and 62 percent thought the statement is rarely or never true. By contrast, 25 percent of male attorneys thought the statement is always or often true, 37 percent thought it true sometimes, and 38 percent thought it rarely or never true. Female attorneys were more certain that the problem exists: 48 percent thought the statement is always or often true, 32 percent thought the statement sometimes true, and only 21 percent thought the statement to be rarely or never true. Domestic relations practitioners, whether male or female, indicated a similar certainty: 58 percent of females and 40 percent of males believed the statement is always or often true.

Court-Mandated Treatment

Several treatment authorities are calling upon courts to require treatment following arrest of a man for wife assault. Most reason that this is important in holding the abuser accountable to both acknowledge and change his behavior. Esta Soler, founder and executive director of the San Francisco Family Violence Prevention Fund, says that because the abuser usually has a continuing relationship with his victim, treatment is necessary to prevent further violence. Even in the case of separation or divorce, there may be other reasons that make a continuing relationship necessary, such as child visitation. Although battered women want justice in these cases, they also want to live safe from further violence.

There are two types of court mandates for treatment. The first is pre-trial diversion or deferred prosecution, whereby the abuser can have his arrest record cleared or the charge reduced upon successful completion of treatment. One problem with pre-trial diversion, according to many advocates, is that the abuser is not required to enter a guilty plea and may not take responsibility for his violence. The other type of mandate is the direct court order to participate in treatment as part of the sentence received after conviction.

Agencies providing treatment for abusers report that without a court mandate or other motivation to attend, such as threat of divorce, one-third to half of the offenders drop out after the first session or during a stressful period of therapy. Most abusers do not desire counseling and will not attend volunteer programs unless motivated by an external factor, such as a court mandate.

Mandated treatment either in the form of diversion or as part of sentencing is becoming increasingly popular among judges. David Adams of the Massachusetts men's program Emerge estimates that 65 percent of men who join his groups are ordered by a judge to do so, compared to about 5 percent five years ago. Alan Rosenbaum, who runs a support group for batterers at the University of Massachusetts Medical School, estimates that 85 to 95 percent of the men he sees are court-ordered.

Batterer Treatment Programs

In the late 1970s, the increased attention on domestic violence and abused wives created a need for services to the abuser. Most treatment programs for men who abuse their partners were developed by community mental health agencies, sometimes with help from the battered women's movement. Many of these programs use former batterers and graduates of the program to run peer groups, much as drug treatment programs have used program graduates.

The first agencies provided diverse services that focused on anger/stress management and control, interpersonal skills, and male socialization. Project Emerge, developed in Boston in 1972, was one of the first agencies to offer services for the batterer using peer counseling. Since then nationwide treatment programs have developed, although there are not as many as needed.

The assumptions when treating abusive behavior are that the abuse follows a cyclical pattern, is resistant to change, is a learned behavior, and can be controlled and changed through intervention and treatment. The goal for the batterer in treatment is to stop his violent behavior by accepting responsibility for his behavior and learning alternate skills for expressing anger.

In 1993 the State of California developed program guidelines for batterer treatment program certification. Only certified programs are eligible as diversion programs that can receive referrals from the courts. There is a movement in other areas toward standardizing treatment and developing certification programs. California's guidelines include the following components that programs must contain:

- Written agreements with the batterer regarding payment, attendance, nonviolence, remaining chemically free
- Strategies to hold the batterer accountable for the violence in a relationship. He must be accountable for both the violence and the impact of the violence.
- Educational programming that examines, at a minimum, gender roles, socialization, the nature of violence, the

dynamics of power and control, and the effects of abuse on children and others
- Communication skill-building: expression of feelings in assertive as opposed to aggressive styles, listening skills
- Community advocacy: working with other men in a supportive role, building a cooperative community base, reaching out to work with others in the larger community to help stop domestic violence

Professionals in the domestic violence movement disagree about the effectiveness of treatment programs for abusers. Some who work with women fear for a woman's safety while her abusive partner is in treatment. The concern is that the abusive man may become angry as a result of a confrontation in the group setting, will repeat his old pattern of blaming his wife for his feelings, and will resort to abuse. Detractors say a batterer's treatment program only makes the abuser more cunning in his violence toward his partner. They believe the treatment may only clear the man's record and conscience rather than change his behavior and that men will go into treatment simply to avoid jail.

Most studies conducted on the effectiveness of treatment are inconclusive. This is due to inadequate research that lacks sound scientific methodology, and inconsistency in methods between studies that make it impossible to allow any solid generalizations. Results of 24 surveys and studies of treatment programs conducted from 1984 to 1990 revealed recidivism rates that range from "not much" to 50 percent. There were no answers to the question "which treatment works best?" The studies varied so in their makeup, process, and reporting that no conclusions could be drawn.

Abusers may stop physical abuse if they face legal consequences, but without effective treatment it is believed they will continue to abuse women and children verbally and emotionally. Eventually, unless attitudinal change has taken place, physical abuse will once again become part of the equation.

Civil Remedies Available to Battered Women

Civil Tort Actions

Victims of domestic violence can file lawsuits in civil court against their abusers based on common law torts. A common law tort is a wrong committed by one person against another person that is satisfied or made right by lawsuit for money damages. Causes of tort action include:

Assault and Battery   Most interspousal tort suits involve some claim of assault by one spouse upon the other. The elements of the causes of action for assault or battery are the same whether the offense was committed by one spouse against the other or by one stranger against another stranger. The elements that must be present are a harmful or offensive physical contact with a person inflicted with the intent of causing suffering, and fear of imminent peril from that attack.

Examples of tort action for assault and battery include:

- *Cain v. McKinnon* (Mississippi 1989)
  This claim was substantiated. The husband was alleged to have "savagely and brutally" assaulted and beaten his wife causing personal injuries, loss of earnings, and medical expenses.

- *Smith v. Smith* (Alabama 1988)
  This claim was substantiated. The wife was battered to such an extent that she suffered a ruptured disc and had to undergo several surgeries, including a fusion of the vertebrae and removal of a rib.

- *Heacock v. Heacock* (Massachusetts 1988)
  This claim was substantiated. The husband, during a heated marital argument, violently grabbed his wife and caused her to repeatedly strike her head against the door frame, resulting in serious physical injuries, including dizzy spells, blackouts, and traumatic epilepsy.

- *Noble v. Noble* (Utah 1988)
  A claim of assault and battery was sustantiated in which the husband shot his wife in the head with a .22 caliber rifle.

- *Simmons v. Simmons* (Colorado 1989)
  The court substantiated a claim of assault and battery in which the husband threw hot coffee on his wife and intentionally kicked, slapped, hit, and tore her ear.

- *Catlett v. Catlett* (Georgia 1989)

  A jury verdict found for the plaintiff and awarded $10,000 compensatory and $20,000 punitive damages for the intentional torts of assault, battery, and false imprisonment. The evidence at trial established that the husband had struck his wife on two occasions and prevented her from leaving his apartment once and from leaving his car once until third parties intervened. It was also found that he had dragged her down a stairway by her feet because he thought it was "comical." The injury to his wife consisted of the aggravation of a pre-existing back injury that she had sustained in an automobile accident.

- *Murray v. Murray* (Alabama Court of Appeals 1992)

  A trial court's award of $5,000 compensatory and $40,000 punitive damages was affirmed to a divorcing woman on her counterclaim against her husband for assault and battery in their divorce action. The appellate court refused to overturn the trial court's acceptance of the wife's testimony that her husband had physically abused her on three occasions during a short marriage, despite the fact that the husband denied that such abuse had occurred.

- *Whittaker v. Dail* (Indiana 1991)

  The appellate court upheld an award of $99,423 compensatory damages and $200,000 punitive damages in a case where the husband severely beat his wife. He had previously been convicted of battery and sentenced to jail.

Marital Rape and Involuntary Deviate Sexual Intercourse   Under common law, rape was defined as the unlawful carnal knowledge of a woman, *not a spouse*, forcibly and against her will. Many jurisdictions have abolished marital rape as an exemption in criminal court. In those jurisdictions there should be no impediments to bringing a lawsuit based upon the rape.

Intentional Infliction of Emotional Injury   Actionable conduct is that which is so outrageous in character and so extreme in degree as to go beyond all possible bounds of decency and to be regarded as atrocious and utterly intolerable in a civilized community. Some examples of conduct that has been actionable in specific cases are death threats against a wife, threat to harm grievously, extreme verbal abuse, and harassment. Since the onset of the AIDS epidemic, wives who have been placed at high risk for contracting the disease due to their husband's adulterous behavior have taken action. One woman who came upon her husband in their bed with another woman successfully sued her husband for emotional distress.

Results of tort action for the intentional infliction of emotional injury include:

- *Massey v. Massey* (Texas Court of Appeals 1991)

  The appellate court affirmed a $362,000 jury award in damages to a wife for the infliction of emotional distress caused by her husband during their marriage. Evidence at trial established that during their marriage the husband was abusive, explosive, and rageful. He engaged in verbal abuse, including criticism, blaming, and belittling his wife in front of the children. The husband had temper tantrums and physical outbursts that sometimes involved the destruction of property. Although he never physically assaulted his wife, the husband's outbursts caused his wife intense anxiety and fear. He maintained a tight control over all financial matters and threatened his wife by telling her she would be penniless if she divorced him. The wife was not allowed any voice in decisions that affected her, including financial matters. The wife testified that she felt viciously attacked by her husband's threats to tell her children and her friends of her extramarital affair and his threat to take custody of her youngest daughter. He belittled her numerous charitable activities and was rude to her friends, often embarrassing her in front of them.

  The wife's psychologist diagnosed the husband as having an explosive personality disorder and lacking impulse control. The wife was characterized as emotionally battered and the psychologist described her as paralyzed, passive, and intimidated. She experienced extreme fear and learned to deal with her husband through avoidance, "walking on egg shells" so as not to trigger his rage. It was the psychologist's opinion that a good deal of the husband's behavior stemmed from "a malicious intent to harm" his wife and that the wife needed extensive future psychotherapy.

Although the husband denied most of the wife's allegations, the jury found that he had intentionally and negligently inflicted emotional distress on his wife, but had neither assaulted her nor acted with malice.

- *Curtis v. Firth* (Idaho 1990)

  In Boise, Idaho, a state district court jury awarded a woman $1 million in damages against her live-in lover, who engaged in a cycle of physical and emotional abuse and domination. The plaintiff argued that her abusive boyfriend's sexual and psychological abuse caused her to develop the battered woman's syndrome, resulting in post-traumatic stress disorder.

- *Weisman v. Weisman* (New York 1985)

  This case involved a man who destroyed the windows of the house where his wife and children were residing, leaving them without protection. He also threatened his spouse's life by displaying a bullet while she was involved in a religious divorce ceremony. His conduct was held to be sufficient to sustain a cause of action for the intentional infliction of emotional distress.

- *Chandler v. Chandler* (Illinois Appellate Court 1992)

  The appellate court held that an unsuccessful attempt to arrange for the murder of a former wife by a husband during their pending divorce was sufficient to give rise to an action by the former wife. The husband argued that it was not his intention to cause emotional distress because he intended for his ex-wife to be killed, in which case there would be no psychological effect on her.

- *Hakkila v. Hakkila* (New Mexico Court of Appeals 1991)

  The appellate court recognized the claim of intentional infliction of emotional distress in the context of a divorce case, but reversed the damage award on the basis that the husband's conduct failed to meet the standard of outrageousness. The husband's misconduct consisted of the following: assault and battery, in which he slammed part of a camper shell on his wife's head and the trunk lid on her hands, grabbed her and threw her face down into a pot full of dirt, grabbed her wrist and severely twisted it, and used excessive force during sex; insulted his wife in the presence of guests, friends, relatives, and foreign dignitaries; screamed at his wife at home and in the presence of others; locked his wife out of the house overnight in the middle of winter while she was wearing nothing but a robe; made repeated demeaning remarks about his wife's sexuality; continuously called his wife crazy, insane, and incompetent; refused to allow his wife to pursue education and hobbies; refused to have sexual relations with his wife; blamed his sexual inadequacies on his wife.

The appellate court emphasized that when determining when "the tort of outrage should be recognized in the marital setting, the threshold of outrageousness should be set high enough . . . that the social good from recognizing the tort will not be outweighed by unseemly and invasive litigation of meritless claims."

False Arrest and Imprisonment Imprisonment is defined as illegal restraint of movement. This cause of action requires that the restraint be a total one rather than a mere obstruction of the right to go where the woman pleases. Actionable conduct might be if a woman is locked in her home or a room in her home, or forced into the car and taken to a place where she is kept against her will. The restraint can be brief. Actionable restraint can be accomplished by threats of force or intimidation; confinement can be imposed by psychological as well as physical means. The following example of tort action is one that was combined with an action for assault and battery.

- *Catlett v. Catlett* (Georgia 1989)
  A Georgia jury returned a verdict for $10,000 compensatory and $20,000 punitive damages against a husband for striking and physically preventing his wife from leaving his apartment on one occasion and his car on another occasion until another person intervened.

Defamation, Slander, and Libel Defamation, slander, and libel are torts concerning the opinions that others in the community may have. A cause of action may be communication about the plaintiff using words, pictures, signs, statues, film, or video that are derogatory, defamatory, and insulting in nature to a third party and that may affect the plaintiff's good name and reputation. This is seldom used between spouses.

Negligent Infliction of Emotional Distress A cause of action for negligent infliction of emotional distress is usually allowed only against a defendant whose negligence causes mental disturbance *and* physical consequences or illness. One such action might be a case in which a woman sees her abuser inflicting severe abuse on their child or inflicting pain and torture on others. The following is an example of the result of tort action for negligent infliction of emotional distress.

- *Twyman v. Twyman* (Texas Court of Appeals 1990)
  The court upheld a trial court's award of $15,000 plus interest for a wife's claim of negligent infliction of emotional distress against her husband. Evidence at the trial established that the wife suffered emotional harm and mental anguish as a result of her husband's activities and repeated demands that continuation of their marriage was conditional upon his wife's participation in sexual bondage activities. It was established that the husband had knowledge of the wife's previous violent rape at knife-point and her inability to handle or cope with bondage activities, and that the husband repeatedly pressured her to engage in sexual bondage nonetheless. Other activities included his participation in sexual acts with extramarital partners, cruelly describing such partners and experiences to his wife, derogatorily comparing the wife's sexual abilities with his other partners, and exposing their ten-year-old son to graphic depictions of sexual acts. This caused his wife emotional feelings of utter despair, devastation, and humiliation. She sustained physical injury and lost approximately 30 pounds, was treated by three mental health counselors, and feared exposure to AIDS and other venereal diseases.

Actions under Wrongful Death Statutes In the case of the death of a battered woman, most wrongful death statutes would apply. In this case, a suit may be brought by the deceased woman's estate for wrongfully causing the death of the woman. On June 12, 1995, the family of Nicole Brown Simpson filed a wrongful death suit against O. J. Simpson. A similar suit was filed by the family of Ron Goldman two weeks earlier. These suits were filed within the one-year statutory time required in California. An example of a successful wrongful death suit follows.

- *Parman v. Price* (South Carolina 1988)
  The parents of a wife who was shot and killed by her husband brought action against the husband for wrongful death. The husband had been charged criminally with murder but subsequently pled guilty to involuntary manslaughter. The jury awarded $10 million to the plaintiffs, including $7.4 million in punitive damages.

Use of Excessive Force: When Battered Women Retaliate If a battered spouse acts in self-defense, she can use only such force as is necessary to defend herself against harm. If she waits until after the beating and then attacks the assailant or uses more force than is necessary, she may be liable for an action against her. It is possible in a case like this for each party to have an action against the other. The case of Francine Hughes as told in the book and film *The Burning Bed* is an example of a case where liability *may* have been found for the use of excessive force. In that case Hughes, a severely battered woman, killed her husband by setting fire to the bedroom where he was asleep.

Until 1962 no states allowed tort action by one spouse against another. Spousal immunity has now been abolished in most states and tort action is now permitted by either spouse against the other. Civil lawsuits are sometimes used by attorneys in divorce cases where no-fault divorce laws have denied the woman equitable property settlement and in cases involving battered women whose husbands have substantial means.

Divorce

Divorce is an action most believe is readily available to women in an abusive marriage. However, in addition to the danger of separation assault discussed earlier (violent and coercive attempts by a batterer to keep his victim from leaving him), separation and divorce can present different kinds of problems for a woman if there is an order of mediation or conflict over custody of the couple's child or children.

Mediation Domestic violence professionals have been concerned over the use of mediation in cases where domestic violence has been present. In her 1984 article on mediation for the *Harvard Woman's Law Journal*, L. Lerman linked wife assault with mediation. She says that mediation not only doesn't work in cases where domestic violence is an issue, but it perpetuates the woman's continued victimization. She asserts that many mediators ignore past marital behavior, assume that responsibility for the violence lies with both the victim and the abuser, give priority to facilitating agreements rather than stopping the violence, facilitate the signing of agreements that legitimate wife abuse, and trivialize the violence by using euphemisms when referring to the abuse.

The history of mediation is one that began in 1906 when jurist Roscoe Pound called for social experimentation with alternate conflict resolution processes that could solve people's legal problems. In 1939 the Los Angeles Conciliation Court was formed, its primary objective to reconcile spouses in marital conflict. In 1963 the Association of Family and Conciliation Courts was formed; its primary orientation changed to solving conflicts associated with separation and divorce. By 1980 court-based mediation services were available in most major cities. Private mediation services started to grow in the mid-1970s and had become a major growth industry by 1985.

Several reasons for the rapid increase in both court and private mediation services in the past 30 years are the rapid increase in the divorce rate combined with a lack of accompanying increases in resources allocated to family courts, judges who prefer to apply determinate standards in reaching their decisions, no-fault divorce that makes the past less important than the present and future, changes in the psychological field that favor mediation over adversarial processes, and legislative changes that have made family mediation legitimate.

Because the mediation process relies on good-faith bargaining between two parties who possess equal bargaining power, and because that condition doesn't exist in abusive relationships between intimate partners, feminist attorneys believe that mediation is contraindicated when domestic violence is involved. There is no process in mediation by which the abuser is held accountable for his violent behavior. The focus in mediation is to reach agreement and not assess blame, which can neither stop the violence nor protect the victim in an abusive relationship. The process therefore implies that the violence is acceptable and that the victim is partially responsible.

In 1994 the Academy of Family Mediators appointed a task force to draft a policy statement on mediation of disputes involving domestic violence. The academy board had not acted on the draft at the time of this writing. Major policy elements include:

- A case with a history of domestic violence should be mediated by an experienced mediator.
- If the victim cannot feel safe, the case should not be mediated.
- There should be no mediation concerning the violence itself.
- The clients should be encouraged to find an alternative to mediation when safety is an issue and a safe environment cannot be assured.
- Mediators must be knowledgeable about domestic violence.
- Above all—safety must be ensured.

Custody What happens if a battered woman tries to leave a relationship with her children's father in order to protect herself and her children? Unfortunately, many women suffer re-abuse by the court system and lose custody of their children to the father.

In recent years abusive husbands have increasingly used custodial access to the children as a tool to terrorize the mother or to retaliate for separation. They may use the threat of gaining custody, or even kidnapping, to keep her from leaving. And their threats of gaining custody aren't so difficult to carry out. Domestic violence professionals are finding that women are losing custody of their children because many courts do not consider a father's abuse of the mother evidence of unfitness as a parent.

Although a father usually has no problem with the mother's parenting ability until she tries to leave him, he may go into court proclaiming himself the most fit parent at time of separation or divorce. A father's fitness may be based on an ability to provide economic stability that includes a home in a better neighborhood as well as increased educational and recreational advantages.

Many times the woman is penalized by the court for a lifestyle that is a direct result of the abuse. She may live in poorer circumstances than she did previously. She may be unable to work for a variety of reasons, including harassment by the abuser at her place of employment, and be forced to live on welfare. Courts do not routinely take into account the abuse that directly led to the mother's economic circumstances.

Although there have been many studies that reveal that children suffer emotional abuse when witnessing the beatings of their mothers, courts usually won't deny visitation or custody on the basis of the father's violence toward the mother unless it is proved that abuse has also been directed at the children. A problem that has gained attention in recent years is the issue of child abuse, often revealed by the child only after separation. Most children do not feel safe revealing abuse, especially sexual abuse, until the abuser is no longer in the home. Or abuse may begin during visitation, due to the abuser's need to regain some control over his family or his desire for vengeance.

Men's rights groups have charged that women falsely allege child sexual abuse at the time of separation, either as an attempt to retaliate or as an attempt to deny the father his rights of access to his children. In cases where there is a pending custody dispute and the mother alleges that the father is sexually abusing the child, some child protective service agencies give the case low priority unless there is strong corroborating evidence.

In a report released in February 1988, the American Bar Association's National Legal Research Center for Child Advocacy and Protection, in conjunction with the Association of Family and Conciliation Courts, found that "deliberately false allegations of child sexual abuse are exceedingly rare . . . on the contrary, most allegations (95 percent) have a legitimate basis." Ironically, many women end up losing custody to the father as a result of their efforts to protect their children. When they make allegations of child sexual abuse they are perceived as mentally unstable, and therefore unfit parents. They have been labeled by judges and mental health evaluators as hysterical, emotional, vindictive, psychotic, or liars. A gender bias study conducted by the state of California found that it is much easier for the courts to believe that a woman is mentally unstable than to believe that a man who seems to be quite normal in all other respects would commit such acts against his own child.

Child sexual abuse is often difficult to prove because there are rarely witnesses and often no physical evidence. Since the majority of sexual abuse occurs to children under the age of three, the victim is unable to testify in a court case. Although these children have communicated to someone through their words and/or behavior that this abuse is occurring, the testimony is excluded because it is classified as hearsay.

Domestic violence professionals believe abusers should not be perceived as equally fit parents and their violence should be the first grounds for termination of unsupervised parental rights (visitation, joint custody, full custody). Many domestic violence professionals believe that when abusers get custody of their children, the children lose their right to legal protection from violence. It also sends a message to abusers that they can continue to abuse and it punishes mothers who have taken proper legal action to protect themselves and their children from abuse. When battered women hear these results, they are discouraged from escaping violence.

What Does the System Do If It Perceives a Mother Is Failing To Protect Her Child?

In recent years a common response to the revelation of child maltreatment by a batterer has been to charge the mother with "failure to protect." This response is founded on the prevalent belief that a mother has primary responsibility for ensuring the safety of her children, the assumption being that she should have the power, ability, and resources to protect her children even when she is repeatedly battered.

In 1989, when Joel Steinberg went on trial in New York for the battering murder of his illegally adopted daughter, Lisa, the public was horrified when it heard the terrible abuse this six-year-old had endured. Public outrage, however, refocused on Steinberg's battered live-in partner of 11 years, Hedda Nussbaum, for failing to protect Lisa. Nussbaum agreed to testify against Steinberg in return for immunity from prosecution and became the target of outraged anger when she testified she had done as Joel told her—straightened out his legal files instead of calling 911 for their comatose daughter. What most media reporters and legal experts did not understand was that Nussbaum was totally unable to act because she had been so brutally battered over a 13-year period and had no will of her own left.

Courts reacted, however, and began prosecuting battered women as murderers or accessories when they did not actively prevent husbands or boyfriends from murdering their children. Since 1989 women have been convicted in such cases in at least a dozen states and received sentences of anywhere from 5 to 60 years in prison, sometimes receiving as much time as the man who committed the murder. In these cases the remaining children are placed in foster care.

The courts ignore or are ignorant of the reality of the woman's life, that she is unable to stop the batterer or protect her child because of the nature of the batterer and her relationship with him. The courts label her a bad mother who is not following (or does not possess) her natural maternal instinct. In such cases the courts fail to recognize the woman's victimization, or that the abuser may be depriving her of the ability or resources to protect her children.

Women are now receiving the message that if they report domestic violence they may find themselves in a no-win situation. Even if they have done everything possible to keep the batterer out of the home or if the children are not the targets of abuse, they may lose the children to foster care. Some women are considered by child protective service workers and the courts as too paralyzed by victimization to protect their children from violence in the home. A woman is considered unfit as a mother if she cannot act promptly to stop her own beating or take her child to safety. The battered mother is blamed for the consequences of her partner's actions and deprived of the support she needs to protect her children as well as herself.

What Action Do Some Women Take When the System Fails Them?

Protective Parents Who Go Underground

Some mothers who have exhausted all legal avenues open to them have taken their children or hidden them away in violation of court orders and become a part of a "mother's underground movement," an unofficial and unstructured group of women in hiding.

Some mothers have taken this drastic step in order to protect their children from sexual abuse or because they have suffered abuse themselves and fear for their own and their children's lives.

Going underground is extremely difficult and most women eventually get caught. A woman must be willing to give up everything—her identity, her friends and family, her home, and often a career. She can have no contact with anyone from her past and she must change her lifestyle, live with strangers, and give up all that's familiar. Poverty, emotional stress, depression, feelings of isolation, and paranoia are common. She will always worry when her child is out of her sight and will constantly be looking over her shoulder.

Once a woman flees with her children, the father can go to court and obtain full custody. Once this is done, a warrant is issued for the mother's arrest and the authorities, including the Federal Bureau of Investigation (FBI), will often help find her. When the woman and children are found, the father (now the custodial parent) gets his children and the mother goes to jail, many times for felony child concealment or kidnapping.

Protective parent Paula Oldham was found guilty of child concealment by a Marin County, California, court in June 1994 and sentenced to two years in prison on May 17, 1995. Oldham, a former bank executive with no prior record, was a battered wife who moved to San Francisco from Los Angeles with her two-year-old daughter to escape battering by her husband. He followed her and they became involved in a protracted custody battle. Sexual acting out and bizarre behavior by her daughter following visits with her father caused Oldham to believe the child was being sexually abused during these visits. Eventually, after two years of unsuccessful attempts to get the courts to order an investigation, Ms. Oldham, who had sole legal custody, fled underground with her daughter. After 15 months in southern France, she was tracked down by a private investigator. Ms. Oldham's then-four-year-old daughter was forcibly taken from her and given to her father, who now has sole legal custody. He has never been investigated. Ms. Oldham is serving her sentence in California.

Most mothers who are captured after hiding in the underground, even if they are not jailed, are allowed only limited supervised visits under the guise that they pose a continuing threat of abduction. Often the court names a supervisor who is a high-priced professional to whom the mother must pay hundreds of dollars for each visit. If she cannot pay the supervisor, she doesn't see her child. In some cases these mothers are further penalized by exorbitant child support awards to the father.

Battered Women Who Kill Their Abusers

On 18 September 1992, the *New York Times* ran a full-page ad asking for letters of protest regarding four California women sentenced to prison for killing the men they had believed loved them.

Brenda A.'s husband broke her jaw, cracked her ribs, blackened her eyes, and pulled her hair so hard she thought he was going to break her neck. He threatened to harm her and her family if she ever called the police. She left with her three daughters many times, only to be tracked down and beaten. The last time he beat her he said she wouldn't live until morning. She got a gun, shot and killed him, and was sentenced to 15 years to life in prison.

Brenda C. was stabbed and beaten by her husband. She called police numerous times, obtained a temporary restraining order against him and later a warrant for his arrest. She was turned away by the local shelter due to a lack of space. She hit her husband with a bottle and killed him. She was sentenced to 15 years to life in prison.

Christy was a 14-year-old with no family when she married her 25-year-old husband. He grabbed and choked her on many occasions and once she nearly lost consciousness. With two babies and no job skills, she described feeling economically trapped and completely powerless to change her situation. Her one attempt to work at a supermarket didn't last long. Her husband threatened that if anything happened to the children while they were in day care they'd find her in the parking lot with her uniform on, cut-up into little pieces. One night she defended herself with a knife, killed her husband, and was given 16 years to life in prison.

Glenda was stabbed and choked by her boyfriend. The police were contacted several times to stop him from beating her. Even though he received psychiatric help to stop his violent behavior, he still beat her with a gas can, held her hostage with a shotgun, and threatened to kill both of them. When she got the gun away from him she shot and killed him and was sentenced to 17 years to life in prison.

These women are only 4 of the approximately 2,000 battered women in America serving prison time for defending their lives against their batterers. Although governors in a few states have reviewed cases and granted clemency, there are many women who are still sitting in prison without much hope for release anytime soon.

Women are faced with a no-win situation. As Richard Gelles acknowledges in *The Violent House,* it seems to make no difference whether or not the assaulted woman fights back. A woman's failure to fight back can leave her passively at the man's mercy for as long as he has the strength to keep hitting her. Conversely, if a woman does try to fight back, she is likely to be punished for it with an even more vicious beating. When women kill, the vast majority kill men who have battered them for years. As many as 90 percent of the women in jail today for killing men had been battered by those men (Bass 1992).

- Self-defense is involved in seven times as many cases when women kill men than when men kill women. The various studies consistently show that the victim initiates the violence significantly more often when a man is killed by a woman than when a woman is killed by a man. Thus, when women kill they are far more likely than men to be responding to, rather than initiating, violence (Campbell 1986).
- Marital homicide differs significantly by gender: for the homicidal husband the act is nearly always offensive; for the wife it is usually defensive. This supports the popular contention that marital homicide, regardless of who inflicts the fatal blow, is typically a reflection of wife abuse (Goetting 1989).
- A study conducted in Georgia of 226 (96 percent) of the 235 female inmates currently serving sentences for homicide revealed a history of domestic violence in more than half (57 percent) of the cases when the woman has killed her intimate partner. In 60 percent of the cases of partner homicide, the woman claims the victim assaulted or abused her at the time of the crime (Haley 1992).
- Forty percent of the women in the Chicago Women's Correctional Center in 1977 were serving time for killing a husband or lover who had repeatedly beat them. A study conducted in Dayton, Ohio, found a history of abuse against the women in 79.3 percent of the cases of a woman killing a man with whom she was having or

had had an intimate relationship, only two involved mutual violence between the partners, and none involved husband abuse (Campbell 1986).

Why Do Some Women Kill the Men Who Batter Them?

Many who have conducted studies of battered women who kill (Angela Browne, Lenore Walker, Ann Jones, Cynthia Gillespie, Charles Ewing, and others) refer to the act of homicide as an act of desperation, committed because there seems to be no escape from the violence. The fear, rage, continual terror, and feeling of entrapment the battered woman lives with can lead her to strike out against the batterer for sheer survival. Unfortunately, killing is often a woman's safest alternative, given the absence of police protection and the ineffectiveness of the legal system in protecting a woman from domestic violence.

Browne's study revealed that many women had stayed with their abusers because they had been beaten after trying to escape or because they believed an attempt to escape would cause their partners to retaliate with further violence. Almost all of the battered women she studied thought the abusers could or would kill them; and many, especially in the homicide group, were convinced that they could not escape this danger by leaving (Browne 1987).

How Are the Women Charged?

Many of these women were charged with serious felonies (first- or second-degree murder rather than manslaughter). Because of this, plea bargains seem the safest option for many women, since the penalties if convicted would be correspondingly severe. In Angela Browne's study of battered women who had killed their abusive partners, the women in the study had to choose whether to go to trial on the charges against them or attempt to negotiate a plea and plead guilty to lesser charges. Most of the women had no prior experience with the criminal justice system and relied heavily on their attorneys for guidance. The most common plea arrangement was voluntary manslaughter, with an agreement that the woman would be given a reduced jail sentence or would spend several years on probation but no time in jail. Many of the women were so emotionally fragile after the homicides that the thought of going through a public trial was too stressful to consider. Even when their attorneys believed the possibility of winning an acquittal was strong, some women preferred to negotiate a plea and end the process as quickly as possible (Browne 1987).

Use of the Battered Woman Syndrome as a Legal Defense

As has been previously described, the Battered Woman Syndrome is what psychologists have named the group of typical behaviors and emotional responses experienced by women who have been beaten repeatedly by the man they live with and love. Because a battered woman's perception is shaped by her experience of battering, and because it is so difficult for a jury to understand how a woman could be severely battered and yet stay with the man, defense attorneys feel it necessary to get information about the Battered Woman Syndrome before the jury. This is normally done by a recognized expert, usually a psychologist who has experience working with battered women. The explanation of the syndrome is offered in a self-defense trial to give information on the reasonableness of the defendant's behavior.

Following is an example of a case in which the Battered Woman Syndrome was used successfully.

- *People v. Wilson* (Michigan Court of Appeals 1992)
  The appellate court recognized, for the first time, the validity of evidence of Battered Woman Syndrome to support a self-defense claim. This was a so-called sleeping spouse case where the defendant shot and killed her husband while he slept, following 48 hours of abuse and death threats, and years of battery. The court permitted the evidence to rebut the prosecution's suggestion that the defendant could have left the house rather than kill her spouse.

How Many Women Are Convicted, and of What?

Although the Battered Woman Syndrome has been used in self-defense cases and sometimes women such as Francine Hughes have been found not guilty due to temporary insanity, these defenses can only be successful if evidence of past abuse is allowed. Many courts have not allowed any evidence of previous abuse, nor do some courts allow expert testimony on the effects of battering on a woman. The previous practice of the particular court in which a woman will be tried can affect her decision regarding the negotiation of a plea bargain.

- Studies show that only 20 percent of battered women who are charged with killing their partners are acquitted; the rest are convicted or plea-bargain to avoid a trial (Chittum et al. 1990).
- Two studies suggest that battered women who kill are either being convicted or taking a plea at a rate of between 72 percent and 78 percent nationally (Ewing 1987).
- Among the 100 cases of homicides by battered women reviewed in Ewing's appendix, 9 women pleaded guilty to murder, manslaughter, or criminally negligent homicide and received sentences ranging from conditional discharge or probation to 20 years in prison, 3 entered pleas of not guilty by reason of insanity and were acquitted on that basis, and 3 had the charges against them dropped before trial. The remaining 85 all went to trial on homicide charges and claimed self-defense; 22 were acquitted and the other 63 were convicted of various forms of criminal homicide: 7 of first-degree murder, 15 of second-degree murder, 1 of third-degree murder, 12 of unspecified murder, 11 of voluntary manslaughter, 5 of involuntary manslaughter, 8 of unspecified manslaughter, 1 of manslaughter with a firearm, and 3 of reckless homicide.

Twelve of these women, all convicted of murder, received sentences of life in prison, one without a possibility of parole for 50 years. Sentences for the others convicted after trial ranged from 4 years' probation (with the first year to include periodic incarceration) to 25 years in prison. Seventeen of these women received prison sentences potentially in excess of 10 years.

Among the 63 women convicted at trial, 55 appealed. The appellate courts affirmed 29 of these convictions, reversed and remanded 22 of them for new trials, and dismissed 4 of them for insufficient evidence to support a conviction (these last ones cannot be retried). In 9 of the 22 cases remanded for new trials the verdict was reversed on appeal because the trial court erroneously excluded expert testimony regarding the Battered Woman Syndrome. Four of the women whose convictions were reversed on appeal waived new trials and pled guilty to the original charge or some lesser form of criminal homicide (Ewing 1987).

Studies show that many women convicted of killing their husbands draw longer sentences than men convicted of killing their wives. Why? Captain Janice Wilson, who heads the women's reception center at Gates, Texas, said she believes it is the fact that a woman almost invariably uses a deadly weapon like a knife or a gun—whereas men use their hands to kill their wives, and that's not considered a deadly weapon (*Houston Chronicle*, 7 May 1989). Others have offered the opinion that many judges have a difficult time with women who have committed a violent act. This seems counter to a woman's gentle and nurturing nature, and these women are seen as aberrant. The sentencing is seen as gender bias, the reinforcement of the traditional gender roles women are supposed to fill. For these women it looks like revictimization by society.

- Women charged in the death of a mate have the least extensive criminal records of any people convicted. However, they often face harsher penalties than men who kill their mates. FBI statistics indicate that fewer men are charged with first- or second-degree murder for killing a woman they have known than are women who kill a man they have known (Browne 1987).
- In 1991 there were 34 women on death row in the United States. Of these women, 14 were condemned for the murder of a husband or partner. While the conviction rate of women for murder has remained steady over the last ten years, the rate of death sentencing of women has undergone some dramatic increases, including the sudden doubling of the rate in 1984 and again in 1989 and 1990. Of these 34 women, there are indications of significant physical, sexual, and/or emotional abuse in 12 cases. For the women who killed their partners, there is evidence of battering in nearly every case researched by the National Coalition to Abolish the Death Penalty. For several of the women there is little or no social

history available, and the incidence of battering could in fact be much higher (Dingerson 1991).

What Can Be Done To Reduce the Number of Homicides?

Women who kill do so as a last resort. They have been battered, tortured, and terrorized for years, and have no hope of escape. Most battered women have tried to leave but have failed, many times due to a lack of victim services or information about available services, lack of adequate law enforcement, and a legal system unresponsive to their needs.

- A 1986 study found that the number of male partners killed by women actually decreased by over 25 percent from 1979 to 1984. It was felt this might have reflected, in part, improvements in alternatives available to women involved in threatening or assaultive relationships (Browne and Flewelling 1986). Further investigation of this issue revealed that those states having more domestic violence legislation and extra legal resources (e.g., funding for shelters, crisis lines, legal aid) had lower rates of total homicides by women against their male partners and that the presence of these resources was associated with the decrease in female-perpetrated partner homicides from 1976 to 1984 (Browne and Williams 1990).
- According to an official at the Washington Corrections Center for Women in Purdy, it costs $32,000 a year to keep a female inmate in prison (figures from July 1991).

Using that figure, we spend $6.4 million per year imprisoning battered women who killed their batterers in self-defense. That money could pay for a substantial amount of victim services and professional training.

The Quincy Model

In Cohasset, Massachusetts, in 1978, Joan Quirk was beaten by her husband. She called police and was brought to the police station, where she was advised to file a formal complaint on Tuesday when the courts reopened. The police then returned her to her home. On Monday James Quirk shot and killed his wife, their three children, and the family dog, then killed himself.

The public was outraged, and as a result the state legislature passed the Abuse Prevention Act, creating civil restraining orders and criminalizing violations of those orders. The Norfolk County District Attorney's Office worked with civic organizations and established the Quincy area's first shelter for battered women. The police developed procedures for their response to domestic violence calls.

From this beginning grew a comprehensive program that coordinates civil and criminal courts, law enforcement, battered women's advocates, children's advocates, and batterer's treatment programs. The program aims to hold batterers accountable, empower victims, and work with children to break the cycle of violence.

How Effective Is It?

- There has not been a domestic killing of a court-involved woman in Quincy in six years. This is in a state where domestic violence claimed the life of a woman every 14 days in 1992.
- The number of women seeking protective orders from the Quincy court has more than doubled since 1985.
- Quincy has the lowest rate of women who drop their restraining orders before expiration. Women drop restraining orders when they find them ineffective, when the batterer violates with no consequence.
- The Gender Bias Commission of the Massachusetts Supreme Judicial Court found that while many courts handed out trivial sentences to restraining-order violators, the Quincy court consistently sentenced the majority to jail and/or formal probation.

In reporting on a study of the Quincy Model, James Hardeman, the corporate counseling manager for Polaroid Corporation, made the following statements: "The most heavily populated area of Plymouth County, Brockton, has advocates against spousal abuse through the local shelter, police department, and district attorney's office, but their strengths are not integrated to support one another." In contrast, the Quincy

Model, due to its permanent interagency partnerships, "has afforded victims improved accessibility within the system, education about their rights under the Abuse Prevention Act, and emotional support and clinical treatment, among other benefits." Most importantly, Hardeman found that victims in the comparison court were re-abused more than twice as often as those in the Quincy court.

The Quincy Model has received recognition and awards from numerous organizations, including the Ford Foundation, the National Council of Juvenile and Family Court Judges, the Family Court Judges Family Violence Project, the National Institute of Corrections, the Massachusetts Supreme Judicial Court, the Harvard School of Public Health, the Massachusetts Women's Legislative Caucus, and numerous battered women's groups.

The Quincy Model is one example of how the tragic results of domestic violence can be reduced when a community integrates its services and works together toward a common goal.

References

Bass, Allison. "Women Far Less Likely To Kill Than Men; No One Sure Why." *The Boston Globe*, 24 February 1992.

Berrios, D. C., and D. Grady. "Domestic Violence: Risk Factors and Outcomes." *The Western Journal of Medicine* (August 1991).

Bowker, Lee H. "The Importance of Sheltering in the Lives of Battered Women." *Response* (Winter 1985).

Browne, Angela. *When Battered Women Kill.* New York: The Free Press, 1987.

———. "Testimony to the U.S. Senate Judiciary Committee." 29 August and 11 December 1990.

Browne, Angela, and R. Flewelling. "Women as Victims or Perpetrators of Homicide." Paper presented at the American Society of Criminology, Atlanta, 1986.

Browne, Angela, and K. R. Williams. "Trends in Partner Homicide: By Relationship Type and Gender: 1976–1987." Paper presented at the annual meeting of the American Society of Criminology, Baltimore, November 1990.

Campbell, Jacquelyn. "Nursing Assessment for Risk of Homicide with Battered Women." *Advances in Nursing Science* (July 1986).

———. "If I Can't Have You, No One Can: Power and Control in Homicide of Female Partners," in J. Radford and D. E. G. Russell, eds., *Femicide: The Politics of Woman Killing* (New York: Macmillan, 1992).

Casanave, N., and M. Zahn. "Women, Murder, and Male Domination: Police Reports of Domestic Homicide in Chicago and Philadelphia." Paper presented at the annual meeting of the American Society of Criminology, Atlanta, October 1986.

Chittum, Samme, Mark Bauman, and Irene Nyborg-Andersen. "No Way Out." *Ladies' Home Journal*, April 1990.

The Commonwealth Fund. *First Comprehensive National Survey of American Women Finds Them at Significant Risk* (news release). New York: The Commonwealth Fund, 14 July 1993.

Dingerson, Leigh. "Women on Death Row," *Response to the Victimization of Women and Children* 14, no. 2 (1991).

Dutton, Donald G., and Barbara M. S. McGregor. "The Symbiosis of Arrest and Treatment for Wife Assault: The Case for Combined Intervention," in Michael Steinman, ed., *Woman Battering: Police Responses* (Cincinnati: Anderson, 1991).

Ewing, Charles P. *Battered Women Who Kill: Psychological Self-Defense as Legal Justification.* Lexington, MA: Lexington Books, 1987.

Family Service of Philadelphia and The Legal Center of Women Against Abuse. *Report of the Task Force on Mandated Counseling for Domestic Violence Offenders.* Philadelphia, July 1991.

Ferraro, Kathleen J., and Lucille Pope. "Irreconcilable Differences: Battered Women, Police, and the Law," in N. Zoe Hilton, ed., *Legal Responses to Wife Assault* (London: Sage Publications, 1993).

Finn, Peter. "Civil Protection Orders: A Flawed Opportunity for Intervention," in Michael Steinman, ed., *Woman Battering: Policy Responses* (Cincinnati: Anderson, 1991).

Follingstad, Diane, Larry Rutledge, Barbara J. Berg, Elizabeth Hause, and Darlene Polek. "The Role of Emotional Abuse in Physically Abusive Relationships." *Journal of Family Violence* 5, no. 2 (1990).

Frieze, Irene Hanson, and Angela Browne. "Violence in Marriage," in Lloyd Ohlin and Michael H. Tony, eds., *Family Violence* (Chicago: University of Chicago Press, 1987).

Gelles, Richard. "Constraints against Family Violence: How Well Do They Work?" Paper presented at the annual meeting of the American Society of Criminology, San Francisco, November 1991.

Gelles, Richard, and Claire Pedrick Cornell. *Intimate Violence in Families.* Newbury Park, CA: Sage Publications, 1990.

Gillespie, Cynthia. *Justifiable Homicide: Battered Women, Self-Defense, and the Law*. Columbus: Ohio State University Press, 1989.

Glazer, Sarah. "Violence against Women." *CQ Researcher* 3, no. 1 (February 1993).

Goetting, Ann. "Patterns of Marital Homicide: A Comparison of Husbands and Wives." *Journal of Comparative Family Studies* 20, no. 1 (Autumn 1989).

Gondolf, Edward W. "The Effect of Batterer Counseling on Shelter Outcome." *Journal of Interpersonal Violence* 3, no. 3 (September 1988).

Grossman, Jody. *Domestic Violence and Incarcerated Women: Survey Results*. New York: State Department of Correctional Services, October 1985.

Haley, Judith. *A Study of Women Imprisoned for Homicide*. Georgia: Department of Corrections, June 1992.

Hamberger, L. K., D. G. Saunder, and M. Hovery. "Prevalence of Domestic Violence in Community Practice and Rate of Physician Inquiry." *Family Medicine* 24, no. 4 (May/June 1992).

Hart, Barbara. "Testimony on the Family Violence Prevention and Services Act." Reauthorization Hearing, U.S. Senate, Washington, D.C., July 1991.

Holtz, Howard, and Kathleen Furniss. "The Health Care Provider's Role in Domestic Violence." *Trends in Health Care, Law & Ethics* 8, no. 2 (Spring 1993).

Hotaling, Gerald T., and David B. Sugarman. "An Analysis of Risk Markers in Husband to Wife Violence: The Current State of Knowledge." *Violence and Victims* 1 (Summer 1986).

Hotaling, Gerald T., David Finkelhor, John T. Kirkpatrick, and Murray A. Straus. *Coping with Family Violence: Research and Policy Perspectives*. Newbury Park, CA: Sage Publications, 1988.

Huling, Tracy. *Breaking the Silence*. New York: The Correctional Association of New York, March 1991.

Jaffe, Peter G., David A. Wolfe, and Susan Kaye Wilson. *Children of Battered Women*. Newbury Park, CA: Sage Publications, 1988.

Johnson, Anne T. "Criminal Liability for Parents Who Fail To Protect." *Law and Inequality* 5, no. 2 (July 1987).

Jones, Ann. *Next Time She'll Be Dead*. Boston: Beacon Press, 1994.

Knapp, Caroline. "A Plague of Murders: Open Season on Women." *The Boston Phoenix*, August 1992.

Kylen, Helene. "Understanding Family Violence: A Legal and Psychological Approach. *Court Review* 28, no. 4 (Winter 1991).

Martin, Del. *Battered Wives*. Volcano, CA: Volcano Press, 1976. Rev. ed. 1981.

Mederer, Helen J., and Richard J. Gelles. "Compassion or Control: Intervention in Cases of Wife Abuse." *Journal of Interpersonal Violence* 4, no. 1 (March 1989).

Morgan, Kay. "Reassessing the Battery of Women: A Social and Economic Perspective." *Fōuinist Jurisprudence* (May 1992). Available from National Clearinghouse for the Defense of Battered Women.

National Woman Abuse Prevention Project. "Understanding Domestic Violence: Fact Sheets." Washington, D.C., 1989.

Roy, Maria. *Children in the Crossfire*. Dearfield Beach, FL: Health Communications, Inc., 1988.

Saunders, Daniel, and Angela Browne. "Domestic Homicide," in Robert Ammerman and Michel Hersen, eds., *Case Studies in Family Violence* (New York: Plenum Press, 1991).

Schecter, Susan. *Women and Male Violence*. Boston: South End Press, 1982.

Sohl, Kay. *Homeless Children and Youth in Oregon, Executive Summary*. North Bend, OR: The Oregon Shelter Network, 1988.

Stark, Evan. "Rethinking Homicide: Violence, Race, and the Politics of Gender." *International Journal of Health and Services* 20 (1990).

Stark, Evan, and Anne E. Flitcraft. "Spouse Abuse." Paper presented at the Surgeon General's Workshop on Violence and Public Health, Leesburg, Virginia, October 1985.

———. "Violence among Intimates: An Epidemiological Review," in Vincent B. Von Hasselt et al., eds., *Handbook of Family Violence* (New York: Plenum Press, 1988).

Steinman, Michael, ed. *Woman Battering: Policy Responses*. Cincinnati: Anderson Publishing Co., 1991.

Straus, Murray A., and Christine Smith. "Family Patterns and Primary Prevention of Family Violence." *Trends in Health Care, Law & Ethics* 8, no. 2 (Spring 1993).

Straus, Murray A., Richard J. Gelles, and Suzanne K. Steinmetz. *Behind Closed Doors: Violence in the American Family*. Newbury Park, CA: Sage Publications, 1981.

Strube, Michael J. "The Decision To Leave an Abusive Relationship," in Gerald T. Hotaling, David Finkelhor, J. Kirkpatrick, Murray A. Straus, eds., *Coping with Family Violence: Research and Policy Perspectives* (Newbury Park, CA: Sage Publications, 1988).

Thyfault, Roberta K. "Self-Defense: Battered Woman Syndrome on Trial." *California Western Law Review* 20 (1984).

Thyfault, Roberta K., Angela Browne, and Lenore E. A. Walker. "When Battered Women Kill: Evaluation and Expert Testimony Techniques," in Daniel J. Sonkin, ed., *Domestic Violence on Trial: Psychological and Legal Dimensions of Family Violence* (New York: Springer, 1987).

U.S. Department of Justice. *Bureau of Justice Statistics.* Washington, DC: U.S. Government Printing Office, August 1986.

Walker, Lenore. *Terrifying Love: Why Battered Women Kill and How Society Responds.* New York: Harper and Row, 1989.

Organizations 5

National Organizations

Battered Women's Justice Project
206 West 4th Street
Duluth, MN 55806
(800) 903-0111

The Battered Women's Justice Project focuses on battered women and the criminal justice system and supplies information to attorneys, advocates, and battered women. As part of a network of four resource centers funded by the U.S. Department of Health and Human Services to advance research, services, and public information in the area of family violence, the project provides training, technical assistance, and other resources through a partnership of three nationally recognized organizations. These are Domestic Abuse Intervention Project of Duluth, addressing the criminal justice system's response to domestic violence, including the development of batterers' programs; National Clearinghouse for the Defense of Battered Women, addressing battered women's self-defense issues; Pennsylvania Coalition against Domestic Violence, addressing civil court access and legal representation issues of battered women.

165

Center for the Prevention of Sexual and Domestic Violence
1914 North 34th Street, Suite 105
Seattle, WA 98103
(206) 634-1903
(206) 634-0115, Fax

The Center for the Prevention of Sexual and Domestic Violence was founded in 1977 as an educational resource working specifically with religious communities on issues of sexual abuse and domestic violence. The center works with clergy and laity to break the silence surrounding sexual and domestic violence, to provide support to victims and survivors, and to promote cooperation between religious and secular agencies. The center has developed multimedia materials—combining training manuals, video resources, handouts, and study guides—with a perspective that is interreligious, multicultural, and multiracial.

The Clothesline Project–National Network
P.O. Box 727
East Dennis, MA 02641
(508) 385-7004

The Clothesline Project, which grew out of the tradition of women meeting and talking across the lines of laundry in their backyards, memorializes abused women. The project collects and strings together T-shirts illustrated by women survivors of abuse in a dramatic display of the effects of domestic violence. The clothesline may hang in a mall, college women's center, town center, courthouse, or at a march, demonstration, or conference. Communities all over America have developed these powerful displays with the help of The Clothesline Project–National Network in Massachusetts.

Family Violence Prevention Fund
383 Rhode Island Street, Suite 304
San Francisco, CA 94103-5133
(415) 252-8900

Founded in 1980 by Esta Soler, the Family Violence Prevention Fund (FUND) is a national, nonprofit organization that focuses on domestic violence education, prevention, and public policy reform. FUND's mission is to stem the epidemic of domestic violence. Throughout its history FUND has developed pioneering prevention strategies in the justice, public education, and public health fields. FUND's publications and model programs have been distributed to every state and several foreign countries. FUND also addresses the legal rights of battered immigrant and refugee women.

Family Violence and Sexual Assault Institute
1310 Clinic Drive
Tyler, TX 75701
(903) 595-6600

The Family Violence and Sexual Assault Institute (FVSAI) was established in 1984 by Robert Geffner, Ph.D. It became an independent, nonprofit corporation in 1991. FVSAI is a national resource center and maintains an international clearinghouse of references and unpublished papers concerning aspects of family violence and sexual abuse, reviews information and materials, and then disseminates the information in the *Family Violence and Sexual Abuse Bulletin,* published quarterly and distributed internationally, in order to improve networking among researchers, practitioners, and agencies. FVSAI, in cooperation with crisis centers, agencies, and counseling clinics, is also involved in developing treatment programs for spouse/partner abuse and sexual abuse. It has published two treatment manuals and four bibliographies and is working on others. Its research has focused on victims and offenders of spouse/partner abuse and incest. FVSAI conducts seminars, workshops, educational programs, and conferences nationwide. It also serves as a consultant to various organizations and agencies, providing program evaluation, research, and technical assistance.

Health Resource Center on Domestic Violence
1001 Potrero Avenue
Building One, Suite 200
San Francisco, CA 94110
(800) 313-1310

Funded by a grant from the U.S. Department of Health and Human Services, the Health Resource Center on Domestic Violence is part of a network of four resource centers designed to advance research, services, and public information in the area of family violence. The center provides resource and training materials, library services, and technical assistance to all those interested in strengthening the health care response to domestic violence. Assistance and library materials include general information packets and materials specifically designed for a variety of health care specialties; program specialists who can help set up a training program on domestic violence, develop protocols for responding to victims, or answer other related requests; and information specialists who can provide customized computer literature searches, research studies, and other published materials from the library's domestic violence collection.

National Battered Women's Law Project
National Center on Women and Family Law
799 Broadway, Suite 402
New York, NY 10003
(212) 674-8200

The project serves as an information clearinghouse for advocates, attorneys, and policymakers on legal issues facing battered women. The project produces manuals, handbooks, public education materials, and resource packets on legal issues facing battered women; analyzes federal and state legislative and administrative developments and other legal issues that affect battered women; assists advocates, policymakers, and attorneys on specific issues faced by battered women in their communities; and contributes to and distributes *The Women's Advocate,* the bimonthly newsletter of the National Center on Women and Family Law, which reports on legal and legislative developments with respect to family law issues, with particular emphasis on battery.

National Clearinghouse for the Defense of Battered Women
125 South 9th Street, Suite 302
Philadelphia, PA 19107
(215) 351-0010

The National Clearinghouse for the Defense of Battered Women was established in 1987 as a resource and advocacy center providing information and resources to attorneys, battered women's advocates, expert witnesses who are assisting battered women charged with crimes, members of the media, students, and other concerned community members. The clearinghouse collects information about many aspects of domestic violence, homicide, and prisoner issues from many sources and coordinates a national network of advocates working with women in prison.

National Coalition against Domestic Violence
P.O. Box 18749
Denver, CO 80218
(303) 839-1852

The National Coalition against Domestic Violence (NCADV) is dedicated to the empowerment of battered women and their children and to the elimination of personal and societal violence. NCADV's work includes coalition-building at the local, state, regional, and national levels; support for the provision of community-based, nonviolent alternatives for battered women and their children; public education and technical assistance; policy development and innovative legislation; caucuses and task forces developed to represent the concerns of organizationally underrepresented groups; and efforts to eradicate social conditions that contribute to violence against women and children.

National Resource Center on Domestic Violence
6400 Flank Drive, Suite 1300
Harrisburg, PA 17112
(800) 537-2238

Funded by the U.S. Department of Health and Human Services, the center is part of a network of resource centers designed to advance research, services, and public information in the area of family violence. The center provides comprehensive statistics, information, technical assistance, and access to expert opinion while also promoting research, policy analysis, and development of programs on all aspects of domestic violence response and prevention. It strives to strengthen the existing support system for battered women and their children as well as to identify and fill information and resource gaps that may perpetuate domestic violence.

National Victim Center
2111 Wilson Boulevard, Suite 300
Arlington, VA 22201
(703) 276-2880

The National Victim Center is a nonprofit organization founded in 1985. Its mission is to reduce the consequences of crime on victims and society by promoting victims' rights and assistance and through education about the effects of crime on our society. The center also serves as a resource for public policymakers, criminal justice officials, and other professionals looking for sample laws, model language, and legal guidance at the state and federal levels. The center accomplishes its mission through:

- **Research.** In 1992 the center, in conjunction with the Crime Victims Research and Treatment Center at the Medical University of South Carolina, released the results of two nationwide studies concerning forcible rape, *Rape in America: A Report to the Nation.* The center participates in many such research projects.
- **Public policy development and implementation.** The center is developing a computerized database of victim-related legislation that will permit comprehensive assessment of victims' rights nationwide, comparison of such rights, tracking of current trends in legislation, and evaluation of the response to victims' needs. The center was instrumental in the passage of constitutional amendments that grant victims the right to be present at, heard from, and informed of key proceedings in the criminal justice process. It has also provided information, resources, and support in organizing public awareness efforts related to the 1990 Hate Crime Statistics Act, the 1990 Child Protection Act, the 1990 Victims' Rights and Restitution Act, the 1990 Violence against Women Act, legislation to reduce crimes against the elderly, stalking laws, identity protection for victims of sexual assault, and to advance legal remedies for victims in civil and criminal courts.
- **Victim services.** The center provides crime victims and witnesses with direct assistance in their communities through information and referral.
- **Coalition building.** The center works to build coalitions between organizations that serve victims, professionals whose work affects the outcome of criminal cases, professionals who serve victims, media professionals who do not sensationalize or intrude on victims, and concerned citizens.
- **Training and technical assistance.** The center educates professionals, volunteers, and concerned citizens in areas such as public policy, victims' rights and the media, and HIV testing in cases of assault.

- **Public awareness and education.** The center conducts public awareness campaigns through surveys, the media, and publications it disseminates to members and citizens.
- **Library and resource services.** The center offers the public a large collection of information related to crime victims and criminal justice.

Nursing Network on Violence against Women International
Daniel Sheridan, Trauma Program, UHN 66
Oregon Health Sciences University
3181 SW Sam Jackson Park Road
Portland, OR 97201-3098

The Nursing Network on Violence against Women International (NNVAWI) was formed to encourage the development of a nursing practice that focuses on health issues relating to the effects of violence on women's lives. NNVAWI was founded in November 1985 during the first National Nursing Conference on Violence against Women held at the University of Massachusetts at Amherst. The network's ethic fosters the ideal of a nursing practice designed to provide assistance and support to women in the process of achieving their own personal empowerment. NNVAWI's ultimate goal is to provide a nursing presence in the struggle to end violence in women's lives.

Resource Center on Child Custody and Child Protection
National Council on Juvenile and Family Court Judges
P.O. Box 8970
Reno, NV 98507
(800) 527-3223

The Resource Center on Child Custody and Child Protection, a division of the National Council on Juvenile and Family Court Judges, features several libraries and databases of resources related to the topic of child protection and custody in the context of domestic violence. It is part of a network of resource centers on domestic violence funded by the U.S. Department of Health and Human Services. Through the resource center, the Family Violence Project provides training, training assistance, and technical assistance on the topic. Reference materials, working materials from courts and programs, training aids, and a network of experts are available through the center.

State Domestic Violence Coalitions

State coalitions serve as advocates for legislative change, provide consultation and technical assistance to programs for battered women and their children, and perform community outreach. Some provide referrals and operate crisis lines. State coalitions have information regarding ongoing projects designed to address domestic violence in their states.

Alabama
Alabama Coalition against Domestic Violence
P.O. Box 4762
Montgomery, AL 36101
(334) 832-4842

Alaska
Alaska Network on Domestic Violence and Sexual Assault
130 Seward Street, Room 501
Juneau, AK 99801
(907) 586-3650

Arizona
Arizona Coalition against Domestic Violence
100 West Camelback Road, Suite 109
Phoenix, AZ 85013
(602) 279-2900

Arkansas
Arkansas Coalition against Violence to Women and Children
7509 Cantrell Road, #205
Little Rock, AR 72207
(501) 663-4668

California
California Alliance against Domestic Violence
Marin Abused Women's Services
1717 5th Avenue
San Rafael, CA 94901
(415) 457-2464

Southern CA Coalition against Domestic Violence
P.O. Box 5036
Santa Monica, CA 90405
(213) 655-6098

Colorado
Colorado Domestic Violence Coalition
P.O. Box 18902
Denver, CO 80218
(303) 573-9018

Connecticut
Connecticut Coalition against Domestic Violence
135 Broad Street
Hartford, CT 06105
(203) 524-5890

District of Columbia
DC Coalition against Domestic Violence
P.O. Box 76069
Washington, DC 20013
(202) 783-5332

Florida
Florida Coalition against Domestic Violence
P.O. Box 1201
Winter Park, FL 32790
(407) 682-3885

Georgia
Georgia Advocates for Battered Women and Children
250 Georgia Avenue SE, Suite 308
Atlanta, GA 30312
(404) 524-3847

Hawaii
Hawaii State Committee on Family Violence
98-939 Moanalua Road
Aiea, HI 96701-5012
(808) 486-5072

Idaho
Idaho Coalition against Sexual and Domestic Violence
1050 Memorial Drive
Idaho Falls, ID 83402
(208) 529-4352

Illinois
Illinois Coalition against Domestic Violence
730 East Vine Street, Suite 109
Springfield, IL 62703
(217) 789-2830

Indiana
Indiana Coalition against Domestic Violence
2511 East 46th Street, Suite N3
Indianapolis, IN 46205
(317) 543-3908

Iowa
Iowa Coalition against Domestic Violence
1540 High Street, Suite 100
Des Moines, IA 50309
(515) 244-8028

Kansas
Kansas Coalition against Sexual and Domestic Violence
820 SE Quincy, Suite 416-B
Topeka, KS 66612
(913) 232-9784

Kentucky
Kentucky Domestic Violence Association
P.O. Box 356
Frankfort, KY 40602
(502) 875-4132

Louisiana
Louisiana Coalition against Domestic Violence
P.O. Box 3053
Hammond, LA 70404-3053
(504) 542-4446

Maine
Maine Coalition for Family Crisis Services
128 Main Street
Bangor, ME 04401
(207) 941-1194

Maryland
Maryland Network against Domestic Violence
11501 Georgia Avenue, Suite 403
Silver Spring, MD 20902
(301) 942-0900

Massachusetts
Massachusetts Coalition of Battered Women's Service Groups
210 Commercial Street, 3rd Floor
Boston, MA 02109
(617) 248-0922

Michigan
Michigan Coalition against Domestic Violence
P.O. Box 16009
Lansing, MI 48901
(517) 484-2924

Minnesota
Minnesota Coalition for Battered Women
1619 Dayton Avenue, Suite 303
St. Paul, MN 55104
(612) 646-6177

Mississippi
Mississippi Coalition against Domestic Violence
P.O. Box 4703
Jackson, MS 39296-4703
(601) 981-9196

Missouri
Missouri Coalition against Domestic Violence
331 Madison Street
Jefferson City, MO 65101
(314) 634-4161

Montana
Montana Coalition against Domestic Violence
1236 North 28th Street, Suite 103
Billings, MT 59101
(406) 256-6334

Nebraska
Nebraska Domestic Violence and Sexual Assault Coalition
315 South 9th, #18
Lincoln, NE 68508
(402) 476-6256

Nevada
Nevada Network against Domestic Violence
2100 Capurro Way, Suite E
Sparks, NV 89431
(702) 358-1171

New Hampshire
New Hampshire Coalition against Domestic and Sexual Violence
P.O. Box 353
Concord, NH 03302-0353
(603) 224-8893

New Jersey
New Jersey Coalition for Battered Women
2620 Whitehorse/Hamilton Square Road
Trenton, NJ 08690
(609) 584-8107

New Mexico
New Mexico State Coalition against Domestic Violence
P.O. Box 25363
Albuquerque, NM 87125
(505) 246-9240

New York
New York State Coalition against Domestic Violence
The Women's Building
79 Central Avenue
Albany, NY 12206
(518) 432-4864

North Carolina
North Carolina Coalition against Domestic Violence
P.O. Box 51875
Durham, NC 27717-1875
(919) 956-9124

North Dakota
North Dakota Council on Abused Women's Services
State Networking Office
418 East Rosser Avenue, Suite 320
Bismarck, ND 58501
(701) 255-6240

Ohio
Ohio Domestic Violence Network
4041 North High Street, #101
Columbus, OH 43214
(614) 784-0023

Oklahoma
Oklahoma Coalition on Domestic Violence and Sexual Assault
2200 North Classen Boulevard, Suite 610
Oklahoma City, OK 73106
(405) 557-1210

Oregon
Oregon Coalition against Domestic and Sexual Violence
520 NW Davis Street
Portland, OR 97209
(503) 223-7411

Pennsylvania
Pennsylvania Coalition against Domestic Violence
6400 Flank Drive, Suite 1300
Harrisburg, PA 17112
(717) 545-6400

Rhode Island
Rhode Island Coalition against Domestic Violence
442 Post Road, Suite 104
Warwick, RI 02888
(401) 467-9940

South Carolina
South Carolina Coalition against Domestic Violence and
  Sexual Assault
P.O. Box 7776
Columbia, SC 29202
(803) 254-3699

South Dakota
South Dakota Coalition against Domestic Violence and
  Sexual Assault
3220 South Highway 281
Aberdeen, SD 57401
(605) 225-5122

Tennessee
Tennessee Task Force against Domestic Violence
P.O. Box 120972
Nashville, TN 37212
(615) 386-9406

Texas
Texas Council on Family Violence
8701 North Mopac Expressway, Suite 450
Austin, TX 78759
(512) 794-1133

Utah
Domestic Violence Advisory Council
c/o Diane Stuart
120 North 200 West
Salt Lake City, UT 84103
(801) 538-4308

Vermont
Vermont Network against Domestic Violence and
  Sexual Assault
P.O. Box 405
Montpelier, VT 05601-0405
(802) 223-1302

Virginia
Virginians against Domestic Violence
2850 Sandy Bay Road, Suite 101
Williamsburg, VA 23185
(804) 221-0990

Washington
Washington State Coalition against Domestic Violence
2101 4th Avenue East, Suite 103
Olympia, WA 98506
(206) 352-4029

West Virginia
West Virginia Coalition against Domestic Violence
P.O. Box 85
181B Main Street
Sutton, WV 26601-0085
(304) 765-2250

Wisconsin
Wisconsin Coalition against Domestic Violence
1400 East Washington, Suite 232
Madison, WI 53703
(608) 255-0539

Wyoming
Wyoming Coalition against Domestic Violence and
   Sexual Assault
341 East E Street, Suite 135A
Casper, WY 82601
(307) 235-2814

Selected Print Resources 6

Anthologies

Atlanta Bar Association. **The Law and Psychology of Domestic Violence.** Manual from the Bar Association's conference held on 7 April 1989. 200p.

The Law and Psychology of Domestic Violence publishes 18 articles on a variety of subjects, including civil and criminal issues involving battered women. There are writings by Barbara Hart, Myra Sun, Nancy Hunter, and others; it can be ordered from the Atlanta Bar Association, 2500 The Equitable Building, 100 Peachtree Street, Atlanta, GA 30303.

Bart, Pauline B., and Eileen Geil Moran, eds. **Violence against Women: The Bloody Footprints.** Newbury Park, CA: Sage Publications, 1993. 294p. ISBN 0-8039-5045-4.

The editors provide introductions to the four parts, each of which contains five chapters that vary considerably in length, depth, and style. Each part explicates an important aspect of violence against women. It includes contributions from many well known writers on the issue, including J. Caputi, Judith Herman, Elizabeth Stanko, Andrea Dworkin, and others.

Finkelhor, David, Richard Gelles, Gerald Hotaling, and Murray Straus, eds. **The Dark Side of Families: Current Family Violence Research.** Newbury Park, CA: Sage Publications, 1983. 384p. ISBN 0-8039-1934-4.

This book contains brief reports by many of the major family violence researchers in the country. Many of the book's papers deal with measurement techniques and other methodological concerns.

Hampton, Robert L., et al. **Family Violence: Prevention and Treatment.** Newbury Park, CA: Sage Publications, 1993. 344p. ISBN 0-8039-5247-3.

Addresses issues including identification of factors that contribute to family violence, the role of substance abuse in family violence, the relationship of psychological abuse to physical abuse, and more. Leading researchers and clinicians from sociology, psychology, and social work explore the roots of family violence. They cover elder abuse, child abuse, violence in families of color, ways to assess and treat violent families, methods for preventing abuse, and legal perspectives.

Hampton, Robert L., ed. **Violence in the Black Family: Correlates and Consequences.** Lexington, MA: D.C. Heath & Company, 1987. 274p. ISBN 0-669-14584-X.

Contributors from a variety of disciplines discuss violence in black families: its prevalence, correlates, and consequences. The book explores the impact of individual and institutional racism as an important contextual variable.

Hansen, Marsali, and Michele Harway, eds. **Battering and Family Therapy: A Feminist Perspective.** Newbury Park, CA: Sage Publications, 1993. 302p. ISBN 0-8039-4320-2.

The book highlights the difficulties of treating batterers and their victims and provides strategies designed to change individual behaviors and the social environment that perpetuates violent behavior.

Hilton, N. Zoe, ed. **Legal Responses to Wife Assault: Current Trends and Evaluation.** Newbury Park, CA: Sage Publications, 1993. 330p. ISBN 0-8039-4552-3.

This collection of essays on police intervention and the court system offers in-depth coverage of four major themes central to the issue of wife assault: a historical framework of the legal response to wife assault; police attitudes and action; prosecution, mediation, and treatment within the court system; and victims as defendants and participants in the legal system. The section on victims includes two chapters on women as defendants, an essay by Lenore Walker on battered women as defendants, and another by Alan Tomkins on self-defense jury instructions in trials of battered women who kill their partners. The authors have compiled recent evaluations of research and present them well. Human resource and legal professionals, students, and researchers will find the book useful.

Lobel, Kerry, ed. **Naming the Violence: Speaking Out about Lesbian Battering.** Seattle: Seal Press, 1986. 233p. ISBN 0-931188-42-3.

Numerous feminists break the silence on what has been considered a taboo subject, challenging stereotypes with concrete personal experience and providing support for the victim. This anthology includes articles and essays written by lesbians active in the battered women's movement that explore the dynamics of abuse and describe community organizing strategies around the country. This title opens the door to discuss lesbian battering and challenges the domestic violence activist to face the meaning of violence between women. This book is valuable for shelter workers and battered women activists.

Peled, Einat, Peter Jaffe, and Jeffrey L. Edleson, eds. **Ending the Cycle of Violence: Community Responses to Children of Battered Women.** Newbury Park, CA: Sage Publications, 1994. 264p. ISBN 0-8039-5368-2.

This anthology covers the varied and complex arena of intervention with children of battered women. It provides an overview of current practice, including strategies and program models. The expert contributors present an accessible look into four major areas: living in a violent culture, shelters and domestic violence counseling, child protection services and the criminal justice system, and prevention and education in schools and communities. This book is useful for practitioners who work with battered women and their children, educators, child protective service workers, youth workers, health and mental health professionals, and child care workers in group homes and foster homes.

Sherrill, J. M., and D. G. Siegel, eds. **Responding to Violence on Campus: New Directions for Student Services Series, No. 47.** San Francisco: Jossey-Bass, 1989. 112p. ISBN 1-55542-856-8.

This book includes essays on the heritage of campus violence, violence in residence halls, campus domestic violence, sexual violence, and counseling victims and perpetrators of campus violence, and lists additional sources of information. Appendices include copies of questionnaires used in the *Intra-university Violence Survey* and the *Campus Violence Survey.*

Sonkin, Daniel J., ed. **Domestic Violence on Trial: Psychological and Legal Dimensions of Family Violence.** New York: Springer, 1987. 288p. ISBN 0-8261-5250-3.

The contributors explore the conjunction of psychological and legal issues surrounding battered women, abusers, and children. The book includes discussions of Battered Woman Syndrome, legal and courtroom procedures, jury selection, expert and child witnesses, and a chapter on battered women who kill.

Steinman, Michael, ed. **Woman Battering: Policy Responses.** Cincinnati: Anderson Publishing Co., 1991. 236p. ISBN 0-87084-807-0.

This anthology assesses how well different types of interventions are working to end woman battering. It introduces the basic concepts of public policy and woman battering and examines the many problems encountered in making battering a public, criminal problem and in developing interventions that satisfy the public, the criminal justice system, the police, advocates, and the women themselves. Included are chapters that focus on conceptualization and measurement of battering, police response, prosecution, counseling and shelter services, arrest and treatment, coordinated community responses and interventions, civil protection orders, coordinated criminal justice interventions and recidivism among batterers, and primary prevention.

Yllo, Kersti, and Michele Bograd, eds. **Feminist Perspectives on Wife Abuse.** Newbury Park, CA: Sage Publications, 1988. 320p. ISBN 0-8039-3052-6.

Brings together works by a well-known group of academicians, activists, and clinicians from a variety of disciplines who approach violence against women from a distinctly feminist perspective. The research is based on the premise that gender inequality is the source of violence against women. The book is divided into four sections: The Politics of Research; Feminist Research; Rethinking the Clinical Approach; and Theory and Practice, Academics and Activists.

Books

Ageism and Battering Project. **Old Women: Breaking the Silence.** Union City Mission, MN: Ageism and Battering Project, 1990. 110p. No ISBN.

Old Women: Breaking the Silence publishes seven stories about older women and domestic abuse. Chapters include essays on older women's issues, institutional and cultural supports for battering, advocating for older women, shelter program accommodations, and other resources. The book can be ordered from the Minnesota Coalition for Battered Women, 1619 Dayton Avenue, Suite 303, St. Paul, MN 55104; (612) 646-6177.

Agtuca, Jacqueline, and The Asian Women's Shelter. **A Community Secret: For the Filipina in an Abusive Relationship.** Seattle: Seal Press, 1994. 80p. ISBN 1-878067-44-3.

Written in easy-to-read English, this book offers support, understanding, and practical information. Three Filipinas tell their stories. Topics include why men batter, what to do about the children, immigration and the law, and resources for ending the cycle of abuse.

Baker, Sally. **Family Violence and the Chemical Connection.** Deerfield: Health Communications, 1991. 152p. ISBN 1-55874-069-4.

A very accessible, easy-to-read book with a mixture of theoretical information, personal experiences, narratives, and poetry. Describes what constitutes abuse and what constitutes addiction, the connections between them, and how to break free of both. For professionals and nonprofessionals.

Barnett, Ola, and Alyce La Violette. **It Could Happen to Anyone: Why Battered Women Stay.** Newbury Park, CA: Sage Publications, 1993. 200p. ISBN 0-8039-5309-7 (cloth); ISBN 0-8039-5310-0 (paper).

This work will be particularly useful to anyone trying to understand why battered women do not leave their abusive situations. Empirically based, this work argues against blaming women for their victimization. It provides comprehensive and current theories on why women stay and why they leave, as well as many case histories outlining the difficulties and dangers of both leaving and staying.

Bauschard, Louise, and Mary Kimbrough. **Voices Set Free: Battered Women Speak from Prison.** St. Louis: Women's Self Help Center, 1986. 162p. No ISBN.

This book contains actual case histories of battered women who have been incarcerated for crimes related to their abuse, including the murder of abusive husbands or lovers. The stories, told in the women's own words, are taken from interviews at Renz Correctional Center, Cedar Hill, Missouri, and from statements by offenders who addressed a public hearing at Bedford Hills Correctional Facility, New York, where they are incarcerated. Louise Bauschard was motivated to write this book when she heard of a Missouri woman who was sentenced to 50 years without parole for killing her abusive husband in self-defense.

Blackman, Julie. **Intimate Violence: A Study of Injustice.** New York: Columbia University Press, 1989. 261p. ISBN 0-231-05094-1.

This book analyzes family abuse in white middle-class America. Blackman explodes the myth of suburban family tranquility and challenges theorists of social injustice, feminism, and the law as she looks into the psychology of the violent home. The book opens with an overview of policymaking and the emergence of intimate violence as a social problem. Blackman presents academic perspectives used to explain observers' and victims' reactions to intimate violence and concludes that a better understanding of victim characteristics is the only solution to the puzzle. She then introduces her own research of intimate violence, derived from a newspaper survey, face-to-face interviews, and observational data based on her experiences as an expert witness. The interplay between scholarly research and its practical application is an interesting approach, but Blackman's analysis of intimate violence as a social problem is weak because she ignores much of the accepted literature available on the subject. This book is appropriate for upper-division undergraduates and above.

Bowker, Lee. **Considering Marriage: Avoiding Marital Violence.** Santa Cruz: Network Publications, 1987. 13p. $1 each (price decreases when greater numbers are ordered, to 60 cents for over 100 copies), plus 15 percent postage. No ISBN.

This booklet describes different ways that women who are dating may judge the violence potential of their dates, and it provides examples of what can happen if the warning signs are ignored and they marry violent or pre-violent men. This booklet may be ordered directly from Network Publications, P.O. Box 1830, Santa Cruz, CA 95061-1830.

Browne, Angela. **When Battered Women Kill.** New York: The Free Press, 1987. 240p. ISBN 0-02-903880-4.

Although Browne's book focuses on the small proportion of battered women who kill their spouses, it is a must for persons concerned with battered women, generally. In addition to offering a composite of the case histories of 42 women who killed their batterers, Browne considers problems of why battered women stay with their abusive partners, social attitudes toward domestic violence, how the legal system has failed battered women, and how one can both predict and prevent abusive behavior patterns. Browne's book is the culmination of six years of interviews with 250 battered women, including the 42 who killed abusive partners. These in-depth interviews provide a unique insight into the many problems faced by battered women. Browne has gathered together much valuable information for the legal, social service, or health professional as well as the layperson and has furthered our understanding of the issue of domestic violence.

Buzawa, Eve S., and Carl G. Buzawa. **Domestic Violence: The Criminal Justice Response.** Newbury Park, CA: Sage Publications, 1990. 160p. ISBN 0-8039-3575-7.

The authors provide an overview of the police and court response to domestic violence. They critically examine the criminal justice system's changing approach to domestic violence and the opportunities and limitations of the new approaches, the growth and value of mandatory and presumptive arrest approaches to domestic assault, and the Minneapolis Police Experiment.

Campbell, Jacquelyn C. **Assessing Dangerousness: Violence by Sexual Offenders, Batterers, and Child Abusers.** Newbury Park, CA: Sage Publications, 1994. 160p. ISBN 0-8039-3747-4.

A discussion of the different models for assessing dangerousness that have appeared since the 1950s and 1960s up until the present provides up-to-date approaches to tackling such assessment areas as physical and sexual abuse, sexual assault, and wife assault. The text draws on the research and clinical expertise of prominent professionals in its description of the importance of and limitations to assessing the risk of dangerousness.

Chalofsky, Margie, Glen Finland, and Judy Wallace. **Changing Places: A Kid's View of Shelter Living.** Mt. Rainier, MD: Gryphon House, 1992. 61p. ISBN 0-87659-161-6.

This book, intended for children, gives the view of eight children living in a family shelter. Each child has a different story about his or her feelings on leaving home, living in a shelter, and finally leaving the shelter. It gives readers an understanding of the problems facing people in shelters and is intended to inspire readers to become involved in helping the homeless. The end of the book gives children and adults ideas about how they can make a difference to people who are without a permanent home.

Chesler, Phyllis. **Mothers on Trial: The Battle for Children and Custody.** New York: Harcourt Brace Jovanovich, 1987 & San Diego: Harvest/HBJ, 1991. 558p. ISBN 0-15-662167-3.

In a series of contemporary portraits of custody battles, Dr. Chesler exposes some of the problems with the family law system. She asserts that the system operates on a double standard for mothers and fathers; awards custody to the father, when he chooses to fight, in 70 percent of the cases, regardless of whether he was an abusive or absentee parent; and is so deeply biased that paternal attentiveness is considered worthy of reward, while maternal care is viewed as an obligation. Incorporating findings from her years of research and hundreds of interviews, as well as information from international surveys about child-custody arrangements, the author argues for new guidelines to resolve custody disputes and to prevent the continued oppression of mothers in custody situations. In the introduction written for the 1991 edition, Chesler discusses recent trends in custody battles that guarantee that custody rights will be one of the paramount women's issues through the 1990s. This book is important reading for anyone concerned with custody rights.

Coontz, Stephanie. **The Way We Never Were: American Families and the Nostalgia Trap.** New York: Basic Books, 1992. 391p. ISBN 0-465-09097-4.

This book examines two centuries of American family life and dispels a series of myths and half-truths about the "good old days." Coontz sheds new light on such contemporary concerns as parenting, privacy, love, the division of labor along gender lines, the black family, feminism, and sexual practice. She concludes that today's so-called crisis of the family is really only a small part of the much larger need for economic, political, and demographic social change.

Dobash, R. Emerson, and Russell P. Dobash. **Violence against Wives.** New York: The Free Press, 1979. 339p. ISBN 0-02-907810-5.

The Dobashes approach the problem of wife abuse from historical, sociological, and psychological perspectives. They have provided statistical data in addition to case histories of violent marriages. Each case history is based on a thorough assessment of the marriage, the violent events within it, and the response to it of friends, relatives, and social agencies. The authors offer an interpretation of wife beating from the perspective of its victims and document why it has been possible to keep violence against women a private act that is not subject to public policy. The Dobashes support the feminist perspective that wife abuse is a social problem that has been allowed to continue virtually untouched because of the patriarchal institutions within our society.

————. **Women, Violence and Social Change.** New York: Routledge, 1992. 366p. ISBN 0-415-02921-X.

This is a comparative study of the British and American responses to the problem of violence against women. The authors show how feminist activists created an international social movement and describe the responses of the state, the justice system, therapeutic professions, and academic research. The Dobashes analyze the development of new therapeutic approaches aimed at abused women and violent men, and show how these have detracted from efforts to assist women and end violence. They show how differing national research agendas have affected the identification and definition of the problem of violence against women and in some cases have actually hampered efforts to assist abused women and challenge male violence.

Edleson, Jeffrey L., and Richard M. Tolman. **Intervention for Men Who Batter: An Ecological Approach.** Newbury Park, CA: Sage Publications, 1992. 164p. ISBN 0-8039-4264-8.

This book examines the individual, social, and cultural factors perpetuating abuse toward women and provides an ecological approach to working with men who batter. Clearly outlines the processes involved in assessing abusive men and discusses the methods and effectiveness of different intervention techniques: men's treatment groups, individual and couple's counseling, working with the abusers' families, community intervention, and the criminal justice system. Ethnic and cultural differences are also discussed.

Ewing, Charles Patrick. **Battered Women Who Kill: Psychological Self-Defense as Legal Justification.** Lexington, MA: Lexington Books, 1987. 192p. ISBN 0-669-14827-X.

Ewing, a psychologist and a lawyer, presents psychological studies of battered women who have killed their abusive partners. He analyzes over 100 cases and examines the kinds of abuse suffered by these women, the characteristics of relationships that led them to kill their batterers, and the legal defense used by battered women who kill. He advances the idea that some women who have suffered severe abuse, resulting in extreme loss of self-esteem, and who see no way out of their situation face a moment when—rather than face psychological "death"—come to believe that killing the abusive partner is their only alternative. Ewing advocates the use of this loss of the psychological self as a legal defense for some women accused of killing abusive partners.

Faludi, Susan. **Backlash: The Undeclared War against American Women.** New York: Crown, 1991. 544p. ISBN 0-517-57698-8.

This book explores the real status of American women as they go into the 1990s and shatters the myths that were products of the backlash to the women's movement of the seventies. The trouble, claims Faludi, is not only that the myths aren't true, but that through deliberate action or passive collusion the government, media, and popular culture have ensured their overpowering influence on the public. Faludi goes on to uncover what she calls the unacknowledged but frighteningly widespread backlash against feminism that has taken place under the surface of the eighties' careerism. Faludi takes the reader step by step through the creation of the eighties' anti-feminist myths in popular culture, politics, popular psychology, the workplace, and health. Faludi concludes that the underlying message of the eighties is that women's problems are a direct result of too much independence and no one but feminists are to blame. Faludi points out the necessity in the nineties to see behind today's post-feminist apathy to the injustices still being done.

Fedders, Charlotte, and Laura Elliott. **Shattered Dreams.** New York: Dell, 1987. 256p. ISBN 0-06-015716-X.

The true story of Charlotte Fedders, the wife of a powerful young attorney and rising star in the Reagan administration. A mother of five sons living in upper middle-class suburban Washington, D.C., she finally spoke out about her experience as the victim of 17 years of battering by her husband, John. The book chronicles her life growing up in a traditional upper middle-class family, meeting the man of her dreams in college, and settling in to live her life for her family. The story tells of her emotional, physical, and economic struggle to break free of the relationship. The book provides an intimate look behind the closed doors of a seemingly happy and beautiful suburban home.

Felson, Richard, and James Tedeschi. **Aggression and Violence: Social Interactionist Perspectives.** Washington, DC: American Psychological Association, 1993. 278p. ISBN 1-55798-190-6.

The first three sections of this book deal with the theory on aggression, control, and social conflict. The last section, on violence against women, includes a chapter on domestic violence. Social interactionist theory states that a crucial part of understanding domestic violence is recognizing the role played at every stage by people other than the aggressor and victim. Domestic violence cannot occur unless the social context in which family members find themselves encourages or allows it. The drawback to this perspective is that social interaction is portrayed as the sole cause of domestic violence, implying that all domestic violence is caused and provoked by a third party.

Ferrato, Donna. **Living with the Enemy.** New York: Aperture, 1991. 176p. ISBN 0-89381-480-6.

Ferrato chronicles domestic abuse with her camera, producing dramatic and haunting black and white photographs. Over a ten-year period she chronicled violence and its aftermath in the home, in emergency rooms, at women's shelters, in the courtroom, in a prison for women, and in the streets. She tells the in-depth story of eight battered women. The reader will see the women's faces—the black eyes, broken noses—covered with blood and fear. The reader will also see the children's fear, anger, and confusion and the abusers' faces full of contempt and contorted with anger. The book's narrative is excellent and provides statistics and stories to accompany the graphic photographs.

Finkelhor, David G., Gerald Hotaling, and K. Yllo. **Stopping Family Violence: Research Priorities for the Coming Decade.** Newbury Park, CA: Sage Publications, 1988. 136p. ISBN 0-8039-3215-4.

This book publishes results of extensive surveys of researchers in the field, with special emphasis on prevention, physical child abuse, child sexual abuse, and spousal violence.

Floyd, Maita. **Don't Shoot!: My Life Is Valuable.** Phoenix: Eskualdun Publishers, Ltd., 1994. 116p. ISBN 0-9620599-2-7.

In this autobiographical story, Marguerite—who spent her teenage years in Nazi-occupied France—tells another story of survival as an adult, of an attack by her armed husband, the "nice guy" who turned violent after separation. It is a compelling story of trauma and its aftermath.

Fortune, Marie M. **Keeping the Faith: Questions and Answers for the Abused Woman.** San Francisco: HarperSanFrancisco, 1987. 94p. No ISBN.

This booklet is written specifically for victims/survivors of domestic violence and is a valuable resource for shelters, counselors, and Christian ministers. It contains a concise response to common religious questions raised by Christian victims of domestic violence. The author says this book "is written to . . . remind you that God is present to you even now and that there are Christians who do understand your pain, your fear, and your doubt. It is written so that we in the Christian community can keep the faith with you during this time of your life." A valuable resource for shelters, clergy, and counselors. This booklet can be ordered directly from the Center for the Prevention of Sexual and Domestic Violence, 1914 North 34th Street, Suite 105, Seattle, WA 98103; (206) 684-1903.

French, Marilyn. **The War against Women.** New York: Ballantine Books, 1993. 223p. ISBN 0-345-38248-X.

Feminist scholar Marilyn French's analysis of the history of women's political, cultural, physical, and economic repression is controversial and somewhat disturbing. The book is divided into four parts: Systemic Discrimination, Institutional Wars, The Cultural War, and Men's Personal War. French probes each of these areas, supports her assertions with statistics and facts, and concludes that women are currently repressed by a male-dominated society whose underlying goal is the total subjugation of women.

Gaines, B. **Hell Is My Husband.** Pompano Beach, FL: Paragraph Publications, 1992. 416p. ISBN 0-9363005-0-8.

This autobiographical book documents the experience of the author's life with an emotionally abusive husband. Gaines takes the reader through the experience from its beginning, when she was unable to understand the abuse, to its sudden and devastating end. She points out the signals along the way that she was unable to recognize at the time and reveals how her husband used "protection" and "caring" to maintain control over her life and to abuse her emotionally. The dedication page tells the story: "This book is dedicated to my abusive ex-husband, without whom I could not have written it. He taught me what anger, hate, pain, and abuse were all about."

Gelles, Richard J. **Family Violence.** Newbury Park, CA: Sage Publications, 1987. 224p. ISBN 0-8039-2886-6.

A research-based book that offers literature reviews, empirical evidence of the author's conceptual model, and a section on methodology.

Gelles, Richard J., and Claire Pedrick Cornell. **Intimate Violence in Families.** Newbury Park, CA: Sage Publications, 1990. 159p. ISBN 0-8039-4795-6.

This is the second edition of the Family Studies Text Series. It is a good course text. Topics include the findings of the Second National Family Violence Survey, experiments with arrest as a deterrent to violence, and the long-term effects of violence on victims.

Gelles, Richard J., and Donileen R. Loseke. **Current Controversies on Family Violence.** Newbury Park, CA: Sage Publications, 1993. 390p. ISBN 0-8039-4673-2.

This is a compilation of essays that deal with some of the most controversial issues regarding domestic violence, written from the perspectives of noted feminists, sociologists, and psychologists in the field. Contributors include K. C. O'Leary, R. J. Gelles, K. Yllo, Murray A. Straus, D. Kurz, M. P. Koss, S. L. Cook, N. Gilbert, Lenore E. A. Walker, Lee H. Bowker, J. Flanzer, B. Egeland, J. Kaufan, E. Zigler, Suzanne K. Steinmetz, K. Pillemer, D. Besharov, David Finkelhor, C. A. Plummer, N. D. Reppucci, J. Haugaard, R. A. Berk, E. S. Buzawa, and C. G. Buzawa.

Gillespie, Cynthia K. **Justifiable Homicide: Battered Women, Self-Defense, and the Law.** Columbus: Ohio State University Press, 1989. 245p. ISBN 0-8142-0521-6.

Gillespie draws on an analysis of over 300 case studies to illustrate that the self-defense law is so biased against women as to often provide them with no effective right to self-defense at all. This book explores the historical, legal, and societal reasons why women are rarely granted the right to act in self-defense. Gillespie traces the concept of self-defense and posits that the law has come to embody masculine assumptions, and therefore in its present form does not apply to women. In addition, women are in a no-win situation because of society's ambivalent and biased attitudes about them as victims of violence.

Gondolf, Edward, and Ellen Fisher. **Battered Women as Survivors: An Alternative to Treating Learned Helplessness.** Lexington, MA: Lexington Books, 1988. 123p. ISBN 0-669-18166-8.

The focus of this work is seeing women who are abused by their male partners not as victims who give in or give up, but as survivors who actively seek help, even though sufficient help is not always available. The book explores survivor theory, causal models of help-seeking, racial differences among shelter residents, intervention with batterers, and the impact of shelter services. The study's point of departure is Lenore Walker's classic work *The Battered Woman.* Although Walker theorized that learned helplessness is a response to battering, these authors provide the alternative hypothesis of survival theory, which suggests that women's help-seeking responses increase with the severity of battering and their degree of independence. The book includes findings, statistical analysis, and discussion of a survey of 6,000 women in 50 Texas shelters. The authors provide policy recommendations for both social agencies and government. The book is technical but readable and clear.

Gordon, Linda. **Heroes of Their Own Lives: The Politics and History of Family Violence.** New York: Penguin Books, 1989. 383p. ISBN 0-670-81909-3.

Although this book focuses on the history of family violence in Boston from 1870 through 1960, it provides important insight into the problem through case records from social work agencies. The records speak to the sadness of the family members and also to the heroic measures they take to escape poverty and violence as they struggle for better lives. Gordon's thorough investigation of child abuse, child neglect, wife beating, and incest reveals that, although the existence of family violence has not changed over the years, society's attitude toward the problem has.

Herman, J. L. **Trauma and Recovery: The Aftermath of Violence from Domestic Abuse to Political Terror.** New York: Basic Books, 1992. 276p. ISBN 0-465-08765-5.

This book begins with an interesting historical analysis and looks at the healing of psychological, physical, and sexual traumas in the twentieth century. The discovery of concepts such as post-traumatic stress disorder, suffered by Vietnam veterans, has carried over to assist the victims of domestic battering, rape, and childhood sexual abuse. This book discusses all victims of violence, including survivors of Hiroshima, the Holocaust, natural disasters, traffic accidents, hostage situations, and other atrocities. It shows the parallels between private terrors, such as domestic violence, and public traumas, such as terrorism. At the heart of the book is a unique approach to recovery that demands that the therapist depart from a stance of moral neutrality, working slowly toward integration rather than catharsis. Highly technical and intended for therapists dealing with trauma.

Hoff, Lee Ann. **Battered Women as Survivors.** London and New York: Routledge, 1991. 289p. ISBN 0-415-04395-6.

This highly researched book was written by a nurse-anthropologist and crisis specialist and moves beyond the question "Why do battered women stay?" and proposes that we ask "Why should victims be expected to leave?" Other topics addressed in an urban American field study of battered women and their social network members include why violent partners are allowed to stay, how abused women move from the role of victim to survivor, and the connection between victimization, society's values, and its policies and practices. The book reveals the relationship between personal crisis and traditional attitudes toward women, marriage, the family, and violence. It helps the reader understand battered women as survivors who manage multiple crises without public support for their situation. Although at times the book is quite technical, it provides new insight into battered women as capable survivors rather than helpless victims.

Horsfall, Jan. **The Presence of the Past.** North Sydney, Australia: Allen & Unwin, 1991. 167p. ISBN 0-04-442326-8.

Horsfall believes that both violence and masculinities are socially constructed. In her book she investigates patriarchal structures and practices: the law, the social security tax system, the employ-ment-unemployment-wage system, and what she believes are male ideologies that are imbedded in professional practices. The book also examines spousal power relations, low self-esteem in men created by emotional distance between fathers and sons, and men with high emotional dependencies. Horsfall concludes that men need to begin taking responsibility for their actions, both individually and collectively. Because this book is focused primar-ily on Australian culture, some of it seems irrelevant to domestic violence in America; however, the historical perspective and analysis of the patriarchy may be of interest.

Hotaling, Gerald T., David Finkelhor, John T. Kirkpatrick, and Murray A. Straus. **Coping with Family Violence: Research and Policy Perspectives.** Newbury Park, CA: Sage Publications, 1988. 336p. ISBN 0-8039-2722-3.

Topics include the growth of shelters and batterers' programs, the changing response of the criminal justice system, the effectiveness of child protection, foster care programs, responses of medical and health authorities to family violence cases, and current prevention efforts.

Jaffe, Peter G., David A. Wolfe, and Susan Kaye Wilson. **Children of Battered Women.** Newbury Park, CA: Sage Publications, 1990. 132p. ISBN 0-8039-3383-5.

This book is extremely important in considering the effects of domestic violence on children. It is the first to focus exclusively on the characteristics and the needs of children of battered women. The authors, all with long-standing histories of work with children who have witnessed violence, explore the scope of the problem, the effect of violence on children's development, the impact of traumatic events in the lives of children, issues in assessment and intervention strategies, and implications for related children's services. Although this is written from a clinical perspective, it is an important work for all persons concerned with the effects of domestic violence on children.

Johann, Sara Lee. **Domestic Abusers: Terrorists in Our Homes.** Springfield: Charles C. Thomas Publisher, 1994. 144p.

This book for battered women and the people who work with them is passionate, sincere, and not always in line with domestic violence experts. The author's style attempts lyricism, but is more often tiring and disjointed.

Jones, Ann. **Everyday Death: The Case of Bernadette Powell.** New York: Holt, Rinehart and Winston, 1985. 202p.

This book meticulously explores the case of Bernadette Powell, a battered woman who shot and killed her husband in 1978 and remains in jail today. It examines how race, sex, and class affect the judicial system's treatment of individuals.

————. **Women Who Kill.** New York: Fawcett Crest, 1988. 457p.

An excellent resource for anyone working with battered women who have killed, this book is a social history of women driven to kill for a multitude of reasons. The author discusses connections between sexual stereotyping, criminal law, criminology, feminism, class and race, and the treatment of women who kill.

————. **Next Time, She'll Be Dead.** Boston: Beacon Press, 1994. 288p. ISBN 0-8070-6770-9.

Jones explains how society unwittingly encourages violence against women in America and how this could be changed. She exposes the stereotypes, attitudes, and institutions that foster the problem. Jones explores and documents her beliefs that the law generally further contributes to a battered woman's abuse; the public is generally ignorant of the real nature and seriousness of battering; our society commingles sex, anger, aggression, and violence; and battered women are generally blamed for their own abuse. She says that the Hedda Nussbaum case was an extreme example of all of these elements, which are present (generally to a lesser extent) in the cases of all battered women. The Nussbaum case, with its extreme battering and child murder, is important in that the public commentary surrounding it illustrated the extent of the public ignorance. Jones concludes by citing the need for massive change in society's institutions, the criminal justice system, legislation and politics, the health care system, child protective services, religious institutions, education, shelters, the disbursement of research money, and individual action. She approaches domestic violence from a feminist perspective, saying the feminist analysis of male violence against women and children is the most accurate and the only one that offers hope for change.

Jones, Ann, and Susan Schechter. **When Love Goes Wrong: What To Do When You Can't Do Anything Right.** New York: Harper-Perennial, 1993. 359p. ISBN 0-06-092369-5.

This is a personal book containing strategies for women with controlling partners. The authors, who have over 15 years of experience working with battered and abused women, give a new analysis of controlling partners and information for women who want to change their lives. Contains numerous first-person stories that show women what their options are in or out of the relationship. The book provides concrete information on finding safety and support for women and their children and includes a comprehensive list of agencies offering information and assistance.

Kirkwood, Cathy. **Leaving Abusive Partners: From the Scars of Survival to the Wisdom for Change.** Newbury Park, CA: Sage Publications, 1993. 218p. ISBN 0-8039-8685-8.

Kirkwood's book makes a contribution to a key issue in feminist theory, going beyond victims and survivors to offer new insights into the multifaceted nature of woman abuse. Kirkwood focuses on the concept of emotional abuse and the experiences of leaving and surviving abuse. She analyzes emotional abuse and the dynamic of control, the obstacles to women securing independence, the effects of the abuse, and the issues that are central to a woman's healing and change.

Kivel, Paul. **Men's Work: How To Stop the Violence That Tears Our Lives Apart.** Center City, MN: Hazelden, 1992. 240p. ISBN 0-345-37939-X.

This book, based on the work of the Oakland's Men's Project, deals directly with some of the hard issues in men's lives: family violence, sexual assault, racism, anger, addiction, and sexuality. Kivel uses his own experiences as a counselor, son, father, and man to illustrate how men are taught about women, other men, traditions, and culture. Every chapter includes practical exercises to help men rebuild their lives, families, and communities without violence.

Levy, Barrie, ed. **Dating Violence: Young Women in Danger.** Seattle: Seal Press, 1991. 315p. ISBN 1-878067-03-6.

This book both calls the reader to action and provides practical tools needed to implement change. Following an introduction by Levy, who outlines the problem, *Dating Violence* is divided into four sections. In the first section, teens and their parents tell their own stories of dating violence; the second section contains essays that provide a cultural and social context for dating violence; the last two sections provide examples of successful intervention strategies as well as education and prevention projects. This is an important book for advocates, teachers, counselors, and anyone working with young people.

————. **In Love and in Danger: A Teen's Guide to Breaking Free of Abusive Relationships.** Seattle: Seal Press, 1993. 120p. ISBN 1-878067-26-5.

This book is for teenagers who have questions about abusive dating relationships. It presents clear information about emotional, physical, and sexual abuse in dating relationships. It includes first-person accounts from teenagers who describe how their romantic relationships became hurtful and dangerous and how they were able to break free from them. The book can help teens confront the problem of abusive relationships and build healthier relationships.

McNulty, Faith. **The Burning Bed.** New York: Avon Books, 1989. 320p. ISBN 0-380-70771-3.

This book is the true story of Francine Hughes, who in 1977 killed her abusive husband by setting fire to the bedroom in which he was sleeping. The book chronicles Hughes's life up to and through the murder and subsequent trial. It tells a tale of terrifying physical and emotional abuse over a period of 14 years, her many attempts to become independent and leave, and the total loss of hope that drove her to end the abuse by killing her husband. The book was made into a television movie by the same name, which aired in 1987.

Martin, Del. **Battered Wives.** Volcano, CA: Volcano Press, 1976. Rev. ed. 1981. 281p. ISBN 0-912078-70-7.

The first introduction to the problem of spousal abuse, this book includes critical summaries of the legal and political status of battered wives and the extent to which their immediate predicament must be understood in broad political terms. The basis of the problem, Martin argues, is not in husband/wife interaction or immediate triggering events, but in the institution of marriage, historical attitudes toward women, the economy, and inadequacies in legal and social service systems. Martin asserts that police and prosecutor functions should be constrained, proposes specific legislation prohibiting wife abuse, and suggests that judges protect wives by closing the door to probation and de-emphasizing reconciliation. Other recommendations concern gun control, equal rights, and marriage contract legislation.

Miedzian, Myriam. **Boys Will Be Boys: Breaking the Link between Masculinity and Violence.** New York: Doubleday, 1991. 337p. ISBN 0-385-42254-7.

Miedzian addresses the nurture or nature issue as it pertains to male violence and comes up with solid, realistic answers. She argues that teaching our boys to give up aggressive behavior will not cause them to become wimps. She analyzes the ways in which violent toys, TV shows, sports, music, and even history lessons have contributed to the aggressive socialization of males. She gives concrete information about methods that can stop the problem of male violence.

NiCarthy, Ginny. **Getting Free: You Can End Abuse and Take Back Your Life.** Seattle: The Seal Press, 1986. 316p. ISBN 0-931188-37-7.

Getting Free explores making the decision to leave or stay in an abusive relationship, getting professional help, and self-help survival issues. The book includes special exercises designed to help women understand their situations and decide what they want in their relationships. Some of the questions it answers are: What is battering? What is emotional abuse? Where can I go? Is it right to break up my family? How can I protect my children? How can I get help from police and lawyers? How can I learn to reach out to others? This revised edition includes new chapters on teen, lesbian, and emotional abuse issues.

————. **The Ones Who Got Away: Women Who Left Abusive Partners.** Seattle: Seal Press, 1992. 329p. ISBN 0-931188-49-0.

This book takes the reader directly into the lives of more than thirty women who left abusive partners and started fresh.

NiCarthy, Ginny, and Sue Davidson. **You Can Be Free: An Easy-To-Read Handbook for Abused Women.** Seattle: Seal Press, 1989. 120p. ISBN 0-931188-68-7.

This how-to book designed specifically for abused women includes exercises and text on identifying abuse, addictive love, child protection, getting help from police and lawyers, reaching out to others, and teen and lesbian abuse.

Okun, Lewis. **Woman Abuse: Facts Replacing Myths.** Albany: State University of New York Press, 1986. 298p. ISBN 0-88706-079-X.

This book provides an extensive review of the domestic violence literature and research as of the mid-1980s in order to determine which beliefs about battered women and abusers are substantiated by empirical evidence and which have been debunked as fallacies or myths. The book is composed of three parts: a report of a descriptive survey based on a sample of clients in two battered women's treatment programs; a review of existing literature on spouse abuse; and a chapter advancing a theory that spouse abuse stems from brainwashing and coercive control. The theory is not supported by the review of literature or the data gathered in the research project. While it may be useful for understanding one kind of spouse abuse, it is probably not suitable as a model to explain the broad range of phenomena presented in the review of the literature. The study is comprehensive, covering both historical and contemporary issues. The writing is clear, and good use is made of a limited number of tables.

Pleck, Elizabeth. **Domestic Tyranny: The Making of American Social Policy against Family Violence from Colonial Times to**

the Present. New York: Oxford University Press, 1987. 273p. ISBN 0-19-504119-X.

The author provides a historical overview chronicling the history of family violence and the rise and demise of legal, feminist, and medical campaigns against it from colonial times to the present. Pleck places domestic violence in a rich historical context, vividly re-creating its history and analyzing the contributions of both radical and conservative feminists, child protective reformers, psychiatric social workers, pediatricians, politicians, and others. This study reveals our inherited domestic beliefs and the impact they have had in shaping and distorting social policy.

Redmond, Lula Moshoures. **Surviving When Someone You Love Was Murdered: A Professional's Guide.** Clearwater, FL: Psychological Consultation and Education Services, Inc., 1989. 171p. ISBN 0-9624592-0-8.

Explores the needs and emotions of survivors, therapy approaches that include peer and individual support groups, and training of professionals (including step-by-step session outlines). For therapists and counselors.

Renzetti, Claire. **Violent Betrayal: Partner Abuse in Lesbian Relationships.** Newbury Park, CA: Sage Publications, 1992. 201p. ISBN 0-8039-3888-8.

Violent Betrayal explores a common theme expressed by subjects of a nationwide study of violence in lesbian relationships: the sense of having been betrayed, first by their partners and subsequently by the lesbian community, which has tended to deny the problem's existence. Renzetti addresses several issues, including consequences for victims, batterers, and the community as a whole. There is extensive use of quantitative data. This book is one of the first to provide empirical data about battered lesbians and is an important resource for gaining an accurate perspective on the issue.

Russell, Diana E. H., and Nicole Van de Nen. **Crimes against Women: Proceedings of the International Tribunal.** Millbrae, CA: Les Femmes, 1976. 298p. ISBN 0-89087-921-4.

The first International Tribunal on Crimes against Women was held in Brussels, Belgium, from 4 to 8 March 1976. Over 2,000 women from 40 countries gathered for this historic event. They were not sent by their countries or any political or economic groups, but came as individual women. This book is the story of what happened at the tribunal. The authors re-create the events, publish a record of the personal testimony, discuss the resolutions and proposals for change, analyze the media's response, and assess the impact of the event that gave birth to an international feminist movement.

Schechter, Susan. **Women and Male Violence: The Visions and Struggles of the Battered Women's Movement.** Boston: South End Press, 1982. 367p. ISBN 0-89608-160-5.

An excellent resource book that takes an in-depth look at battering, the social movement against it, and the institutional and cultural realities that maintain and perpetuate male violence. Schechter examines a wide range of topics, including the struggle for police, judicial, and social service reforms; the role of academic sociologists and professionals; racism; state and national coalitions; the particular roles of lesbians and men; the backlash; and government response. The book provides a comprehensive history of the battered women's movement.

Simon, Rita, and Jean Landis. **The Crimes Women Commit, the Punishments They Receive.** Lexington, MA: D.C. Heath and Company, 1991. 137p. ISBN 0-669-20236-3.

An update of the original work *Women and Crime* (1975), this book consists of the following chapters: Women and Crime in Review, The Contemporary Women's Movement, American Women: Their Demographic and Status Characteristics, Arrest Statistics, Women in Court, and Women in Prison. An otherwise comprehensive index includes no reference to battered women or the Battered Woman Syndrome. Although the book acknowledges feminism, it maintains that its impact has been minimal.

Stanko, Elizabeth. **Intimate Intrusions: Women's Experience of Male Violence.** London: Routledge and Kegan Paul, 1985. 211p. ISBN 0-7102-0069-2.

Examines women's experiences of male violence and the reactions of those to whom women complain about male violence, including police and judges, in both the United States and Britain.

Straus, Murray A., Richard J. Gelles, and Suzanne K. Steinmetz. **Behind Closed Doors: Violence in the American Family.** Newbury Park, CA: Sage Publications, 1981. 301p. ISBN 0-8039-3292-8.

Behind Closed Doors publishes the results and conclusions of the first national survey on family violence in American homes, a seven-year study of over 2,000 families. The authors provide their conclusions on the phenomenon of violence and what causes Americans to inflict it on their family members. Since this book was published, there have been numerous clarifying updates on the data and critical reviews regarding the measuring instrument, the Conflict Tactics Scale (CTS); the fact that only intact families were studied; and the fact that only one adult was interviewed. This book is valuable to an understanding of a major premise for the claim that husbands are battered as often as wives.

Switzer, M'Liss, and Katherine Hale. **Called To Account: The Story of One Family's Struggle To Say No to Abuse.** Seattle: Seal Press, 1987. 145p. ISBN 0-931188-55-5.

After 20 years of being battered by her husband, M'Liss Switzer decided one day that the abuse had to stop. With the help of new mandatory arrest laws for domestic violence in Minnesota and the special Domestic Abuse Project (DAP) that included batterer treatment and ongoing individual and family counseling, the Switzers began the difficult task of overcoming Chuck's violence and its effect on the marriage. This is the story of their journey, from M'Liss's first walk into a police station to demand her husband's arrest through the difficult and painful therapeutic interventions to the present. Although this book presents a hopeful picture, it is clear that the DAP and its many components were necessary to make the intervention work.

Tifft, Larry L. **Battering of Women: The Failure of Intervention and the Case for Prevention.** Boulder, CO: Westview, 1993. 230p. ISBN 0-8133-1391-0.

Battering is a phenomenon located in the structural and cultural dynamics of society, according to Tifft. In the first chapters the author reviews the structural and interpersonal aspects of battering. Next he evaluates existing programs, finding both therapeutic and legal interventions deficient because they tend to ignore the social structural supports for violence, such as sexism, hierarchical family organization, and work alienation. Tifft's book offers an excellent assessment of existing programs and a clear argument of the social structural roots of violence and battering in American society. He concludes that prevention is the only way to stop the violence, and provides a comprehensive plan for prevention that includes all levels of action, from individual to global.

Walker, Lenore E. A. **The Battered Woman.** New York: Harper and Row, 1979. 270p. ISBN 0-06-090742-8.

This book, one of the first on battered women, is a classic. It describes the myths and realities of battering and explains Walker's cycle theory of violence and coercive techniques in battering relationships. Walker's study suggests that battering is not only a crime of the "drunken, ethnic working classes" but that battered women are also far more common in the middle- and upper-income homes where economic power is in the hands of the husband.

————. **The Battered Woman Syndrome.** New York: Springer, 1984. 272p. ISBN 0-8261-4620-2.

The Battered Woman Syndrome explores the range of psychological issues in the domestic violence field. Walker's analysis of the syndrome includes susceptibility factors, relationship dynamics, demographics, sexual and psychological abuse, and information about batterers. Walker maintains that battered women undergo a process of victimization, acquiring a learned helplessness that leaves them vulnerable to further abuse and unable to either blame their abusers or leave them. Using numerous case histories, she traces the cycle of violence. Walker includes sections on preventive education, practical remedies, and a careful discussion of psychotherapy.

————. **Terrifying Love: Why Battered Women Kill and How Society Responds.** New York: Harper and Row, 1989. 342p. ISBN 0-06-092006-8.

This book provides clinical analysis and personal narratives regarding why battered women kill, sexual violence, incest, women in prison, expert witnesses, sexism and the law, and learned helplessness. Case histories are given, as are explanations of the stresses and frustrations that lead battered wives to resort to violence. Walker recounts her experience as an expert witness in a series of precedent-setting court cases and vividly relates the terror and violence in battered women's lives. She explains how women become trapped in abusive relationships and how, pushed to the edge out of fear for their own or their children's lives, these women find the strength to defend themselves. The book looks at the battered woman's experience in court, prison, and with her local law enforcement system.

White, Evelyn C. **Chain, Chain, Change: For Black Women Dealing with Physical and Emotional Abuse.** Seattle: Seal Press, 1985. 77p. ISBN 1-878067-60-5.

Chain, Chain, Change is written for the black woman who is or has been abused, or who is concerned about the existence of abuse in her life. With its step-by-step approach, it makes reaching out for help easier. The book is also important for domestic violence activists, to help them gain an understanding of the issues that black women must handle in abusive situations, exposing the cultural and institutional barriers that they face and offering a new understanding of their life experiences.

Zambrano, Myrna M. **Mejor Sola Que Mal Acompanada: For the Latina in an Abusive Relationship/Para la Mujer Golpeada.** Seattle: Seal Press, 1993. 242p. ISBN 0-931188-26-1.

A bilingual handbook in Spanish and English, this book offers Spanish-speaking victims of domestic violence encouragement, sensitive understanding, and important information. The book defines abuse and addresses family and cultural expectations; getting police, medical, and legal assistance; where to go after leaving home; what the church may say; protecting one's children; and dealing with discrimination. This book also discusses special problems of women who are undocumented, have few resources, and/or speak little or no English. This book is a valuable resource for counselors, shelter workers, and activists, and an empowering handbook for the Latina who wants to break free from the cycle of abuse.

———. **No Mas! Guia para la Mujer Golpeada.** Seattle: Seal Press, 1994. 60p. ISBN 1-878067-50-8.

This is the first handbook entirely in Spanish for the Latina in a physical or emotionally abusive relationship. This book addresses itself to the Latina in a crisis situation and to those who work with her. In direct and easy-to-read Spanish, this guide covers topics such as recognizing abuse, characteristics of men who batter, physical and sexual abuse of children, legal support, and where to get help. For the Latina who is trying to understand and change her situation.

Articles

Allard, Sharon Angella. **"Rethinking Battered Woman Syndrome: A Black Feminist Perspective."** *UCLA Women's Law Journal* 1, no. 1 (Spring 1991): 191–207.

The concept of Battered Woman Syndrome, which has been used as a legal defense in criminal cases in which battered women have attacked or killed chronically abusive spouses or mates, relies on a stereotype of women as weak and passive. This stereotype, however, is not usually applied to black women, who are typically portrayed as strong and aggressive. Thus black women are less able to avail themselves of a defense based on Battered Woman Syndrome. Allard argues for a broader definition of Battered Woman Syndrome that encompasses the experience of black women.

Avni, Noga. **"Battered Wives: Characteristics of Their Courtship Days."** *Journal of Interpersonal Violence* 6, no. 2 (June 1991): 232–236.

Interviews with battered women in Israel indicate that the best predictor of spousal abuse during courtship is a patriarchal attitude displayed by the future husband, not premarital violence.

Bandy, Carole, Dale Richard Buchanan, and Cynthia Pinto. **"Police Performance in Resolving Family Disputes: What Makes the Difference?"** *Psychological Reports* 58 (1986): 15–29.

Examines the efficacy of police training in resolving domestic disputes, finding that officers trained in intervention techniques performed significantly better in simulated interventions than did officers without training.

Barnett, Ola, and L. Kevin Hamberger. **"The Assessment of Maritally Violent Men on the California Psychological Inventory."** *Violence and Victims* 7, no. 1 (1992): 15–28.

Examines personality differences between maritally violent and maritally nonviolent men. Violent men differ from nonviolent men in three areas of personality: problem-solving ability, impulsiveness, and intimacy. The differences in maritally violent men are often associated with experiences with violence in childhood.

Berk, Richard A., and Phyllis J. Newton. **"Does Arrest Really Deter Wife Battery? An Effort To Replicate the Findings of the Minneapolis Spouse Abuse Experiment."** *American Sociological Review* 50 (1985): 253–262.

Reports that incidents of wife battering are significantly reduced by the arrest of the husband.

Bonifaz, John. **"Broken Dreams: Battered Women Choosing between Violence and Homelessness."** Harvard Law School paper, May 1991. 27p.

The definition of homelessness needs to be broadened to include battered women, who are effectively homeless if their home is not safe. Currently, many battered women are not eligible for a place in a homeless shelter, either because they are not receiving welfare benefits or because they are viewed as being intentionally homeless. Available from the National Clearinghouse for the Defense of Battered Women, 125 South 9th Street, Suite 302, Philadelphia, PA 19107; (215) 351-0010.

Branan, Karen. **"A Matter of Murder and Survival: The Fate of Women Who Strike Back."** *Ladies Home Journal* (October 1991): 130–133.

Examines the case of Joyce Steiner, a battered woman who, after killing her abusive partner, was tried and convicted of second-degree murder.

Browne, Angela. **"Assaults between Intimate Partners in the United States: Incidence, Prevalence, and Proportional Risk for Women and Men."** Testimony before the U.S. Senate Judiciary Committee. 11 December 1990.

In the United States, male partners are the likeliest assailants of women victims of violent crimes, including assault, battery, rape, and murder. Calls for a national program to prevent abuse of women by spouses and other partners. Available from the National Clearinghouse for the Defense of Battered Women, 125 South 9th Street, Suite 302, Philadelphia, PA 19107; (215) 351-0010.

Buel, Sarah. **"The Dynamics of Violence Cases in the United States: An Overview."** American Bar Association paper, 1993.

Examines the frequency, escalation, and lethality of domestic abuse of women; the dynamics of family violence; the relationship between domestic violence, juvenile delinquency, and child abuse; and the position of battered women as defendants, particularly in cases in which battered women are tried for violent acts against an abusive partner. Available from the National Clearinghouse for the Defense of Battered Women, 125 South 9th Street, Suite 302, Philadelphia, PA 19107; (215) 351-0010.

Caputi, Jane, and Diana E. H. Russell. **"Femicide: Speaking the Unspeakable."** *Ms. Magazine* (September/October 1990): 34–37.

Examines the social and cultural underpinnings of the murder of women by men in a sexist society. The increasing incidence of femicide and other forms of violence against women is an aspect of the male backlash against feminism.

Cohn, Ellen. **"Changing the Domestic Violence Policies of Urban Police Departments: Impact of the Minneapolis Experiment."** *Response* 10, no. 4 (1987): 22–25.

The Minneapolis Domestic Violence Experiment found in 1984 that arrest was far more effective in stopping domestic violence than was mediation or separation. The study influenced many urban police departments to prefer arrest as a means for dealing with domestic violence cases.

Coker, Donna. **"Heat of Passion and Wife Killing: Men Who Batter, Men Who Kill."** *Southern California Review of Law and Women's Studies* 2, no. 1 (Fall 1992): 71–130.

Examines the California Supreme Court case of *People v. Berry*, in which the defendant's conviction for first-degree murder for the killing of his wife was overturned on the grounds that the trial court did not instruct the jury regarding voluntary manslaughter. The case reveals how current law tends to separate wife killing from wife battering. The former is often regarded as a crime of passion—the man losing control over himself—while the latter is typically seen in light of wife abuse theory—the man losing control over his wife. Argues for the integration of these two perspectives, whereby wife killing would be recognized simply as the most extreme form of wife battering.

Colasuonno, Jennifer. **"One Woman's Survival of the California Justice System."** *Yale Journal of Law and Feminism* 4 (1991): 51–56.

Recalls the author's conviction and imprisonment for the 1993 killing of her abusive husband, noting particularly the author's participation in a program that allowed her to serve her sentence in a community setting with her two children.

Congressional Quarterly Researcher. **"Violence against Women: Is the Problem More Serious Than Statistics Indicate?"** *Congressional Quarterly Researcher* 3, no. 8 (26 February 1993): 169–192.

This is an overview of issues surrounding violence against women, presenting statistics and other information on rape, date rape, spousal abuse, women's shelters, sexual violence in the media, and related topics.

DeMaris, Alfred. **"The Efficacy of a Spouse Abuse Model in Accounting for Courtship Violence."** *Journal of Family Violence* 2 (September 1987): 291–306.

Examines the significance of social class, control of household resources between partners, and personal history of family violence as determinants of spousal abuse among white college students.

Ellis, Desmond. **"Marital Conflict Mediation and Post-Separation Wife Abuse."** *Law Inequality* 8, no. 2 (March 1990): 317–339.

Studies the incidence of wife abuse among separated couples and examines the efficacy of post-separation mediation. Separation does not necessarily end abuse, and mediation in such circumstances may actually prolong abuse. However, mediation can serve a positive role in some circumstances.

Erickson, Nancy S. **"Battered Mothers of Battered Children: Using Our Knowledge of Battered Women To Defend Them against Charges of Failure To Act."** *Current Perspectives in Psychological, Legal and Ethical Issues* 1a (1990): 195–216.

Examines the legal responsibility of battered women to act to prevent the abuse of their children by the batterer. Legal defenses in cases in which a woman fails to act include duress, physical incapacity, and others.

Ewing, Charles Patrick. **"Psychological Self-Defense: A Proposed Justification for Battered Women Who Kill."** *Law and Human Behavior* 14, no. 6 (December 1990): 579–594.

Maintains that most battered women who kill their batterers do so to defend themselves from psychological destruction rather than physical harm. The concept of self-defense should encompass the defense of the psychological self.

Fiora-Gormally, Nancy. **"Battered Wives Who Kill: Double Standard Out of Court, Single Standard In?"** *Law and Human Behavior* 2, no. 2 (1978): 133–166.

Examines social and legal standards of self-defense as applied to battered women. While there exists a double standard outside the courtroom, in court the same standard is applied to women and men alike. There should be legal recognition that there are differences between reasonable self-defense as it applies to men and women.

Follingstad, Diane. **"Factors Associated with Patterns of Dating Violence toward College Women."** *Journal of Family Violence* 3, no. 3 (1988): 169–177.

An examination of dating violence reveals that it is not a single pattern of behavior but rather a number of distinctly different patterns of behavior erroneously considered as a single behavioral phenomenon.

Gibbs, Nancy. **"Fighting Back: Do Women Who Turn against Their Abuser Deserve a Special Kind of Forgiveness?"** *Time* 141 (18 January 1993): 38–45.

Discusses problems confronted by abused women, focusing on women who are serving prison sentences for the killing of abusive partners and the controversy over the granting of clemency in such cases.

Gondolf, Edward W. **"The Effect of Batterer Counseling on Shelter Outcome."** *Journal of Interpersonal Violence* 3, no. 3 (September 1988): 275–283.

Reports that a woman who has sought refuge in a battered women's shelter is more likely to leave her abuser permanently if the woman is financially independent. She is less likely to leave her abuser if the abuser participates in counseling.

Goode, Stephen. **"When Fear Is Enough in Defense."** *Insight* 3 (6 July 1987): 56.

Profiles the case of Doris Jen Norman, who was acquitted of killing her partner who had verbally abused her. Norman's defense successfully argued that the extreme verbal abuse in her case had led to her suffering Battered Woman Syndrome.

Hart, Barbara. **"Testimony before the House Select Committee on Children, Youth and Families on the Failure of the Justice System to Protect Women from Male Violence."** U.S. House of Representatives document, 16 September 1987.

Discusses problems with the enforcement of laws designed to protect women from domestic violence, including inadequate definitions of abuse, the failure of protective and restraining orders, failure to prosecute domestic violence cases, and others. Available from the National Clearinghouse for the Defense of Battered Women, 125 South 9th Street, Suite 302, Philadelphia, PA 19107; (215) 351-0010.

Huling, Tracy. **"Battered Women Who Kill: One Man's Opinion."** *Out of Silence* 1, no. 1 (December 1991): 2–4.

Interviews New York State Department of Correctional Services commissioner Thomas Coughlin, focusing on the disparity in the sentencing of women accused of killing abusive partners. Women who opt for a jury trial and are found guilty often receive much longer sentences than do women who plea-bargain a manslaughter charge.

Johnson, Anne T. **"Criminal Liability for Parents Who Fail To Protect."** *Law and Inequality* 5, no. 2 (1987): 359–390.

Examines the development of criminal law regarding child abuse and parents' failure to protect children from such abuse. Current statutes often hold a nonabusive parent responsible for his or her failure to protect, but this victimizes the nonabuser and often is not in the child's interest. Particularly for first offenses, it would be better to commit the nonabusive parent to a course of education and counseling rather than to criminal proceedings.

Kandel-Englander, Elizabeth. **"Wife Battering and Violence Outside the Family."** *Journal of Interpersonal Violence* 7, no. 4 (December 1992): 462–467.

Survey data indicate that violent men tend to be violent toward their wives or violent toward persons outside the family but not both.

King, Patricia. **"Not So Different After All: The Trials of Gay Domestic Violence."** *Newsweek* 122 (September 1993): 75.

Women who are the victims of abuse by their lesbian partners have fewer resources and legal protections than do women who are battered by male partners.

Kochan, Deborah. **"Beyond the Battered Woman Syndrome: An Argument for the Development of New Standards and the Incorporation of a Feminine Approach to Ethics."** *Hastings Women's Law Journal* 1 (Spring 1989): 88–115.

Laws made primarily by men do not fit the experiences of women in abusive relationships. For women who kill abusive partners, even the expanded definition of self-defense inherent to a claim of Battered Woman Syndrome is inadequate. An ethic of caring should be applied to battered women who kill in self-defense.

Kurz, Demie. **"Social Science Perspectives on Wife Abuse: Current Debates and Future Directions."** *Gender and Society* 3, no. 4 (December 1989): 489–498.

Indicates that the study of wife abuse by social scientists is usually informed by one of two major viewpoints: a feminist perspective and a family-violence perspective. The two differ fundamentally in the way they approach gender issues, and these differences have implications for research and public policy relating to domestic violence. The feminist perspective is more accurate in its approach to wife battering.

Levy, Barrie. **"Abusive Teen Dating Relationships: An Emerging Issue for the '90s."** *Response* 13, no. 1 (1990): 5.

Examines the growing problem of violence in dating relationships and discusses services available to victims.

Lundy, Sandy. **"Debra Reid Testifies before Board."** *The Network News* 1, no. 2 (Spring 1993): 5–7.

Discusses the testimony of Debra Reid, who was convicted of killing her abusive lesbian partner, before the Massachusetts Board of Pardons.

Mahoney, Martha. **"Legal Images of Battered Women: Redefining the Issue of Separation."** *Michigan Law Review* 90 (1991): 39–40.

Presents an overview of woman battering, arguing that the way in which a batterer prevents his victim from leaving is a fundamental aspect of abuse.

Marano, Hara Estroff. **"Inside the Heart of Marital Violence."** *Psychology Today* (November/December 1993): 48–53.

Indicates that men's abuse of their partners often arises from the batterers' own feelings of powerlessness. Research by five clinical psychologists suggests that some men become abusive when they are threatened by apparently hostile behavior by their partners.

Marshall, Linda L., and Patricia Rose. **"Premarital Violence: The Impact of Family of Origin Violence, Stress, and Reciprocity."** *Violence and Victims* 5, no. 1 (1990): 51–64.

Assesses the results of a study of undergraduate students, comparing individuals' childhood experiences of violence in their families with the violence they have experienced in their recent relationships.

Martin, Patricia Yancey, and Robert A. Hummer. **"Fraternities and Rape on Campus."** *Gender and Society* 3, no. 4 (December 1989): 457–473.

Argues that college fraternities foster a social climate that encourages the sexual coercion and exploitation of women.

Morgan, Kay. **"Reassessing the Battery of Women: A Social and Economic Perspective."** *Feminist Jurisprudence* (May 1992).

Argues that the failure of many women to leave abusive relationships is based on rational decisions that consider financial well-being, lack of police assistance, and the threat of greater physical violence if they attempt to leave. Social and economic power structures, not the stereotypical helplessness of battered women, are the fundamental causes of continuing abusive relationships.

Pagelow, Mildred Daley. **"Adult Victims of Domestic Violence: Battered Women."** *Journal of Interpersonal Violence* 7, no. 1 (March 1992): 87–105.

Presents a review of recent research on battered women, noting implications of this research both for the persistence of common stereotypes and for public policymaking.

Rasch, Christine E. **"Early Models of Contemporary Thought on Domestic Violence and Women Who Kill Their Mates: A Review of the Literature from 1895 to 1970."** *Women and Criminal Justice* 2 (1990): 31–43.

Examines the historical development of ideas regarding the reasons battered women kill their abusers, ranging from insanity and extreme emotionalism to self-defense.

Rich, Robert, and Robert Sampson. **"Public Perceptions of Criminal Justice Policy: Does Victimization Make a Difference?"** *Violence and Victims* 5, no. 2 (1990): 109–118.

Survey data reveal that age and education have the greatest influence on attitudes toward criminal justice policy; gender, race, and whether or not a respondent has ever been victimized are less important factors affecting attitudes.

Rodriguez, Rachel. **"Perception of Health Needs by Battered Women."** *Response* 12, no. 4 (1989): 22–25.

Examines the health needs of the residents of a battered women's shelter. Many barriers exist to battered women's access to health care, including abusive partners' refusal to permit their victims to seek medical attention.

Rouse, Linda. **"Abuse in Dating Relationships: A Comparison of Blacks, Whites, and Hispanics."** *Journal of College Student Development* 2 (July 1988): 312–319.

A survey of undergraduate students showed no significant difference between races in the incidence of dating violence. Men reported more abusive behavior by women than women did of men.

Schneider, Elizabeth. **"The Violence of Privacy."** *Connecticut Law Review* 23, no. 4 (Summer 1991): 973–1000.

Maintains that the tradition of privacy from government intrusion into the private lives of married couples tends to hide and encourage violence against women.

Sherman, Lawrence, and Richard Berk. **"The Specific Deterrent Effects of Arrest for Domestic Assault."** *American Sociological Review* 49 (April 1984): 261–271.

Reports that among three different kinds of police responses to incidents of domestic assault—arrest, advice, and an order to the suspect to leave the home for eight hours—arrest was the most efficacious in deterring subsequent violence.

Smith, Michael. **"Patriarchal Ideology and Wife Beating: A Test of a Feminist Hypothesis."** *Violence and Victims* 5, no. 4 (1990): 257–265.

Argues that men who believe that women should be subjugated within marriage are more likely to abuse their wives than are men who do not. Men with low-status and low-income jobs and low educational attainment are more likely to subscribe to such beliefs.

Sorenson, Susan B. **"Self-Reports of Spousal Violence in a Mexican-American and Non-Hispanic White Population."** *Violence and Victims* 6, no. 1 (1991): 3.

Examines the occurrence of domestic violence among Mexican-born Americans, Mexican Americans born in the United States, and non-Hispanic whites, finding that spousal abuse is most common in the second group and linking this finding to poor cultural self-image.

Stark, Evan, and Anne H. Flitcraft. **"Spouse Abuse."** Paper prepared for the Surgeon General's Workshop on Violence and Public Health, Leesburg, Virginia, 27–29 October 1985.

Presents an overview of the problem of spousal abuse and examines the efficacy of different interventions. Available from the Centers for Disease Control, (404) 639-3311.

Truesdell, Donna L., John S. McNeil, and Jeanne P. Deschner. **"Incidence of Wife Abuse in Incestuous Families."** *Social Work* 31 (1986): 138–140.

Examines the correlation between wife battering and incest in families. The mother in these cases is, due to her own victimization, typically unable to protect the abused child.

Walker, Lenore E. A. **"Battered Women and Learned Helplessness."** *Victimology: An International Journal* 2 (1977–1978): 525–535.

Argues that childhood sex-role socialization is a root cause of spousal abuse and contributes to the feelings of helplessness that tend to keep many women in abusive relationships.

Curricula, Manuals, and Program Materials

Boulder County Safehouse. **We Can't Play at My House: Children and Domestic Violence.** Boulder, CO: Boulder County Safehouse, 1990.

In 1989, the staff of the Boulder County Safehouse helped create a task force of multidisciplinary health and counseling professionals to help children who live in homes with violence. One result of the task force's efforts is the first two booklets in the We Can't Play at My House series. *Book I: Guidebook for Parents* informs the reader about the ways in which children are affected by verbal and physical abuse they experience or witness in their home. As it points to children's awareness, fears, anger, and sadness, it also helps parents understand how to deal with those concerns and suggests ways to create a safe, abuse-free home. Written for parents who are or have been involved in a violent relationship. *Book II: Handbook for Teachers* serves as a practical guide for teachers on how to detect a child living in an abusive home and work with those children in the classroom. It suggests ways and resources for helping the family deal with the situation. A Spanish version of each book is available. The full program can be ordered from Boulder County Safehouse at P.O. Box 4157, Boulder, CO 90306; (303) 449-8623.

Creighton, Allan, Battered Women's Alternatives, with Paul Kivel, Oakland Men's Project. **Helping Teens Stop Violence.** Alameda, CA: Hunter House, 1990. 152p. ISBN 0-89793-116-5.

This book outlines a program that contains practical workshops for parents, teachers, and counselors. It explores the roots of violence and its effects on young people; discusses issues of race, gender, and age and how they relate to domestic violence and dating violence; provides curricula for the classroom setting and support groups on role-playing techniques and helping abused teens; and includes special sections that address adult expectations and prejudices in relationship to young people. This book is recommended for teachers, youth workers, juvenile correction staff, group leaders, parents, counselors, and therapists who work with young people.

Domestic Violence Intervention Services. **Dating Violence: Intervention and Prevention for Teenagers.** Tulsa: National Resource Center for Youth Services, 1993. 118p. No ISBN.

This group leader's manual provides five complete lesson plans, handouts, and flip-chart samples. The program, for use in group sessions, is designed to help prevent violence and the development of abusive relationships, and will help teenagers understand what dating violence is, what its causes are, the relationship of substance abuse to interpersonal violence, and what implications it has for their own lives. The program is also designed to assist young people already involved in dating violence in getting help. It is recommended for adolescents and available from National Resource Center for Youth Services, University of Oklahoma, 202 West 8th, Tulsa, OK 74119-1419; (918) 585-2986.

Family Violence Project. **Domestic Violence: A Training Curriculum for Law Enforcement.** San Francisco: Family Violence Project, 1988. Rev. ed. 1991. No ISBN.

This two-volume set includes comprehensive course material on domestic violence and law enforcement responses. It includes reference material and handouts and can be ordered directly from Family Violence Project, Building One, Suite 200, 1001 Potrero Avenue, San Francisco, CA 94110.

————. **Domestic Violence Is a Crime.** San Francisco: Family Violence Project, 1988. No ISBN.

This is a manual on domestic violence facts, policies, and procedures. It includes information on police response, prosecution strategies, and diversion and probation guidelines. It can be ordered directly from Family Violence Project, Building One, Suite 200, 1001 Potrero Avenue, San Francisco, CA 94110.

Fortune, Marie M., Rev. **Violence in the Family: A Workshop Curriculum for Clergy and Other Helpers.** Cleveland: The Pilgrim Press, 1991. 278p. ISBN 0-8298-0908-2.

For use by clergy and groups that want to provide continuing education for clergy and assist secular helpers in responding to religious questions. The book contains an extensive appendix, and resource sections offer teaching and worship materials that can be duplicated.

Goodman, Marilyn Shear, and Beth Creager Fallon. **Pattern Changing for Abused Women: An Educational Program.** Newbury Park, CA: Sage Publications, 1994. 204p. ISBN 0-8039-5494-8.

A manual designed for those who are currently facilitating or would like to start a group for abused and formerly abused women. The book is based on the accumulated experience of the authors and groups they have facilitated over the course of eight years. Along with the material for clients, group leaders are provided with easy-to-follow scripts for each session. The program focuses on women and their power to change the course of their lives. Its goal is for women to begin to understand the problem of abuse and its realities for the entire family, to become aware of their lifelong patterns, to set realistic goals, and to learn techniques for developing new patterns of their own choosing. Sessions are not intended to function as group therapy.

Health Education Alliance. **Domestic Violence: A Course in Assessment and Intervention.** San Jose: Health Alliance, 1993.

This training program about domestic violence for persons in the health field includes two courses, each of which comes with a video, workbook, and certificate of completion. *Course I: Living in a Violent Relationship* discusses types of abuse, the cycle of violence, myths vs. facts, the psychological profile of the victim, the psychology of a batterer, and alternatives to violence. *Course II: Breaking the Silence* discusses medical assessment, screening the victim, interacting with the perpetrator, barriers to identification, reporting requirements, cultural contexts, violence among gays and lesbians, and intervention through community resources. Courses include VHS videocassettes, workbooks, and certificates of completion. Additional workbooks may be purchased. The program can be ordered from Health Education Alliance, 7426 Phinney Way, San Jose, CA 95139; (800) 404-3258.

Kivel, Paul. **Men's Work: Comprehensive Violence Treatment.** Center City, MN: Hazelden, 1993.

Men's Work: The Facilitator's Guide provides a complete treatment plan, including practical suggestions for initiating discussion, fostering motivation, and developing new skills. It also provides group exercises and helps facilitate client assessment. The Men's Work Workbooks series consists of three 32-page workbooks used to help men work through their struggle with violence and to document progress. As participants work through the exercises, they begin to identify the roots of male violence and develop their own alternatives to violence. For groups, individuals, and as take-home assignments to reinforce group session work. *Growing Up Male: Identifying Violence in My Life* looks at how boys are raised to become men who hold pain inside and turn anger into violence. The 44 exercises help men explore and assess their attitudes and behaviors toward women and other men. *Anger, Power, Violence, and Drugs: Breaking the Connections* aims to increase the participant's awareness of the psychological and behavioral connections common in violent relationships. Explores how men have been taught to connect anger, power, violence, and alcohol and other drugs, and uses 41 exercises to help participants break the connection, give healthy expression to anger, and improve communication skills. *Becoming Whole: Learning New Roles, Making New Choices* uses 61 exercises focusing on establishing relationships with other men, intervening with other men who may need help with their violent behaviors, helping men develop a spiritual connection, and improving parenting skills. Participants are encouraged to reconstruct their lives and relationships by developing alternatives to violence within their families, friendships, and communities. Used as a tool for prevention programs. The entire program or any part of it may be ordered directly from Hazelden, 15251 Pleasant Valley Road, P.O. Box 176, Center City, MN 55012; (800) 328-9000.

Levy, Barrie. **Skills for Violence-Free Relationships: A Curriculum for Young People Ages 13–18.** Santa Monica: The Southern California Coalition of Battered Women, 1984. 88p.

This curriculum was designed to enable young people to break the cycle of abuse by describing abuse of all kinds, identifying the warning signs, and providing participants with coping, communication, decision-making and conflict-resolution techniques. The text presents strategies for making changes in understanding and behavior so that participants can prevent abuse from being part of their lives, either as a victim or as a perpetrator. Each section contains specific goals and recommends ways to adapt the curriculum for age appropriateness. It is available from Southern California Coalition against Domestic Violence, P.O. Box 5036, Santa Monica, CA 90405; (213) 655-6098.

McCue, Margi. **No Punching Judy: A Program for the Prevention of Domestic Violence.** Portland, OR: Community Advocates, 1994.

No Punching Judy is a comprehensive, culturally sensitive prevention program for children in grades 1–5 designed to break the cycle of domestic violence. The program is a nine-unit, video-based program designed for schools and children's programs. The children explore the facts about domestic violence, gender-role stereotyping, nonviolent conflict resolution, how to handle domestic violence that may be present in their own homes, effective communication and expression of feelings, their unique value as human beings, and their right to live free of violence. The program includes a curriculum for grades 1–2 (90p.), a curriculum for grades 3–5 (114p.), a user's guide, coloring books, "No Punching" pins, a 16-minute staff training video, and a 30-minute *No Punching Judy Puppet Show* video for children. The program can be ordered directly from McCue and Associates, 1543 SE Marion, Portland, OR 97202; (503) 238-7973.

Massachusetts Coalition of Battered Women Service Groups, Inc. **For Shelter and Beyond: An Educational Manual for Working with Women Who Are Battered.** Boston: Massachusetts Coalition of Battered Women Service Groups, Inc., 1990. 217p.

This manual is an excellent resource for all advocates working in the field of domestic violence. Chapters include essays on patriarchy, sexism and violence against women, feminist approaches to supporting battered women and children, understanding diversity and accessibility, legal advocacy, and mental health and addictions. It can be ordered directly from the Massachusetts Coalition of Battered Women Service Groups, Inc., 107 South Street, Boston, MA 02111.

Minnesota Coalition for Battered Women. **Safety First: Battered Women Surviving Violence When Alcohol and Drugs Are Involved.** St. Paul: Minnesota Coalition, 1993.

This program includes a facilitator's guide and a guide for the battered woman. *A Guide for Counselors and Advocates* is a manual specially designed to be helpful to chemical health providers, psychotherapists, and advocates who work with battered women or violent partners who have concerns about alcohol or drug use. *A Guide for Battered Women* is a booklet designed for women who are survivors of battering and are wondering about their chemical use. The booklet is intended to be available to women utilizing chemical health facilities, counseling services, battered women's shelters, or advocacy services. The program is available from Minnesota Coalition for Battered Women, 1619 Dayton Avenue, Suite 303, St. Paul, MN 55104; (612) 646-6177.

The National Council of Juvenile and Family Court Judges–Family Violence Project

The Family Violence Project has a number of publications available. *Family Violence: Improving Court Practice* (1990, 59p.) is a booklet that includes recommendations for improving court practices in family violence cases that were adopted as official policy of the National Council of Juvenile and Family Court Judges. This publication details the policies and procedures necessary to create and maintain an effective court, agency, and community response to family violence. In addition to recommendations concerning criminal and civil courts, there are sections concerning policy recommendations and recommendations for court-related agencies and their personnel, such as law enforcement, prosecutors, court administration, probation officers, advocates, children's protective services, and treatment providers. *Family Violence State-of-the-Art Court Programs* (1992, 100p.) is a publication that examines 18 of the best U.S. court programs dealing with family violence. Various programs are included, such as comprehensive programs, statewide court programs, rural programs, civil protection order programs, and prosecution programs. There are also chapters on offender accountability, coordinating councils, and legislation and policy development. Photographs by Donna Ferrato highlight this book, which offers practical solutions that can assist courts, agencies, and communities wishing to improve the ways in which their justice system deals with such violence. An issue of *The Juvenile and Family Court Journal* (43, no. 4 [1992, 81p.]), titled *State Codes on Domestic Violence: Analysis, Commentary and Recommendations*, by Barbara J. Hart, examines existing state laws regarding civil protection orders, custody codes, mediation, civil damages, social and health services codes, evidence codes and battered women defendants, and the duty to protect children. Each chapter compares and contrasts the state codes, then the author offers recommendations for provisions to be included in state codes concerning domestic and family violence. *The Juvenile and Family Law DIGEST* published two special issues in 1993, *Civil and Marital Tort Cases Concerning Domestic Violence* by Joan Zorza and Robert Spector and *Criminal Cases Concerning Domestic Violence* by Nancy K. D. Lemon. The digests cover case law from across the United States on such current topics as the effect of spousal abuse on children, marital tort cases, and substantive crimes and defenses. These publications may be ordered directly from the National Council of Juvenile and Family Court Judges, P.O. Box 8970, Reno, NV 89507; (702) 784-4829.

National Training Project

Develops, publishes, and distributes books, manuals, educational curriculums, and training materials for use by batterer treatment groups, law enforcement training, and other professional training.

Materials can be ordered from National Training Project, 206 West Fourth Street, Duluth, MN 55806.

National Woman Abuse Prevention Project (NWAPP)

Offers assorted pamphlets and brochures for domestic violence programs to use in their public education and training activities, including *Understanding Domestic Violence: Fact Sheets, Domestic Violence: Understanding a Community Problem, Helping the Battered Woman: A Guide for Family and Friends, Sad Is How You Feel When Mom Is Being Beat, and Physical Abuse: You Don't Have To Take it, You Don't Have To Use It.* The minimum order for any one product is 25 copies. You may order directly from: NWAPP, 2000 P Street, Suite 508, Washington, D.C. 20036; (202) 857-0216.

NiCarthy, Ginny, Karen Merriam, and Sandra Coffman. **Talking It Out: A Guide to Groups for Abused Women.** Seattle: Seal Press, 1984. 165p. ISBN 0-931188-24-5.

This publication is an informative and comprehensive handbook for counselors, mental health workers, and shelter or community activists on starting and sustaining a group for abused women.

Paris, Susan, with illustrations by Gail Labinske. **Mommy and Daddy Are Fighting: A Book for Children about Family Violence.** Seattle: Seal Press, 1986. 24p. ISBN 0-931188-33-4.

Written from a child's perspective, this gentle and supportive illustrated book tells about the confusing experience of living in a violent home. Discussion questions and a bibliography are included as an aid to parents, teachers, counselors, and child care workers.

Patterson, Susan. **I Wish the Hitting Would Stop.** Fargo: Red Flag, Green Flag, 1987. Rev. ed. 1990. ISBN 0-914633-17-1.

Written for those working with children ages 6 to 14 who live in homes where there is violence, each page of the 28-page children's workbook presents the child's worries, concerns, and feelings. The "I Wish" statement on each page helps the child talk about, explore, and learn to cope with his or her feelings of anger, fear, guilt, sadness, helplessness, hurt, and confusion. Children learn that they are not responsible for the violence between others, they are encouraged to express their feelings constructively, and they develop a personal safety plan. *I Wish the Hitting Would Stop* is appropriate for group settings or one-on-one sessions. The 68-page facilitator's guide includes discussion questions, related activities, and a resource section listing books, films, and games for children and adults, as well as sections titled "Cycle of Violence" and "Myths and Realities of Domestic Violence."

Sheehy, Lila, Melissa Reinberg, and Deborah Kirchwey. **Commutation for Women Who Defended Themselves against Abusive Partners: An Advocacy Manual and Guide to Legal Issues.** Philadelphia: National Clearinghouse for the Defense of Battered Women, 1991.

This manual, written for domestic violence activists, attorneys, and advocates, explores the issue of battered women who have been convicted and sentenced for defending their lives against abusive partners. It was written in 1991 and focuses primarily on Massachusetts; however, it is a highly usable resource for those concerned with the issue. Not only does it discuss the failure of the system to help women, but it shows how to build a post-conviction strategy and how to work with women while they are in prison. It also explores many problems women face at trial and suggests strategies for dealing with these problems. Available from the National Clearinghouse for the Defense of Battered Women, 125 South 9th Street, Suite 302, Philadelphia, PA 19107; (215) 351-0010.

Newsletters, Journals and Professional Publications

Alternatives: For Protective Parents in Civil Child Sexual Abuse Cases
National Center for Protective Parents in Civil Child Sexual Abuse
  Cases
1908 Riverside Drive
Trenton, NJ 08618
(609) 394-2574
Quarterly. $25.

This publication contains articles, legal information, book reviews, conference information, and so forth on parents attempting to protect their children from sexual abuse, generally in custodial situations. It provides current information valuable to advocates, attorneys, and parents.

Double-Time
National Clearinghouse for the Defense of Battered Women
125 South 9th Street, Suite 302
Philadelphia, PA 19107
(215) 351-0010
Semi-annually. $35 membership fee.

Double Time contains articles, book reviews, case summaries, resource information, and so on regarding battered women in general and those in prison for killing their abusers. Call for a subscription or a listing of available back issues.

Family Violence and Sexual Assault Bulletin
Family Violence and Sexual Assault Institute
1310 Clinic Drive
Tyler, TX 75701
(903) 595-6600
Quarterly. $25 (individuals); $40 (institutions).

Family Violence and Sexual Assault Bulletin (FVSAB) is a publication dealing with the issues of family violence and sexual assault. Specific topics include spouse/partner abuse, sexual assault/incest survivors, child physical abuse/neglect, and elder/parent abuse. The *FVSAB* provides current classified references, research and treatment articles, information on resource networking, a conference calendar, book and media reviews, new book releases, information on legislative issues, letters to the editor, and announcements.

The Homefront: Research Reports on Intimate Violence
Women's Center of Rhode Island
Box 3300
Providence, RI 02906-0300
(401) 861-2760
Quarterly. $40.

An innovative newsletter designed to help local programs expand their outreach through media, this publication is a two-page, front-and-back, camera-ready newsletter that summarizes research and reports on topics relating to intimate violence. The newsletter is complete with space for logos of local sponsors. The mission is to bridge the gap between research and practice with short, easy-to-read summaries that programs can insert in their own newsletters. This will allow programs to augment their own news with important summaries of topical issues regarding domestic violence. Each issue focuses on one theme so that the reader's grasp of the topic will be deeper and more comprehensive.

Journal of Interpersonal Violence
Sage Publications, Inc.
2455 Teller Road
Newbury Park, CA 91320
(805) 499-0871
Quarterly. $49 (individuals); $129 (institutions).

This professional journal is devoted to the study and treatment of victims and perpetrators of interpersonal violence. With its dual focus on victims and victimizers, the journal publishes material about the causes, effects, treatment, and prevention of all types of violence.

NCADV Voice
National Coalition against Domestic Violence
P.O. Box 18749
Denver, CO 80218
(303) 839-1852
Three times per year. $25 (individuals); $100 (institutions).

The official publication of the National Coalition against Domestic Violence, *Voice* publishes articles on subjects related to the issue of domestic violence. Back issues available.

Violence against Women: An International and Interdisciplinary Journal
Sage Publications, Inc.
P.O. Box 5084
Thousand Oaks, CA 91359
(805) 499-0721
Quarterly. $45 (individuals); $125 (institutions).

First published in March 1995, *Violence against Women* focuses on gender-based violence against women in all forms across cultural and national boundaries. It publishes a wide range of articles, including empirical research, book reviews, research notes, theoretical papers, review essays, and articles by survivors. A primary goal of the journal is to bridge the gaps that exist between academicians, practitioners, clinicians, advocates, and activists; therefore, contributions from diverse disciplines are featured, including ethnic studies, criminology, public health, political science, public policy, social work, gender studies, media studies, law, medicine, psychology, and sociology.

Violence and Victims
Springer Publishing Co.
536 Broadway
New York, NY 10012-9904
(212) 431-4370
Quarterly. $42 (individuals); $79 (institutions).

This is a professional journal of theory, research, policy, clinical practice, and social services in the area of interpersonal violence and victimization. *Violence and Victims* facilitates the exchange of information across professional disciplines and publishes articles from relevant fields, including psychology, sociology, criminology, law, medicine, psychiatry, social work, and nursing. Special emphasis is given to the reporting of original research on violence-related victimization within and outside of the family, the etiology and perpetration of violent behavior, legal issues, and implications for clinical intervention. The journal's most recent addition is a legal reports section covering important developments and issues in the legal-judicial area.

Bibliographies

Geffner, Robert, Mary Gail Milner, K. Ann Crawford, Susan Kreager Cook. **Spouse/Partner Abuse: A Categorized Bibliography and Reference List.** Tyler: University of Texas, 1990. 370p.

This bibliography is a categorized reference tool listing research, treatment, and other related information gathered through December 1989. Included in this reference list are over 3,000 published journal articles, books, manuals, papers presented at conferences, and unpublished manuscripts and research work. Areas covered include treatment approaches, child observers of parental violence, characteristics of both victims and abusers, police/legal issues, support groups, pornography, pregnancy, acquaintance/date rape, and sex roles. Each of these areas is further divided into distinct subcategories, such as alcohol/drug usage, learned helplessness, depression, learned violence, and clergy support. At the back of the book are listings of the abstracts and journals searched to provide these references, as well as a list of conferences reviewed annually. Updated supplements to the bibliography are available yearly. The bibliography is available directly from Family Violence and Sexual Abuse Institute, 1310 Clinic Drive, Tyler, TX 75701; (903) 595-6600.

Michigan Coalition against Domestic Violence. **Working against Violence: A Bibliography.** 2d ed. Lansing: Michigan Coalition against Domestic Violence, 1990. 180p.

Compiled by Ellen Hates and Phillis Mullins for the Michigan Coalition Resource Library, this comprehensive bibliography of printed and audiovisual materials is relevant to all persons committed to ending violence in the lives of women and children. Contact the library directly for information on how to order the bibliography and other material in their library at The Resource Library, 600 South Capitol Avenue, Lower Level, Lansing, MI 48933; (517) 372-4960.

Rosen, Nathan Aaron. **Battered Wives: A Comprehensive Annotated Bibliography of Articles, Books and Statutes in the United States of America.** New York: National Center on Women and Family Law, 1988.

This bibliography can be ordered directly from the center, which also has numerous other publications of interest to battered women and those working with battered women. Of particular interest is *Protecting Confidentiality: A Legal Manual for Battered Women's and Rape Crisis Programs* by Lynn Marks (1987). For a complete listing write to the National Center on Women and Family Law, Inc., 799 Broadway, Room 402, New York, NY 10003; (212) 674-8200.

Selected Nonprint Resources 7

Audiocassettes

Getting Free
Type: Audiocassette
Length: 60 min.
Date: 1986
ISBN: 0-931188-84-9
Source: Seal Press, Seattle

Based on the book *Getting Free* by Ginny NiCarthy, written for women who are being physically battered or emotionally abused in their relationships, this audio tape is excellent for women who don't read, for use in support groups, and for counselors and others working with abused women. *Getting Free* offers support, practical help, and inspiration, and includes special exercises designed to help women understand their situations. An important self-help resource.

Men's Work Audio
Type: Audiocassette
Length: 60 min.
Date: 1992
Source: Hazelden
15251 Pleasant Valley Road
P.O. Box 176
Center City, MN 55012
(800) 328-9000

For men who want to stop their own violence. This audio tape helps listeners trace the roots of violence in their lives. Narrator Paul Kivel's use of role playing and discussion encourages men to take a stand against violence, from questioning assumptions to asking for help. Men learn how to make the decision not to be violent, to listen, to state preferences without anger or blame, to respond to feelings, and more.

Video and Film

Acquaintance Rape
Type: VHS videocassette
Length: 22 min.
Date: 1992
Source: Intermedia
1300 Dexter Avenue North
Seattle, WA 98109
(800) 553-8336

Acquaintance Rape addresses the most common form of sexual assault, rape by a friend. Acquaintance rape, or date rape, continues to occur in part because so many people are misinformed about the crime. *Acquaintance Rape* discusses the many myths surrounding this form of sexual assault, such as confronting the rapist and reducing the risks. The video is appropriate for audiences high school age and older.

Against Her Will: Rape on Campus
Type: VHS videocassette
Length: 46 min.
Date: 1990
Source: Coronet/MTI Film and Video
4350 Equity Drive
Columbus, OH 43228
(800) 321-3106

Hosted by actress Kelly McGillis, this candid documentary explores the shocking problem of rape on campus and examines what parents can do to better prepare their children for the new freedoms that come with contemporary campus life. Designed to raise students' awareness of how they can protect themselves and each other, this program also details educational and security measures colleges and universities can take to stop the epidemic of acquaintance rape. Candid interviews with female rape victims, young male students, security personnel, and counselors help to underscore the growing horror of rape on college campuses. College and above.

Battered Wives
Type: 16mm film and VHS videocassette
Length: 45 min.
Date: 1979
Source: Coronet/MTI Film and Video
4350 Equity Drive
Columbus, OH 43228
(800) 321-3106

This drama focuses on two situations of family violence. In one, the wife of an ambitious lawyer is an easy target for her impatient husband. In the other, a couple finds that alcohol turns their happy marriage into an inferno. High school level and above.

Broken Vows: Religious Perspectives on Domestic Violence
Type: VHS videocassette
Length: 59 min.
Date: 1994
Source: Center for the Prevention of Sexual and
Domestic Violence
1914 North 34th Street, Suite 105
Seattle, WA 98103
(206) 634-1903

A documentary about religious perspectives on domestic violence. The video presents the stories of six formerly battered women from diverse religious traditions, including Jewish, Roman Catholic, Protestant, and Evangelical Christian. *Broken Vows* is a two-part video (Part I is 37 minutes and Part II is 22 minutes) with two separate sessions recommended for viewing and discussion. The video includes introductory information about domestic violence, definitions, myths and facts; the nature and dynamics of abuse; discussion of theological issues, divorce, repentance, Shalom Bayit (peace in the home), and forgiveness; interviews with rabbis, priests, pastors, shelter workers, psychologists, and secular professionals; concrete ideas about how religious institutions can work to end domestic violence; and discussion of how religious and secular groups can work together. Program includes a 40-page study guide and audience brochures.

Date Rape: It Happened to Me
Type: VHS videocassette
Length: 30 min.
Date: 1990
Source: Pyramid Film and Video
P.O. Box 1048
Santa Monica, CA 90406
(800) 421-2304

Date Rape cuts through the rationalizations for date rape by getting to the heart of the matter: "no" means "no," forced sex is rape, and rape is a felony punishable with jail time. This video aims to sensitize teenagers to the emotional, psychological, and legal ramifications of an act of sexual violence. A dramatized incident of date rape is combined with narration by teenage hosts, first-person accounts of date rape victims, and observations by law officers and adult counselors. It covers prevention of, treatment for, and recovery from date rape. This video is intended to get kids thinking and talking before ignorance gets them into trouble. Recommended for junior high school and high school age.

Dating, Sex, and Trouble: Acquaintance Rape
Type: VHS videocassette
Length: 24 min.
Date: 1990
Source: Sunburst Communications
Dept. TH42
39 Washington Avenue
P.O. Box 40
Pleasantville, NY 10570-0040
(800) 431-1934

This program details how sexual attitudes contribute to sexual assault, and points out that sexual assault can be anything from unwanted kissing and touching to rape. It emphasizes every person's right to safeguard her or his own body. Opening with a series of rape myths and common beliefs about dating behavior, the video contrasts the differing interpretations each sex may put on the same sexual cues. A psychologist-narrator points out that rape can happen to anyone, male or female, that half of all reported rapes happen on dates, and that most victims know their attackers. The program notes that in 75 percent of such rapes, alcohol or drug use is involved. The video emphasizes that rape is an act of violence, not passion, lists steps to take to cut the risk of assault, and underscores the fact that rape is never the victim's fault. It describes what to do if rape does occur, stresses the importance of telling someone at once, and stresses that everyone has the right to behave in a way that protects herself or himself from emotional and physical harm. Includes a teacher's guide. Recommended for grades 7–12.

Defending Our Lives
Type: 16mm film and VHS videocassette
Length: 41 min.
Date: 1993
Source: Cambridge Documentary Films, Inc.
P.O. Box 385
Cambridge, MA 02139
(617) 354-3677

This Academy Award–winning documentary features women imprisoned for killing their batterers. Their personal testimonies expose the magnitude and severity of domestic violence in this country. Sarah Buel, a district attorney and head of the Suffolk County Domestic Violence Unit, outlines the problem throughout the video as both a member of the criminal justice system and a formerly battered woman. Every person in this documentary is an expert; each has experienced firsthand the terror of domestic violence. The women in the documentary are members of Battered Women Fighting Back!, a grassroots organization dedicated to exposing domestic violence as a critical human rights violation threatening the majority of our population: women and children. These women have killed in self-defense and this documentary captures the cruel irony of putting them behind bars once they finally escaped their abusers. They share their stories, hoping to inspire creative strategies for ending this violence. High school age and above.

Discussion Openers
Type: VHS videocassette
Length: 27 min.
Date: 1989

Source: Coronet/MTI Film and Video
4350 Equity Drive
Columbus, OH 43228
(800) 321-3106

This overview program consists of a series of six short vignettes to be used as discussion starters for five major private violence issues: domestic violence, acquaintance violence, teen violence, street violence, and violence prevention. Each vignette features individuals who, in one way or another, are involved in interpersonal violence and their efforts to understand their problems. The video describes programs and treatments designed to prevent violent behavior. Junior high and above.

Domestic Abuse: A Challenge to the Media and the Courts
Type: VHS videocassette
Length: 67 min.
Date: 1994
Source: Women's Center of Rhode Island
P.O. Box 3300
Providence, RI 02906

Sarah M. Buel—a formerly battered woman who graduated cum laude from Harvard Law School and became an assistant district attorney and prosecutor in Massachusetts—tells her own story and explains how systems that are supposed to help battered women actually keep them and their children trapped; why child protection agencies concentrating on family reunification must place greater priority on child safety; and what hospitals, courts, educators, and battered women's advocates need to do differently. The video is valuable for training professionals on issues of domestic violence. High school and above.

Domestic Assault: The Police Response
Type: VHS videocassette
Length: 24 min.
Date: 1987
Source: Coronet/MTI Film and Video
4350 Equity Drive
Columbus, OH 43228
(800) 321-3106

This video is designed primarily to educate officers in the techniques used to investigate domestic assault. It emphasizes the importance of officers trusting their own observation skills and feelings when responding to a domestic call. This program grew out of movements in states that enacted laws requiring the mandatory arrest of offenders using only probable cause, and uses dramatized scenarios to underscore the minimal amounts of evidence needed. It demonstrates interviewing techniques, response techniques, and the proper handling of both aggressors and victims. Adult level.

Domestic Violence
Type: VHS videocassette
Length: 17 min.
Date: 1989
Source: Coronet/MTI Film and Video
4350 Equity Drive
Columbus, OH 43228
(800) 321-3106

This documentary presentation profiles a 32-year-old former batterer who has taken responsibility for his actions by getting treatment at a center for men who are violent toward women. Junior high school and above.

Heart on a Chain: The Truth about Date Violence
Type: VHS videocassette and videodisc
Length: 17 min.
Date: 1991
Source: Coronet/MTI Film and Video
4350 Equity Drive
Columbus, OH 43228
(800) 321-3106

This informative program addresses the issue of teenage date violence by speaking directly to young abusers and victims. Dramatically staged, it demonstrates the behaviors of several teenagers as each relates to a dating partner. Viewers will examine a number of dating behaviors, ranging from abusive and controlling to healthy and open. Teenagers get a clear understanding of what constitutes abuse in a relationship, why it happens, and what is a healthy, rewarding relationship. High school and above.

He's No Hero
Type: VHS videocassette
Length: 18.5 min.
Date: Not available
Source: National Resource Center for Youth Services
University of Oklahoma
202 West 8th
Tulsa, OK 74119-1419
(918) 585-2986

This video examines a long overlooked subject, the responsibilities of males in sexual decision making. It focuses on peer pressure, stereotypes, and the problems teens have in developing positive relationships with the opposite sex. The video helps stimulate discussions on feelings about one's sexuality, including the conflicting pressure to have or not have sex. Recommended for adolescents.

Hot Head in the House
Type: 16mm film & VHS videocassette
Length: 16 min.
Date: 1984
Source: Coronet/MTI Film and Video
4350 Equity Drive
Columbus, OH 43228
(800) 321-3106

This program is a realistic presentation of how uncontrolled anger can result in wife beating. Using actual cases and interviews with the couples involved, the film focuses on how this problem is handled by police, courts, and counselors. The program could prove useful for a variety of college courses that deal with domestic violence, such as family and gender role courses. College age and above.

It's Not Always Happy at My House
Type: 16mm film & VHS videocassette
Length: 34 min.
Date: 1987
Source: Coronet/MTI Film and Video
4350 Equity Drive
Columbus, OH 43228
(800) 321-3106

This presentation uses dramatization to cut through barriers of isolation and secrecy to help children from homes with domestic violence understand the feelings they experience as a result of witnessing or becoming a victim of abuse. A thorough teacher's guide, with detailed discussion questions for each scene, designed to help students confront situations in their own families, is provided. Primary age and above.

Journey into Courage
Type: VHS videocassette
Length: 60+ min.
Date: 1995
Source: Kingdom County Productions
Barnet, VT 05821
(802) 633-3240

This documentary, in production at the time of this writing, is based on the acclaimed theater piece *Journey into Courage*, which was written and performed by six Vermont women who survived domestic violence and sexual abuse. From 1992 to 1994, *Journey into Courage* toured as live theater throughout New England, acting as a force for social change in rural communities. It has been an empowering experience for the survivors who had the courage to tell their stories publicly. The video explores the power of theater as a teaching tool for speaking out against domestic violence, how survivors were empowered by taking their stories on the road and speaking out in communities, how *Journey into Courage* was a powerful step in the healing process of survivors, and how domestic violence affects rural women.

Men's Work
Type: VHS videocassette
Length: 60 min.
Date: 1992
Source: Hazelden
15251 Pleasant Valley Road
P.O. Box 176
Center City, MN 55012-0176
(800) 328-9000

Men's Work comes to life on video. Based on the book *Men's Work: How To Stop the Violence That Tears Our Lives Apart* by Paul Kivel, the video actively engages men in a process of personal change.

Viewers will see the impact violence has on their lives and the lives of others. Through narrative, realistic dramatizations and instructive role plays, men learn to understand the social, political, and personal roots of abusive behavior. Suggested activities help participants learn to recognize violence in everyday situations. Viewers are encouraged to develop a new image of male power that replaces violence with love, respect, cooperation, and community involvement. Sections in this video are also arranged to correspond to sections in the three *Men's Work* workbooks (see Chapter 6) to facilitate study.

No Longer Alone
Type: 16mm film and VHS videocassette
Length: 30 min.
Date: 1986
Source: Coronet/MTI Film and Video
4350 Equity Drive
Columbus, OH 43228
(800) 321-3106

Through a series of personal interviews and group discussions, residents and support staff of the Washington State Network share their experiences and findings about domestic violence. Professionals explore the cycle of abuse from the viewpoints of the victim and aggressor and examine its impact on children. High school and above.

No Means No!: Avoiding Date Abuse
Type: 16mm film and VHS videocassette
Length: 19 min.
Date: 1988
Source: Coronet/MTI Film and Video
4350 Equity Drive
Columbus, OH 43228
(800) 321-3106

Young Lisa is nearly raped by her boyfriend. Confused by her fear and inexperience, she feels that the incident may even have been her fault, that if she had just given in, her boyfriend wouldn't be so upset with her, but she just isn't ready for sex. When some older friends discover her dilemma, Lisa gets a lesson in how to recognize and avoid date abuse. Through dramatized examples of typical behavior leading to rape and other forms of date abuse, the program stresses the importance of communicating expectations and sexual limits and helps alleviate the fear of being rejected for standing up for personal rights. The video is also intended to curtail date abuse by teaching young men that, despite the myth, "real" men don't abuse women and that there are serious consequences for such behavior. A good tool for discussion groups for young people. High school and above.

People Like Me: Violence in Dating Relationships
Type: VHS videocassette
Length: 17:22 min.
Date: 1990
Source: Boulder County Safehouse
P.O. Box 4157
Boulder, CO 80306
(303) 449-8623

This video depicts interviews with four teenagers who discuss their experiences with violence in dating relationships, speaking thoughtfully and candidly and making it easy for other teens to identify with them. Two young women talk about their relationships from the standpoint of the victim: how it started, what they did, how they changed, and how they feel now. The two young men were both abusers in dating relationships and tell what they thought, how they failed to control their actions and why, and what they feel today.

Playing the Game
Type: VHS videocassette
Length: 16 min.
Date: 1992
Source: Intermedia
1300 Dexter Avenue North
Seattle, WA 98109
(800) 553-8336

Playing the Game explores the issue of date rape/acquaintance rape from the perspectives of both the victim and the assailant. Mark wants to believe that "no" means "maybe," while Suzanne feels that she has been raped and asks herself, "Why did this happen to me?" This video explores how we interpret the actions of the opposite sex. High school and above.

Preventing Date Violence
Type: VHS videocassette
Length: 13 min.
Date: 1992
Source: Coronet/MTI Film and Video
4350 Equity Drive
Columbus, OH 43228
(800) 321-3106

The "You Can't Be Beat" theater troupe, a group of trained peer leaders who write and perform scenes that illustrate date violence, acts out a situation: Alfred, in a jealous rage, punches his girlfriend, Ronnie, for dancing with someone else at a party. The theater troupe then discusses the reaction of teens to their skit. In the discussion that follows the skit, peer leaders listen to young audience members who say they see the same type of behavior all the time but don't know what to do about it. Together they examine abusive behavior, including constant put-downs, emotional manipulation, and attacks on self-esteem that often escalate into physical abuse. Junior high and above.

Rough Love
Type: VHS videocassette
Length: 50 min.
Date: 1994
Source: National Coalition Against Domestic Violence
P.O. Box 18749
Denver, CO 80218
(303) 839-1852

This provocative program presents a dialogue between actress Gabrielle Carteris of the television show *Beverly Hills 90210* and a studio audience including teens, families, friends, and professionals about the dynamics and consequences of teen dating violence. Through real life stories and interviews, Carteris covers all the bases. Topics include verbal, emotional, physical, and sexual abuse; discussions of jealousy and disrespect; generational patterns of violent behavior; danger signals of abuse; how adults can help; elements of a healthy relationship; and how to break the cycle of violence. The video includes celebrity appearances by Jody Watley, Kelli Martin, and Soleil Moon Frye.

Savage Cycle
Type: VHS videocassette
Length: 30 min.
Date: 1991
Source: Intermedia
1300 Dexter Avenue North
Seattle, WA 98109
(800) 553-8336

Savage Cycle is a candid view of domestic violence told by men and women dealing with violence in relationships. This video talks about abuse, co-dependency, and eventual freedom from the cycle of domestic violence.

Savageman
Type: VHS videocassette
Length: 30 min.
Date: 1992
Source: Intermedia
1300 Dexter Avenue North
Seattle, WA 98109
(800) 553-8336

Savageman explores domestic violence from the male abuser's perspective and deals with the struggle men go through when they are forced to confront their violent behavior and must move from anger and control over others to compassion, caring, and self-control. Considered a sequel to *Savage Cycle* (see above).

Scenes from a Shelter
Type: VHS videocassette
Length: 30 min.
Date: 1992
Source: Pennsylvania Coalition Against Domestic Violence
6400 Flank Drive, Suite 1300
Harrisburg, PA 17112

The Pennsylvania Coalition has produced this program as a tool for adults who work with young children from violent homes. Filmed in two segments (approximately 17 minutes and 13 minutes, respectively), *Scenes from a Shelter* talks about domestic violence honestly and directly. It depicts life in a shelter through the eyes of children. Puppets are used to voice children's feelings and fears. An accompanying workbook and discussion guide can be used by children's advocates, teachers, counselors, and other professionals to direct discussion and initiate reinforcement activities with children. An illustrated storybook, *I Do, and I Don't*, helps children understand their ambivalent feelings about many things that result from their experience with violence in the home. The program tells children that they are not alone, not to blame, and can talk about how home makes them feel—no matter how confused or strange the feelings may seem. Kids are reminded that no one expects them to make it better. They are encouraged to be kids and do kid things while grown-ups begin to help fix what is broken.

Scoring: A Story about Date Rape
Type: VHS videocassette
Length: 19 min.
Date: 1993
Source: Coronet/MTI Film and Video
         4350 Equity Drive
         Columbus, OH 43228
         (800) 321-3106

In this story, Jimmy's attitude toward women is colored by destructive myths. He believes that women need to be pressured into having sex and that some women are teases who deserve their abuse. Though his friends try to convince Jimmy to respect women, he refuses and is eventually arrested for rape. This program provides viewers with facts about physical and emotional sexual abuse and encourages them to examine and change the attitudes that promote disrespect toward and violence against women. High school and above.

Someone You Know: Acquaintance Rape
Type: 16mm film and VHS videocassette
Length: 30 min.
Date: 1986
Source: Coronet/MTI Film and Video
         4350 Equity Drive
         Columbus, OH 43228
         (800) 321-3106

This sensitive documentary, produced and hosted by Collin Siedor, looks at acquaintance rape crime, examines its effects on the victims, probes the underlying causes of these violent acts, and explores what can be done to prevent the crime and aid the victims. Appropriate for courses in introductory sociology, deviance, criminology, and sexual victimization. Junior high school and above.

To Have and To Hold
Type: 16mm film and VHS videocassette
Length: 20 min.
Date: 1981
Source: New Day Films
            22 Hollywood Avenue
            Ho-Ho-Kus, NJ 07423
            (201) 652-6590

This is the first film to examine the problem of woman abuse through the man's experience of it; it is still a timely piece. The piece is composed primarily of interviews with men who have assaulted their wives and lovers, and explores the personal and societal attitudes that lead men to do violence to those nearest them. It also examines the changes in attitude that are essential in order for men to stop their violent behavior. A study guide is included.

The Truth and Trauma of Date Rape
Type: VHS videocassette
Length: 19 min.
Date: 1991
Source: National Resource Center for Youth Services
            University of Oklahoma
            202 West 8th
            Tulsa, OK 74119-1419
            (918) 585-2986

In plain talk, Summer describes her experience of acquaintance rape during her first month in college and the skills and strengths she discovered as a survivor. She offers realistic advice on how to avoid date rape and how to handle the aftermath. Produced by the Santa Fe Rape Crisis Center with Focus Foundation.

Two Million Women: Domestic Violence
Type: 16mm film and VHS videocassette
Length: 29 min.
Date: 1987
Source: Coronet/MTI Film and Video
4350 Equity Drive
Columbus, OH 43228
(800) 321-3106

This documentary, hosted by Collin Siedor, reveals the uncomfortable truths behind battering. In-depth interviews with the women who stay and the men who abuse them show the reasons for both behaviors. The video's real concern is with how the cycle changes, and it introduces some of the people who made the decision to change the pattern of their lives and ask for help. High school and above.

When Women Kill
Type: VHS videocassette
Length: 47 min.
Date: 1994
Source: Filmakers Library
124 East 40th Street
New York, NY 10016
(212) 808-4980

Produced by the National Film Board of Canada, *When Women Kill* is a documentary that places the personal stories of three battered women in a legal/historical context. Ann Jones, an authority on women, domestic violence, and criminal justice, explains the evolution of society's attitudes toward women who murder abusive spouses. The video takes the viewer from eighteenth-century England, when such women were burned at the stake, to the Victorian era, when women who poisoned their husbands were declared insane and acquitted as such, to 1979, when the Battered Woman's Syndrome was formulated. Jones refers to the syndrome as the old insanity argument in new language, saying that by focusing on the "helpless woman" it does not address the many women who try to leave their relationships and continue to be harassed, and it does not focus on the violence of the batterers. Three women who have killed their abusers tell their stories of beatings, torture, humiliation, and violent attacks on their person and property. One speaks from prison, where she is serving a seven-year sentence. There are also sequences of counselling groups for violent men, which provide insight into why male violence continues and why initiatives taken by the police and courts often fail. Appropriate for college students and above. Valuable for service providers.

Without Consent
Type: VHS videocassette
Length: 25 min.
Date: 1987
Source: Pyramid Film and Video
P.O. Box 1048
Santa Monica, CA 90406
(800) 421-2304

This piece is a thought-provoking drama that stimulates serious reflection and discussion about acquaintance rape. The story centers on two young college students whose developing relationship ends explosively. The film does not teach women specific ways to stay safe; rather, it challenges viewers to consider what rape is, why it occurs, how it might be prevented, and who is ultimately responsible. Closed captioned available. Recommended for high school, college, and adult levels.

Index

249